KANT AND ARISTOTLE

KANT AND ARISTOTLE

Epistemology, Logic, and Method

MARCO SGARBI

M.C. Escher's "Bond of Union" © 2015 The M.C. Escher Company-The Netherlands. All rights reserved. www.mcescher.com

Published by State University of New York Press, Albany

© 2016 State University of New York

All rights reserved

Printed in the United States of America

No part of this book may be used or reproduced in any manner whatsoever without written permission. No part of this book may be stored in a retrieval system or transmitted in any form or by any means including electronic, electrostatic, magnetic tape, mechanical, photocopying, recording, or otherwise without the prior permission in writing of the publisher.

For information, contact State University of New York Press, Albany, NY
www.sunypress.edu

Production, Diane Ganeles
Marketing, Kate R. Seburyamo

Library of Congress Cataloging-in-Publication Data

Sgarbi, Marco, 1982-
  Kant and Aristotle : epistemology, logic, and method / Marco Sgarbi.
    pages cm
  Includes bibliographical references and index.
  ISBN 978-1-4384-5997-4 (hardcover : alk. paper) — ISBN 978-1-4384-5999-8 (e-book) — ISBN 978-1-4384-5998-1 (paperback : alk. paper)
  1. Kant, Immanuel, 1724–1804. 2. Aristotle—Influence. 3. Logic. 4. Methodology. I. Title.
  B2798.S43 2016
  193—dc23
                        2015013509

10 9 8 7 6 5 4 3 2 1

CONTENTS

ACKNOWLEDGMENTS	vii
SOURCES AND ABBREVIATIONS	ix
INTRODUCTION	1
The Other Kant	1
Kant in Context	6
Prospectus	16
1. FACULTATIVE LOGIC	19
The Operations of the Mind	19
Gnostology and Noology	25
Habit and Physiology	36
Between Locke and Leibniz	51
2. TRANSCENDENTAL LOGIC	79
Matter and Form	79
Syllogistic and Combinatorics before Kant	94
Syllogistic and Combinatorics in Kant	118
Categories and Judgments	135
Analytic and Dialectic	150

3. METHODOLOGY — 165
Method in the Aristotelian Tradition — 165
Modern Conceptions of Method — 176
Kant's Precritical Conception of Method — 183
The Method of *Critique of Pure Reason* — 193

CONCLUSION — 217
Aristotle in Kant — 217
The Aristotelian Kant — 222

NOTES — 225

BIBLIOGRAPHY — 257

INDEX — 277

ACKNOWLEDGMENTS

I gratefully acknowledge the help and support of numerous people and institutions while I was working on this book. This research has been made possible thanks to a Frances A. Yates Short-Term fellowship at the Warburg Institute (2011), a Fritz Thyssen Stiftung postdoctoral fellowship at the Herzog August Bibliothek, Wolfenbüttel (2012), and an Accademia dei Lincei-British Academy postdoctoral fellowship (2012).

Earlier versions of the contents of this book were presented in a very different form in some of my previous Italian books and articles (cf. Sgarbi 2010a; Sgarbi 2010b; Sgarbi 2010c; Sgarbi 2010d; Sgarbi 2012). Interaction with many scholars and conference presentations prompted me to write a compelling new book in English on the topic to reach a broader audience. In this book, I have used some of the scholarly work of my previous research, especially the investigation of the Königsberg intellectual framework, the analysis of unpublished manuscripts and unknown documents, and the study of the eighteenth-century Aristotelian textbooks.

While any list of reasonable length would be undoubtedly incomplete, I nonetheless wish to acknowledge the great help of Seung-Kee Lee and Riccardo Pozzo. I am particularly grateful to the four peer-reviewers and to Robert Norris for the linguistic revision of my book. Despite the invaluable assistance of many people, any and all errors or shortcomings in this book are mine, and mine alone.

SOURCES AND ABBREVIATIONS

All references to Kant's works are cited in the body of the text according to the volume and page number, given in Arabic numerals separated by a colon in the critical edition of *Kants gesammelte Schriften*, edited by the Royal Prussian (later German, then Berlin-Brandenburg) Academy of Sciences (Berlin: Georg Reimer, later Walter de Gruyter & Co., 1900–). The one exception to this rule is the *Critique of Pure Reason*, where passages are referenced by numbers from "A," the first edition of 1781, and/or "B," the second edition of 1787. The pagination of the Academy Edition is reproduced in almost all modern English translations of Kant's writings.

All Greek and Roman authors are cited in their most familiar single-name form, both in the text and in the bibliography, for example, Cicero (not Marcus Tullius Cicero) and Quintilian (not Marcus Fabius Quintilianus). All the titles of the works are given in the original language, with the exemption of Aristotle and Kant's writings. My general rule has been to preserve original spelling and punctuation, even when erroneous, except where there are critical editions. Sometimes, when fitting quotations around the text, I have silently changed a lowercase initial letter to an upper, or vice versa, as the sentence requires.

Unless otherwise noted, the translations of Kant's writings are from the *Cambridge Edition of the Works of Immanuel Kant* (Cambridge: Cambridge University Press, 1992–) and those of Aristotle's from the *Complete Works* (Princeton: Princeton University Press, 1984).

A   *Leibniz: Sämtliche Schriften und Briefe* (Darmstadt-Berlin: Akademie-Verlag, 1923–).

AT   Charles Adam and Paul Tannery (ed.), *Oeuvres complètes de René Descartes* (Paris: Cerf, 1897–1900).

CL   Louis Couturat (ed.), *Opuscules et fragments inédits de Leibniz* (Paris: Félix Alcan, 1903).

GP   Carl I. Gerhardt (ed.), *Die philosophischen Schriften von Gottfried Wilhelm Leibniz* (Berlin: Weidmann, 1875–1890).

OP   Johann Eduard Erdmann (ed.), *Leibnitii Opera philosophica quae extant Latina, Gallica, Germanica Omnia* (Eichler: Berlin, 1840).

BIBLIOGRAPHICAL NOTE

This book was finished and submitted for publication in April 2015, hence valuable books on related topics that appeared after that date are not discussed.

INTRODUCTION

THE OTHER KANT

There are many ways of reading Kant and his work. One way is to actualize his thought and to find relevant ideas in answer to contemporary questions.[1] Another way is to examine his thought analytically to show his consistency or inconsistency.[2] A third way is to study the impact of Kantian philosophy on the making of Western culture and on the philosophy of the two following centuries.[3] It is also possible to investigate Kant's philosophy through a historical inquiry into the intellectual context that determined his thought.[4] The latter approach has not been widely adopted in Anglo-Saxon Kantian scholarship, which is the reason why my book privileges this latter way of reading Kant and his philosophy. But such a reading of Kant can also be carried out by means of two different hermeneutical and methodological approaches: on the one hand, there is the immanent interpretation of the text (*textimmanente Interpretation*), that is, the close reading of a work, while on the other hand, there is the historical interpretation of sources (*quellengeschichtliche Interpretation*).[5]

The former approach bases the interpretation of the works on the study of inner references to a single text, or more in general to the entire corpus of Kantian writings. This approach is characterized by the fact that it has a higher degree of certainty, because references and analysis are dealt with in such a way that there can be no doubt about the text, the thought, and the intention of the author. However, this approach is often unable to reconstruct the context from which a work emerges, the reasons for the formation of particular ideas rather than others, and the tensions that underlie the philosophical development of an author.

Conversely, a historical approach to the sources seems to provide the tools necessary for compensating for the lack of an immanent interpretation of the text, and despite its reconstructions being no more than probable, they nevertheless seem to me to offer new hints and open up new possibilities for further research. Contrary to the close reading approach, the historical approach is epistemologically weaker, in that it has a lower degree of certainty resulting from the obvious fact that we do not live in Kant's times and cannot be sure with absolute certainty about what he read or who he met. That said, if justified systematically, it has the advantage of being corrective and opening up an interesting dialogue on the formation of a philosophical text, which is—in my view—true to the spirit of philosophy and its historiography. Relying solely on an immanent interpretation entails making the misleading assumption that all the thought of an author can be contained in a text. Anyone fortunate enough to have the experience of writing and thinking is well aware that the written lines and words are not always a faithful reflection of what we have in mind, and that a great deal more lies behind and between the lines. For this reason, I have chosen to follow the methodology of the history of sources. For instance, a close reading of the *Critique of Pure Reason* has never solved questions about its formation, and on certain knotty issues it has in fact given rise to thousands and thousands of readings. Reconstructions based on the history of sources are perhaps only probable, but when carried out systematically they can prove far more revealing while allowing us thoroughly to understand the ideas of an author, thereby transforming our initial persuasion into conviction. Instead of a self-referential and mute text, the historical approach offers the scholar a work that converses not only with our questions, but also with problems and philosophical issues pertaining to the tradition from which it emerges.

Concerning Kant and his relation to Aristotle and the Aristotelian tradition, which is the topic of the present book, we can recognize at least six different kinds of sources: (1) Kant's open statements; (2) references in letters and manuscripts; (3) references in other authors; (4) the university context (i.e., syllabi, lecture catalogs, academic programs, textbooks); (5) lecture notes; and (6) Königsberg intellectual framework. Kant mentions Aristotle and Aristotelian philosophers only a hundred times in all his works (printed and manuscript). This is not so much if we think that most of the times they are only cursory references or are contradictory and ambiguous: we can read praise for Aristotle's logic and ontology, but also harsh criticism against the confusion and asystematic nature of his thought. In this book, I will examine the most relevant passages. In general, we can state that from the very beginning Kant's differing opinions on Aristotle and the Aristotelian tradition reflect, as we shall see, his eclecticism, that is, the contrast and attraction between innovation and conservatism, and the cultural prejudices of his time.

We must confess openly that concerning these kinds of sources we have no evidence in other authors that Kant read Aristotelian works, nor do the textbooks he used during his lessons testify to a good knowledge of the Aristotelian tradition. My work therefore focuses mainly on the reconstruction of the conditions in Königsberg that gave rise to Kantian philosophy. The research follows the methodology of the history of problems and that of the history of concepts. Regarding the history of problems, I have tried to inquire deeply into Kant's philosophical questions in the light of Aristotle, trying to understand whether Kant's answers were in fact a more or less conscious reappraisal of those given by Aristotle. Where this was the case, as it proved to be in particular with the problem of categories and schema, I have provided the sources that I found most appropriate to explaining Kant's thought. My inquiry aims to contextualize Kant's logical works, and in particular the *Critique of Pure Reason*, within the Aristotelian tradition, which does not only mean to ascertain that there are Aristotelian doctrines in his philosophy, but also to understand how he received and elaborated this bi-millenarian tradition.

Many scholars of Kantian philosophy are likely to be disappointed in reading this book, because it shows definitively that Kant is not necessarily the original philosopher so often presented by the historiography and that his thought is a constant reworking of philosophical issues and problems common to many other contemporary thinkers. That is not to say that we should question the genius of Kant, which consists in recasting the material in totally new ways in an attempt to solve problems that until then had remained unresolved. In his recent book, Graham Bird maintains that there is a major division in the interpretation of Kant, between traditionalists and revolutionaries. Traditionalists tend to assimilate Kant to predecessors such as Locke, Leibniz, Hume, and Berkeley, while revolutionaries take more seriously Kant's criticism of all the earlier empiricist, rationalist, idealistic, skeptical, and dogmatic doctrines. He recognizes that the traditionalist position was once dominant, but that in the last thirty years revolutionary interpretations have found more favor.[6] With this book I would like to suggest a third way of reading Kant: as a revolutionary, but within a tradition.

The aim of my research is to reconstruct the intellectual framework and the sources that contributed to the making of Kant's philosophy. In so doing, I examine Kant's philosophical development from his first published work in 1747 up to the *Critique of Pure Reason*. In my view, logic, epistemology, and methodology are the key disciplines to understanding how and why Kant elaborated his new transcendental philosophy, with the *Critique of Pure Reason* standing as an independent eclectic form of philosophy against Wolffian rationalism and British empiricism.

Central to my investigation is the idea that the intellectual environment in Königsberg and its indigenous philosophy had a decisive impact on many aspects in the genesis of a critical philosophy, in terms of both the dissemination of philosophical issues foreign to other traditions and the assumption of particular philosophical positions. Kant's achievements arise from the effort to solve problems in relation to which the responses of the various contemporary philosophical movements were inadequate. Kant's progress in the field of philosophy is the expression of an attitude of partial revision or wholesale rejection of the entire systematic structure of a tradition, or at least some of its elements. Such an attitude should not be regarded as a radical break with the past, as he seems to claim in the "Introduction" of the *Critique of Pure Reason*. This would lead to the misleading idea of a rupture in the history of philosophy that is difficult to accept. The comparison with a philosophical tradition should be seen as the perfect starting point to explain the genesis and the development of Kant's thought, although he may turn away from it.

My opinion, as I shall show, is that the seeds and roots of Kant's philosophy originated between 1766 and 1772, but that they do not find a full expression in either the *Dreams of a Spirit-Seer* or the *Inaugural Dissertation*. From the logical standpoint, the enterprise of criticism began only with the discovery of the Aristotelian doctrine of categories as an essential part in the conception of synthetic a priori knowledge, in other words after 1772. Kant, however, came to this doctrine only after two decades of failed attempts and only, as I have already mentioned, after turning away from Wolffian rationalism and British empiricism. There was an evolution in Kant's thought from the false starts and incomplete projects of the precritical period to the discovery of the key of his transcendental logic.

Historical comparisons between Kant and Aristotle in the fields of metaphysics, logic, and methodology are few and far between.[7] My proposal, following Giorgio Tonelli's suggestion, is to read Kant's *Critique of Pure Reason* not as a treatise on metaphysics or on the theory of knowledge, but as a book on logic and, more specifically, on the "method" of metaphysics, which must be understood within the Aristotelian tradition: "referring the *Critique of Pure Reason* to its logical matrix has the most far-reaching consequences on the very intelligibility, and on the historical and philosophical interpretation of this work [. . .] the whole general structure of the *Critique*, seen in this light, does not appear any more as a personal, and largely obscure and arbitrary, creation of its author, but as the meaningful outcome of some basic traditions in the history of logic."[8] In this sense the whole first *Critique* would have been a propaedeutic tool for metaphysics, while the "critique" would have been a canon for the possibility of knowing an object in general.

Privileging the Aristotelian tradition, however, does not mean reducing the *Critique of Pure Reason* to a work related exclusively to Aristotelianism: such an attempt would be totally misleading. On the contrary, what I am offering is a systematic study that digs deep into the Königsberg Aristotelian tradition of the seventeenth- and eighteenth-centuries, which is where Kant's philosophy arises. It is "another Kant" that I wish to present in this research, a Kant who drew important ideas of his own logic and metaphysical doctrines from the Aristotelian tradition. It would be a mistake to say that in this survey Kant is presented as an Aristotelian: he is in fact treated as such only to the extent that he makes use of Aristotelian doctrines to solve certain, by no means trivial, problems in his philosophy.

KANT IN CONTEXT

Immanuel Kant, it is a well-known fact, lived most of his life in Königsberg, and with its university Königsberg has always been a stronghold of Aristotelianism. Johann Jakob Brucker, probably the most important eighteenth-century historian of philosophy, wrote in his monumental *Historia critica philosophiae* that "a genuine study of Peripatetic philosophy in Königsberg University flourished."[9] Nowadays, the history of the Aristotelian tradition in German territories, in Königsberg especially, is marked by a lack of scholarship. Despite some pioneering inquiries,[10] a detailed survey of Königsberg Aristotelianism remains to be written, due largely to the difficulty of finding primary sources. Nonetheless, some attempt to shed light on the most significant milestones in early-modern Aristotelianism in Königsberg is needed, since this was the philosophical tradition that fostered Immanuel Kant's thought.

During the second half of the sixteenth century, Aristotelianism in Europe benefited from the dissemination of new editions of Aristotelian writings.[11] With the rediscovery of Aristotle's ancient Greek commentators, who offered some guarantee of a faithful reading of the Stagirite's works, Aristotle's original thought made a serious comeback, especially in Padua. From there it spread all over Europe, gaining purchase in Protestant Germany, in particular, where a reading of Aristotle expurgated of Catholic and Scholastic issues was warmly received during the Reformation, thanks primarily to Philipp Melanchthon. This process of purification had a double origin. On the one hand, humanistic and philological studies led to a more thorough reading of the texts in the original language, while on the other hand, Luther's diatribe against the exploitation of philosophy by theology in the schools promoted a direct reading of the text at the expense of the great Latin interpretations. For both these reasons, it was a triumph for Aristotle and definitive defeat for any alternative philosophies, and established a primacy that lasted until the beginning of the eighteenth century, when Aristotelianism began to wane. The "German educator," as Melanchthon was nicknamed, was well aware of the necessity of improving Lutheran theology with a secular philosophy such as Aristotelianism,[12] hence he dedicated himself to saving the fundamental elements of Aristotelian philosophy from Martin Luther's criticism while at the same time showing the intrinsic value and validity of Aristotelian doctrines.[13] Many Protestant universities were founded during his time (Marburg in 1527, for instance, and Jena in 1556), and they all placed the Philippistic interpretation of Aristotle alongside Lutheran theology at the heart of their syllabi.

One such university was the *Albertina* of Königsberg. Since its foundation in 1544, Königsberg University was strongly characterized by Aristotelianism. The resounding success of Aristotelianism was due to the close ties between the first rector, Georg Sabinus, and Philipp Melanchthon: Sabinus was in fact Melanchthon's son-in-law.[14] Early Aristotelianism in Königsberg was thus characterized by the Philippistic interpretation of Aristotle, which also enjoyed the esteem of Duke Albrecht I, the university's founder. Aristotelianism was the official philosophy according to the statute of the university, which in the chapter "doctrinae temporibus et ordine" established Melanchthon as the authority to be followed in the teaching of dialectic, natural philosophy, and ethics.[15] Particular importance was given in Königsberg to the teaching of dialectic as a propaedeutic subject to improve the argumentative skills of future physicians, jurists, and theologians.[16] Besides, dialectics, metaphysics, and natural theology were also an important part of the curriculum, but Philippistic philosophy did not pay much attention to Aristotle's metaphysics, which became a subject of investigation only around the third decade of the seventeenth century, when Königsberg established itself as one of the most important Aristotelian universities in Germany. Königsberg's general view on Aristotle is pithily expressed in the words of one the leading Aristotelians of the time, Christian Dreier, according to whom "we can only praise Aristotle, who dealt accurately with philosophical sciences, whose tools he first found, elaborated, and knew."[17] This period was characterized by the publication of numerous Aristotelian handbooks and companions dealing with the entire body of Aristotelian philosophy with the aim of elucidating the obscurity of the texts and illustrating the superiority of Aristotle's approach,[18] compared to the Baconian and Cartesian doctrines. In particular, it is possible to recognize a shift in interest from dialectics to the methodology of sciences as a result of the widespread dissemination of the ideas of Paduan Aristotelianism at the Albertina, especially those of Jacopo Zabarella.[19] The most important Zabarellean scholar in Königsberg was undoubtedly Melchior Zeidler, who in 1676 published his *Analytica sive de variis sciendi generibus et mediis eo preveniendi libri III*, which made him, as Brucker testifies, the greatest Aristotelian of his time.[20] Zeidler's *Analytica* dealt with the doctrine of method and the problem of analysis and synthesis according to Aristotle's philosophy, which was in opposition to modern methodology,[21] an Aristotelian approach followed also by Christian Dreier and Lambert Steger, who were particularly praised by Daniel Morhof and Johann Jakob Brucker for their attack on and confutation of the Cartesian principle cogito ergo sum.[22]

In this general shift toward methodology, the most significant event in the seventeenth century for the history of the Aristotelian tradition in Königsberg was the birth of two new disciplines, which were propaedeutic to logic and metaphysics: gnostology and noology. The origin is traceable back to the conjunction of Melanchthon's thought with Zabarella's logic and the introduction of Francisco Suárez's ontology. The field of *gnostologia* emerged in Wittenberg with Georg Gutke's *Intelligentia sive habitus primorum principiorum* (1625) and Valentin Fromme's *Gnostologia* (1631), both of which bore the imprint of Zabarella.[23] In the Albertina, Lorenz Weger was the first to follow these pioneering studies,[24] but it was only with the publication of Abraham Calov's *Gnostologia* in 1633 that Königsberg became the center of reference for the study of these two new disciplines.[25]

Aristotelianism remained the dominant movement in Königsberg University up to the fourth decade of the eighteenth century. Also when new philosophies became popular, Königsberg Aristotelianism preserved its main features: its attention to logic and methodology, and its criticism of Cartesian philosophy. A vivid example of the relevance of the Aristotelian tradition in Königsberg is Johann Jakob Rohde's *Meditatio philosophica qua Aristotelem sapientissimum de veritate judicem* (1722), in which he wrote against the modern philosophers in favor of Aristotle: "Aristotle [is] the highest dictator of wisdom, [he is] infallible, rule and example that nature has generated to demonstrate the ultimate human perfection."[26] The most prominent figure in this intellectual framework was Paul Rabe,[27] the first eighteenth-century professor of logic and metaphysics and probably Kant's most important Aristotelian source.[28] His main publications include the *Dialectica et Analytica, scientiarum biga utilissima* (1703),[29] the official logical and rhetorical textbook of the *Collegium Fridericianum* up to the fourth decade of the eighteenth century,[30] the *Cursus philosophicus* (1703),[31] the *Rhetorica civilis* (1704), the dissertation *Primitiae professionis logico-metaphysicae, sive Commentarius in librum categoriarum Aristotelis* (1704), and the *Methodologia nova atque scientifica, sive tractatus de ordine genuine* (1708). With Rabe, Aristotelianism in Königsberg was without doubt the dominant philosophical movement before Pietism and Wolffianism. It was not only the official philosophy according to the university statute, but it was widely recognized, as well as highly regarded, for its opposition to the modern thinkers. A meaningful example is Rabe's dissertation *De novellis philosophis eorumque philosophia* (1678), in which the Königsberg Aristotelian outlines *in nuce* his confutation of Cartesian philosophy, which was included in his *Methodologia* thirty years later. The fact that a young and not so well-established scholar such as Rabe chose in his *disputatio pro loco* to attack Cartesian philosophy so vehemently is clear evidence that anti-Cartesian sentiments were widespread among Königsberg professors.[32]

Aristotelianism was professed also by Rabe's heirs to the chair of logic and metaphysics, even those related to Wolffianism. Rabe's immediate successor was Johann Böse, professor of logic and metaphysics from 1713 to 1715. Böse's work in the logical and metaphysical fields remains unknown to us, but during this same period Christian Gabriel Fischer, a controversial scholar who went from Aristotelianism to Wolffianism,[33] published the *Problemata dialectica quibus extantiora dialecticae capita sub expresio problematis schemate ex logics topicis ventilanda exhibentur* (1716), entirely based on Aristotelian logic. After Böse, Heinrich Oelmann taught logic and metaphysics from 1715 to 1725 as associate professor, and was one of the first to adopt Wolffian textbooks in his lectures. After Rabe, the most important Aristotelian was Johann Jakob Rohde, professor of logic from 1720 to 1727. He professed Aristotelianism throughout his academic life, as his academic program *Meditatione philosophica qua Aristotelica sapientissimus de veritate* shows.[34] From 1725 to 1758, Johann David Kypke was professor of logic and metaphysics, with a short interval between 1728 and 1729, when Johann Gottfried Teske became associate professor. Both scholars were deeply involved in Aristotelian philosophy. After Teske, Daniel Lorenz Salthenius (1729–1731) and Johann Georg Bock (1732–1733) became associate professors, again following in the Stagirite's footsteps. In 1733, Konrad Gottlieb Marquardt, Kant's professor of mathematics, published his *Philosophia rationalis methodo naturali digesta* (1733), which was an eclectic textbook that merged Aristotelian and Wolffian elements.[35] From 1734 to 1751, Martin Knutzen, Kant's mentor, was associate professor of logic and metaphysics. To the field of logic he contributed the *Elementa philosophiae rationalis seu logicae* (1747), the result of a decade of teaching that was studied also by Kant during his university years.[36] In 1759, Friedrich Johann Buck, mathematician and Knutzen's pupil, became professor of logic until he was replaced by Kant.

If we examine the chair of logic and metaphysics, and the teachings given between 1703 and 1770, we can argue that Königsberg University was at once deeply conservative and highly receptive: conservative, because the Aristotelian tradition exercised a particular influence on the teachings during the first half of the eighteenth century; receptive, because all new editorial releases were used in the classes, as was the case for the textbooks of Wolff, Thümmig, and Crusius. This could mean that the teachings at Königsberg were open to new trends, but also that the textbooks themselves were not so important in practice, if they were changed so often, and that lectures were therefore still largely delivered on the basis of knowledge that was generally Aristotelian and Scholastic.

Königsberg, between the end of the seventeenth and the beginning of the eighteenth centuries, is characterized by several philosophical upheavals. Königsberg University was a crucible of hard struggles between the various philosophical movements and schools, and this undoubtedly had an impact on the formation of early Kantian philosophical thought.[37] From 1715 to 1740, Aristotelianism, Eclecticism,[38] and Wolffianism fought to extend their hegemony in philosophy. Of course, the beginning of the eighteenth century was characterized by a strong conservatism both in theology, in which seventeenth-century theological debates were dominant,[39] and in philosophy, in which Aristotelianism maintained its long-standing tradition. The dominant philosophical school was Aristotelianism, even if Scholastic Protestant philosophy was still extremely powerful. Distinguishing between these two philosophical currents, which only in Königsberg, with figures like Abraham Calov, tended to merge, is not simple. We can say, however, that Aristotelianism has its root in the foundation of the university and in the Philippistic interpretation of Stagirite's work, while Scholastic Protestant philosophy follows Francisco Suárez's metaphysics. In the second half of the sixteenth century, there was a renewed interested in Aristotelianism with the dissemination of the works of Jacopo Zabarella. Aristotelianism was characterized by a careful exegesis of Aristotelian works in the original Greek, and by the production of large commentaries and propaedeutic companions, while Scholastic Protestant philosophy aimed to establish methodologically the relations among the various philosophical disciplines, in particular the connection with theology, the queen of all disciplines. Both these philosophical perspectives denied modern science and methodology, preferring to be anchored in their own traditions instead. In this sense, both Aristotelianism and Protestant Scholastic philosophy were conservative. At the beginning of the eighteenth century, however, teachings show that Protestant Scholastic philosophy had lost out to Aristotelianism. The result was that metaphysics was completely absorbed by logic, and lectures were dominated by the Aristotelians at least up until WS 1719/1720. The most used textbooks in logic and metaphysics were those of Abraham Calov, Melchior Zeidler, and Paul Rabe, who gave a nominalistic interpretation of Aristotle's thought.[40]

If in Germany the three decades between 1690 and 1720 were characterized by the expansion of Pietism and Eclectic philosophy, in Königsberg this period was dominated by Aristotelianism, and the influence of Pietism was practically absent. Aristotelianism was so deeply embedded in the University's tradition that it was virtually impossible for the new philosophical movements to supplant it.

It would thus be erroneous to suppose that Königsberg Pietism superseded Aristotelianism.[41] Indeed, Aristotelianism ruled unchallenged up until the third decade of the eighteenth century under the aegis of Johann Jakob Quandt and Johann Jakob Rohde, two of Rabe's former students, although by 1717 Pietism and Wolffianism had come to constitute a genuine threat within the intellectual landscape of Königsberg. From the early 1720s onward, Wolffianism in particular gave Aristotelianism a serious run for its money, firmly establishing itself within the academic corpus.[42] The readiness with which some Königsberg intellectuals reacted favorably to Wolff's German works is evidence of how receptive to new philosophies the intellectual environment in Königsberg was.[43] Even so, ordinary professors such as Georg Thegen and Johann David Kypke were not influenced by Wolffianism. The Wolffians had their moment of glory between 1717 and 1723 when they were allied with the Pietists against Aristotelian conservatism, as evidenced by the widespread dissemination and use of Wolffian manuals during these years.[44] The alliance lasted only a few semesters, however, and already by 1723 the Pietists, who favored Eclecticism, were fomenting unrest in what is known as the "Wolff case," an incident that had repercussions all over Prussia.[45] With a view to undermining Wolffianism, which was garnering support especially among the younger university professors, and contrasting the influence of the Aristotelians, in 1725 the King appointed two Pietists, Abraham Wolf and Georg Friedrich Rogall, as ordinary professors in the theological faculty.[46] Moreover, in 1726, Heinrich Lysius introduced a new statute for Königsberg University, which further marginalized the Wolffians.[47] The core claims of Lysius's reform were the centrality of the Bible and fierce opposition to Wolffianism. Philosophy itself was subordinated to the teaching of the Bible, dogmatics, ethics, and catechism.

The outcome of this Pietist development in the university *curricula* was, on the one hand, the banishment of Wolffians such as Fischer, on the other hand, the widespread use and dissemination of Eclectic authors favored by Pietists. Eclectic textbooks such as those of Thomasius and Budde, previously completely unknown in Königsberg, quickly became very popular. The advent of Pietism in Königsberg, delayed by at least twenty years compared to Halle, resulted in the predominance of Eclecticism.[48]

The two marginalized philosophical movements, Aristotelianism and Wolffianism, were quick to forge an alliance under the leadership of Quandt and rally against the Pietists. The King intervened to resolve the acrimonious situation, appointing Franz Albert Schultz as mediator. Himself a Pietist with a Wolffian past, having once been a pupil of Wolff's in Halle, Schultz's influence on Kant is still a matter of intense debate, but there is no doubt that he played an important role in molding the young philosopher, steering him in his early studies toward a certain kind of Eclecticism.[49]

The Wolffians never recovered their influence, even when the Pietist ban on Wolffian philosophy was lifted in 1740 with the coronation of Frederick II: no Wolffian was appointed as professor, and no ordinary professor could openly proclaim himself a Wolffian.[50] Nonetheless, after 1740, we see that Wolffian texts began increasingly to be used in university courses.

Different was the situation of the Aristotelians, who, though marginalized, had not been banned, and continued to profess their doctrines, albeit filtered through the Eclectic perspective. The result was a rise of an Eclectic-Aristotelian movement, which found its highest expression in the two most important ordinary professors of logic and metaphysics at the Albertina, Rohde and Kypke. In particular, Kypke's influence on the young Kant was not only academic and doctrinal, but also, as already mentioned, personal, Kant having resided as a guest for a period of time in Kypke's house.[51] In the wake of the Eclectic-Aristotelian movement, professors reclaimed Protestant Scholastic philosophy, as represented for instance by Franz Albert Aepinus, which was contrary to Wolffian theological rationalism.

An interesting perspective for a considered analysis of the philosophical setting in Königsberg during the 1720s is that of Rohde, who, in his academic program titled *Meditatio philosophica*, attempted to give an Eclectic reading of Aristotelianism.[52] It is reasonable to assume that the Pietists were more comfortable with a harmless and conservative philosophy such as that of Aristotle than with Wolffianism. Both Pietists and Aristotelians rejected modern science and its philosophical approach. Unlike in Halle, where Eclecticism spread in reaction to Wolffianism and the influence its exponents enjoyed, in Königsberg Eclecticism established itself for a specific philosophical reason, namely to find an agreement between Aristotle and Pietist doctrines without remaining dogmatically closed within his philosophical system.

The Pietists controlled Königsberg University at least until Frederick II's coronation, but even after 1740 their influence was strong. Even so, the lecture catalogs for the 1740s and the '50s, the period when Kant was a student, reveal a renewed interest in Wolffian textbooks such as those of Friedrich Christian Baumeister, Ludwig

Thümmig, and Alexander Gottlieb Baumgarten.[53] There is no exaggeration in speaking of a genuine renaissance for Wolffianism, but once again it lacked a leader. It also bears mentioning that this revival was mediated by a reappraisal of Leibnizian philosophy, such as contained in the works of Marquardt and Knutzen, which explains also the wide and rapid dissemination of Baumgarten's textbooks. Wolffianism in Königsberg in the 1740s, was without question a pale shadow of the philosophical movement that had established itself in the early 1720s giving rise to numerous conflicts and controversies: hence, in its distorted, weakened state, it no longer constituted a threat to the Pietists. Meanwhile, English empiricists such as Locke were gaining popularity, and by the end of 1750s the works of Christian August Crusius were enjoying great success.[54]

Königsberg was undoubtedly one of the foremost Lockean schools in Germany, although Locke's doctrines had been in circulation already for some time, largely in a summarized form in Eclectic manuals. Furthermore, second-generation Wolffian textbooks also incorporated Lockean ideas and doctrines.[55] Locke's philosophy became so important that Knutzen sought to reconcile English empiricism with Wolffian philosophy. He also undertook a new translation of Locke's works that death prevented him from finishing.[56] His project was brought to completion by Georg David Kypke, one of Kant's best friends, who translated *Of the Conduct of the Understanding*. Further impetus to this philosophical movement came from Frederick II's decree in 1770 requiring the study of Locke's *Essay* in Prussian universities, despite the fact that no university course in Königsberg was devoted to it.

Crusius gave rise to a powerful philosophical school in Königsberg, which lasted for at least a decade, from the end of the 1750s to the end of the 1760s, whose main exponents were Friedrich Johann Buck and Daniel Weymann. Far from being simply a philosophical movement opposed to Wolff's philosophy, as Wundt argues,[57] the Crusian school, with its peculiar blend of Eclecticism and English empiricism, offered a genuine alternative. Kant was to some extent influenced by it at least up to 1756, thanks also to the predominance of the Berlin Academy, which favored Crusians over Wolffians.[58] But Kant distanced himself from Crusian philosophy as early as 1759, when Buck took over the chair of logic and metaphysics from him, and when the controversy on optimism with Daniel Weymann began.[59]

The Berlin Academy became particularly influential in Königsberg during the 1760s under the leadership of Pierre-Louis Moureau de Maupertuis, who was firmly opposed to Wolffianism and open to the ideas of the *Lumiéres* and of the French philosophers, as the dissemination of the works of Jean-Jacques Rousseau and Jullien Offray de La Mettrie testifies.

To conclude, in the 1720s, after an early dissemination of Wolffianism, Pietism became dominant, favoring Eclecticism, which included among its exponents the Aristotelians. Eclecticism did not undermine religious authority, being directed primarily toward the investigation of philosophical truth, and overlooking theological issues. The eclectic approach of the Pietists promoted philosophical perspectives opposed to Wolffianism, which, despite something of a comeback in the 1740s and '50s, never again won much support. Meanwhile, Lockean and Crusian philosophy, thanks also to the support of the Berlin Academy, won widespread acclaim at the expense of Wolffian rationalist doctrines, especially among the younger faculty members.

Pietism had the merit of promoting a secular eclectic philosophy and bracketing metaphysical and theological problems that might involve questions of faith. Taking this perspective, Königsberg Pietism encouraged Kant to seek his own "philosophy," in other words, an eclectic philosophy that would "critically" examine all the arguments of the various philosophical movements. The "freedom" accorded by the Pietists, in my opinion, goes some way to explain both the readiness to accept and the receptivity toward new philosophical doctrines in academic circles, as well as the survival of old schools such as Aristotelianism. Baumgarten and Meier themselves, usually considered champions of Wolffianism, were thought of as eclectic philosophers. Indeed, the former acknowledged his indebtedness not only to Wolff, but also to Protestant scholastic philosophers such as Maier, Calov, and Aepinus, while the latter supported clearly heterodox Wolffian positions.[60]

If we look at the Königsberg professors, we see that up until the mid-1720s, Aristotelianism held sway in the university. It was later joined by Eclecticism and, for a short period of time, Wolffianism. Eclecticism, favored by Pietism, took control in the second half of the 1720s, and held it until the second half of the 1740s. Only subsequently was there a significant revival of Wolffianism, yet, as we have seen, Wolffianism never became a dominant movement within the university. The Pietist ban on Wolffian philosophy in a Pietist university and intellectual setting could not but have a profound impact. What is more, of the four professors who were very close to Kant, Kypke and Georg Gottfried Teske defined themselves as Aristotelians, while Karl Gottlieb Marquardt and Martin Knutzen were extremely well-versed in Aristotelian doctrines.

What has all this to do with Kant and his philosophical development? Shedding light on these elements helps us understand how during his college and university years Kant received an eclectic education and acquired a broad knowledge of the multifarious logical and metaphysical positions. His numerous precritical attempts must be seen in the light of the different stimuli to which he was exposed, and about which he would have been called on to form an opinion before taking any serious stance with regard to them. Any study of his early writings must include this varied cultural context, which in fact, in my view, greatly enhances their value and goes a long way toward justifying Kant's philosophical positions. In the following chapters, I will show that all the signs of the struggles between the various philosophical movements are there in Kant's early writings, and I will seek to explain how the Kantian position can be considered "Eclectic and anti-Wolffian,"[61] not on the basis of specific theoretical assumptions, but moving from this context of controversy among schools.

PROSPECTUS

In chapter 1, I contextualize Kant's facultative logic within the Aristotelian tradition. Kant denies that facultative logic can be based on the philosophical attempts of John Locke and Nicolas Malebranche, who were more concerned with psychology or metaphysics. In the first section, I examine facultative logic in Aristotle and the Aristotelian tradition with particular reference to Zabarella and the rise of gnostology and noology. In the second section, I show that Kant can be considered as a part of this philosophical Aristotelian tradition from the time of his early writings up to the *Critique of Pure Reason*. In the third section, I examine Kant's relation to the so-called discipline of physiology, characterizing his Kantian categories as a habit of the mind characteristic of the Aristotelian tradition. In Kant's *Critique of*

Pure Reason there is no general survey of the formation of concepts, for logic deals only with their transcendental use. He narrows his inquiry into the genesis of the structures of the mind to physiology, whose key historical figures were, in his view, Aristotle and Locke. The frequent appeal to physiology explains the recurring metaphors relating to the human mind as an epigenetic system. This is possible because, as we shall see, transcendental logic is grounded in facultative logic, that is a natural acquired logic, which is not a part of the critical investigation but is in fact its actual presupposition. I briefly reconstruct Aristotle's theory of habits in the *Nicomachean Ethics* and its reception in the Aristotelian tradition. Then I focus on the same problem in the Wolffian school. Such a reconstruction serves to characterize the origin of Kant's notion of pure concepts of understanding as acquired concepts. I compare Kant's ideas with those of Locke and Leibniz on the polemic against innatism, especially as regards the controversy with Eberhard.

Chapter 2 is divided into three sections. The first section of the chapter deals with two fundamental concepts of Kantian epistemology, namely the matter and form of knowledge, and outlines their Aristotelian origin. I start by examining the conception of the matter and form of knowledge in the Aristotelian tradition, focusing particularly on the meaning of the conceptual pairs of things considered (*res considerata*) and the way of considering (*modus considerandi*) in Zabarella. Then I move on to investigate the reception of the doctrine in Leibniz, in the Wolffian school and in Königsberg Aristotelianism. Finally, I reconstruct the philosophical significance of this conception in Kant's precritical philosophy and in the transcendental aesthetic and logic of his later years. The forms of knowledge, that is, the way of considering things (*modus considerandi*), are pure intuitions and categories. The second section concerns Kant's appropriation of the Aristotelian syllogism and doctrine of categories. I begin by investigating Kantian positions on syllogistic and Leibnizian combinatorics, and then go on to show how from the failure of a syllogistic and combinatorics Kant elaborated his doctrine of categories. In particular, I suggest that Kant's reawakening from a dogmatic slumber is connected with his rediscovery of Aristotelian categories. Once having established the nature of the categories, I argue that Kant's conception of categories and schema comes from the nominalistic interpretation of categories elaborated by Königsberg

Aristotelianism, and in particular by Rabe. In the third part, I show the reason why Kant divided transcendental logic into analytic and dialectic, and why the former precedes the latter. In particular, I emphasize the epistemological value of analytic and dialectic for Aristotle. Then I suggest the hypothesis that, in the slipstream of the Königsberg Aristotelian tradition, the analytic of concepts corresponds to gnostology, while the analytic of principles corresponds to noology. More specifically, I demonstrate Rabe's influence on Kant's conception of analytic and dialectic in conceiving the former as the logic of concepts and principles and the latter as the logic of probability, or logic of illusion.

Chapter 3 examines Kant's methodological doctrines in the precritical period, shedding some light on the Königsberg Aristotelian school of methodology and the conceptions of the moderns, the Wolffians in particular. From the failure of mathematics as a descriptive tool of reality, Kant makes his first attempts at developing a methodology, leading up to the *Critique of Pure Reason*. In the second section of the chapter, I analyze the methodological elements of the *Critique of Pure Reason*, focusing in particular on the influence of Abraham Calov on Kant's "Doctrine of Method." In this chapter, I devote some space to the examination of the methodological distinction between arguments κατ' ἄνθρωπον and κατ' ἀλήθειαν.

In the conclusion, I show how the failure of the precritical logical and metaphysical projects prompted Kant to develop the *Critique of Pure Reason*. I then summarize briefly the result of my research, thereby providing justification for my thesis that Kant's work must be included within the Aristotelian tradition.

As this prospectus makes clear, I do not proceed by extrinsically comparing Kant with Aristotle. This would be a merely theoretical exercise, which has sometimes produced misleading results. I have tried as far as possible to reconstruct all the most important passages illustrating the transmission of ideas from Aristotle to Kant. Of course, it is not possible to outline the entire history of the doctrine of categories, or the division of logic into analytic and dialectic. I have considered the main turning points in the history of philosophy and Kant's possible sources: only in this way is it possible to understand how Kant received Aristotle's doctrines and then went on to re-elaborate them for his own philosophical purposes.

1

FACULTATIVE LOGIC

THE OPERATIONS OF THE MIND

Facultative logic has been defined as the science of "the principles of the habituated regulation of the mind in the apprehension of truth and the acquisition of knowledge and properly grounded opinion."[1] Although divided on the question of identifying its origin, scholars generally agree that it is a new early-modern conception of logic. Its rise, for James Buickerood, may be traced to the publication of John Locke's *Essay Concerning Human Understanding* (1689), in which the ideas were the result, the product of the operations of the human cognitive faculties of perception, imagination, memory, and judgment in their relation to the world.[2] This opinion is supported also by Paul Schuurman, who nevertheless stresses the importance of Malebranche as the first philosopher to build a new logic around human cognitive faculties,[3] and René Descartes, who provided the basis and first principles, but left it to his followers to apply his new insights in the field of facultative logic.[4] Instead, Sylvain Auroux and Frederick S. Michael trace the birth of facultative logic back to the *Logique de Port-Royal* (1662).[5] Logic, according to Antoine Arnauld and Pierre Nicole, consists in the "reflections of men on the four operations of mind, conceiving, judging, reasoning and ordering."[6] Facultative logic thus concerns the operations of mind, serving to rightly conduct human reason to the knowledge of things. A closer view, however, shows that this conception comes from Bartholomeus Keckermann's *Systema Logicae* (1601), where logic is defined as the "art of directing mind in the cognition of things," in particular, in "understanding, knowing, and thinking,"[7] which in turn is derived from Renaissance Aristotelians, in particular from Jacopo Zabarella's logical writings. For this reason, in this chapter I propose to contextualize the origin of facultative logic within the Aristotelian tradition. The subjects of facultative logic are concepts rather than terms, judgments rather than propositions, reasonings rather than syllogisms.[8] It emerged from the combination of psychology and logic at the end of the sixteenth century, departing from Scholastic syllogistic.[9]

In this sense, facultative logic differs from both "epistemic logic" and the "logic of ideas." "Epistemic logic" does not cover the psychological dimension of the problem of knowledge, rather it "has to do with necessary and sufficient conditions of knowing and with the inferential relations involving epistemic and other propositional-attitude statements."[10] The "logic of ideas," on the other hand, concerns the various possible combinations among the manifold mental contents, rather than the certainty and the truth of the discourse, as epistemic logic does.[11] Instead, facultative logic is concerned with the origin and the logical use of the natural powers of the mind in knowing an object. It was born from the discussions on the theory of habits, especially the habit of understanding, which became the main faculty of the human mind for knowledge, namely, that which differentiates human beings from animals.[12] In particular, I support the provocative thesis that the real Copernican revolution in the field of epistemology was possible only from a reconsideration of Aristotelian logic in early modernity with a new understanding of the dialectic between the knowing subject and the known object. In this chapter, I would like to suggest the impact of this revolution on Kant's logic.

There was no genuine facultative logic in Ancient Greece because, to start with, there was no corresponding concept to that of "faculty." The term most widely used to define it, δύναμις, denoted in a most meaningful way a force more than a capacity, for which at least an "intentional" activity of the subject is necessary.

In *Republic* IV, 440E, Plato deals with three parts of the soul: (1) the rational part, which thinks and suppresses the instincts; (2) the irrational or concupiscible part, which rules the impulses and needs;

and (3) the irascible part. Thereafter, in the fifth book, Plato outlines a distinction between two different cognitive powers or forces and their objects,[13] ἐπιστήμη and δόξα, "by which human beings are able to do what they are able to do."[14] Plato uses the term δύναμις to denote these kinds of cognitive faculties, but he often uses the cognitive verbs γιγνώσκω and νοέω in its place. Clearly Plato does not use terminology in a careful and technical way, but sometimes "he uses more than one term to refer to the same element in the theory, or the same term to refer to different elements in the theory."[15]

In Aristotle, things change quite drastically. First of all, Aristotle does not deal with parts, but with functions of the soul: vegetative, sensible, rational, and locomotive. All these functions have in themselves a characteristic force thanks to which the human being can grow, sense, think, and move. Only the rational part of the soul, however, is properly called "faculty." Aristotle in fact states that "to think depends on the subject, when it wants to exercise his knowledge, but sensation does not depend upon itself because a sensible object must be there."[16] Imagination itself, which mediates knowledge between sensation and understanding, is a force, not a faculty. On the one hand, Aristotle states, imagination "is not of the same kind of thought of apprehension,"[17] because it does not depend totally on the subject but on the affection of the sensation; on the other hand, however, it seems to involve active thought.[18] Imagination is properly a force or disposition in virtue of which human beings discern and judge whether something is erroneous or not, and is not of the kind of sense, opinion, science, intelligence.[19] Imagination cannot be sensation, because sensation is in all animals, whereas imagination is not. It is neither science nor intelligence, because these are always true, while imagination can be false. Imagination cannot be opinion because it is in some animal, while opinion is not. It must be a force, that is "a movement resulting from an actual exercise of a power of senses."[20]

If facultative logic in Aristotle was not primarily concerned with either sensation nor imagination, it would deal with the understanding. In *On the Soul*, however, Aristotle describes physiologically how the sensible object becomes intelligible, and he outlines only a few epistemological reflections. Kant himself defines Aristotle's attempt as a kind of physiology, which is akin to Locke's standpoint, as we will see later in this chapter (17: 554).

The only place in the entire Aristotelian corpus where an attempt at drafting a facultative logic is made is the thirty-nine lines in *Posterior Analytics*, II.19.[21] Aristotle states that there "exists a discriminative innate force in all animals that is sensation."[22] Sensibles then, Aristotle adds, in some animals, rest in the mind. If sensibles do not rest in the mind for these animals, there is no other knowledge than the sensible one. In other animals, the sensible object rests in the mind, and after various sensations a kind of conceptualization is possible. From this kind of sensation originates memory and, subsequently, experience. From experience a general concept (καθόλου) is formed that rests in the mind. In this way, it is possible to acquire the disposition for scientific knowledge. The mental process, which infers from the various particulars to what is the same in all of them, is a kind of induction (ἐπαγωγή). The mental process of assent to the product of this induction is called intellection (νοεῖν). The process of acquiring general concepts and principles is therefore twofold: on the one hand, we have the formation of knowledge, which relies on experience and is mainly discursive; then, on the other hand, we have the actual cognition, which is a kind of an intuitive act of grasping what is given and generated by experience. The inductive process is necessary for the cognition of immediate and first principles, from which every scientific demonstration begins, and which is at the outset qualitatively different from the cognition after the conclusions of the demonstration. This marks a passage from a general indeterminate concept to a determinate universal concept. In fact, the formation and intellection of general concepts and principles produces only temporary knowledge, which must be proven discursively by means of demonstration to make of it scientific knowledge.

Aristotle's "facultative logic" plays with the discriminative force of sensation and with memory, on the one hand, and on the other hand, with understanding, so as to determine how sensible knowledge could become universal and epistemic. Aristotle's brief outline of facultative logic was almost the only example in the Aristotelian tradition until the Renaissance on which the Greek commentators first, and then the medieval thinkers, based their investigations. The question of the *intellectus adeptus*, *acquisitus*, and *speculativus*, for example, first outlined by Alexander of Aphrodisias and then fully developed by Averroes, is a development of Aristotle's theory of the understanding.[23]

In Germany, the problem of facultative logic in the Renaissance reemerges with Philipp Melanchthon and his *Liber de anima*. Melanchthon writes that the mind is usually credited with three operations: (1) simple apprehension; (2) composition and division; and (3) discourse.[24] They correspond, within the Aristotelian canon, to (1) induction (simple term); (2) synthesis and analysis (proposition); and (3) reasoning (syllogism). Melanchthon then specifies in detail all the operations of the mind. They are simple cognition, enumeration, composition and division, reasoning (complex logical inferences), memory, and judgment.[25]

Melanchthon's legacy in German Scholastic philosophy is long lasting and is even very vivid in Kant's *Critique of Pure Reason* and logic lectures, so much so, in fact, that Brandt writes: Kant "will employ the concept of consciousness in his long-standing search for the proper form of logic. However, in the edition of 1781, Kant no longer speaks of consciousness, but rather of the Aristotelian tradition's *operationes mentis*."[26] Indeed, on closer examination, Kant's transcendental logic is modeled on the three operations of the mind. Transcendental logic, however, finds its parallel in general logic, therefore, "general logic is constructed on a plan that corresponds quite precisely with the division of the higher faculties of cognition. These are: **understanding, the power of judgment,** and **reason**. In its analytic that doctrine accordingly deals with **concepts, judgments,** and **inferences**, corresponding exactly to the functions and the order of those powers of the mind, which are comprehended under the broad designation of understanding in general."[27] Traces of Melanchthon's conception are scattered throughout the Kantian corpus. Again, in the *Critique of Pure Reason*, Kant establishes that the form, abstracting from the content (or matter) of cognition, has no other task than that "of analytically dividing the mere form of cognition into concepts, judgments, and inferences, and thereby achieving formal rules for all use of the understanding" (A 132–33/B 171–72). In *The Vienna Logic*, Kant asks himself: "how many operations of the mind are there? Response. Three. Simple apprehension, judgment, and inference" (24: 904). From *The Busolt Logic* we know that "logic has to do with the understanding: the *operationes mentis* were already divided by the ancients, that is: *apprehensio simplex* or *conceptus, iudicium et ratiocinium*" (24: 653). Kant clearly has the Aristotelian tradition in mind: "one should deal with the three operations of thought before inferences. This was the way strictly followed by Aristotle. Wolff left it" (24: 763).[28] Kant could read Melanchthon directly, however, his nearest available source being Martin Knutzen's logic, which clearly establishes that: "there are only three fundamental operations of the mind or of understanding. The first one is simple apprehension, the second one is judgment and the third is reasoning."[29] However, as we will see, Kant could read this partition in many other eighteenth-century logicians such as Baumgarten, Crusius, and Reimarus. Nonetheless the fact that he recognizes that his classification belongs to Aristotle allows us to surmise that his reference was the Königsberg Aristotelians.

On the tripartition of the cognitive faculties of Melanchthonian derivation Kant founded his attempt to build up a logic as science that could identify the laws of the mind in an exhaustive system.[30] Thus, in Kant, the system of the forms of logic is nothing other than a reflection of the natural system of the forms of thought, which is for him immediately evident, rendering superfluous any further attempt at analysis and foundation.[31] Kant defends this thesis in *The Blomberg Logic*, where he aims not only to found logic on the natural operations of the mind, but also his philosophical system on mental processes (24: 31), as we may see also from the above mentioned passage from the *Critique of Pure Reason* (A 130/B 169).

His attempt to build up an entire philosophical system on cognitive faculties also in the critical period is manifest in "Introduction" to the *Critique of the Power of Judgment*, where Kant structures his philosophy according to the three inferences of the mind: concept, judgment, and syllogism.[32] Reinhard Brandt maintains that facultative logic is pivotal to understanding Kant's transcendental logic, indeed the three operations of the mind are recognizable in the table of judgments and constitute its deduction: "the triad of quantity, quality, and relation refers to the *tres operationes* of the understanding: the doctrines of concepts, judgments, and inferences, to which the doctrine of method is added as a fourth member."[33] Erich Adickes also suggests that "Kant's enterprise was an investigation on human cognitive faculties [. . .] a logic of the research of cognitive activities."[34] This perspective, however, seems to suggest an identification between natural logic, namely, the logic of inborn faculties of the mind, and formal logic, which one can question.[35] In this chapter, we shall see that general or formal logic does not coincide with natural logic, but the former is *based on* a particular kind of natural logic that Kant calls physiology of the mind, whose main theoretical reference is Locke, and which has to do with the origin of the logical elements, not with their use. Kant divides the origin and use of logical elements, and in this way can separate natural logic from both general and transcendental logic.

GNOSTOLOGY AND NOOLOGY

Besides Melanchthon, the Paduan Jacopo Zabarella was the Aristotelian logician who made the most important contribution to the rise of facultative logic. His writings on the cognitive powers of the mind such as *De sensu agente, De mente humana, De specibus intelligibilibus,* and *De ordine intelligendi* were very popular in Germany. Probably the most significant book in developing this new logic is the *Liber de tribus praecognitis*. This book deals with the conditions of the mind in acquiring scientific knowledge as exposed by Aristotle in *Posterior Analytics*. According to Zabarella, the object of speculative science is twofold. The first part, the material one, is the *res considerata*, while the second part, the formal one, is the *modus considerandi*. Since in the Aristotelian framework science deals only with necessary things, while matter is always contingent and accidental, science is concerned only with the form, that is the *modus considerandi*, which is a priori to the object of knowledge (*res considerata*) and makes it knowable, whatever it is.[36] The investigation of the science is therefore for Zabarella an inquiry into the condition of possibility of cognition in relation to a possible object in general. The conditions of possibility of a cognition are what Zabarella calls precognitions (*praecognita*). Since the speculative science is preceded by precognition, to investigate the condition of possibility of cognition of an object means simply to investigate this kind of precognition. But again, precognition, on which the speculative science is based, cannot be accidental, otherwise scientific knowledge would ultimately be accidental too. Precognition must be grounded in first, true, and immediate principles, in other words logical principles that make cognition possible. Investigating the condition of possibility of a cognition in general means, therefore, to investigate the first principles of sciences.

There are various first principles that are not demonstrable but are used in demonstrations, like syllogisms.[37] In relation to precognition, first principles are of two kinds: (1) supposition or hypotheses, if they deal with the "that is"; and (2) definitions, if they deal with the "what is."[38] Principles can be either *principia cognoscendi* or *principia essendi*. *Principia cognoscendi* are those propositions that are not cognizable in themselves, and are hypotheses insofar as they are special requirements of scientific argumentation.[39] *Principia essendi*, on the other hand, are not propositions, but rather principles that are unknown at the beginning and the object of the discovery.[40] In the history of facultative logic, *principia cognoscendi* play a key role at the start of the seventeenth century, characterizing the subjectivity of the mind in cognition.

The early reception of Zabarella's *Liber de tribus praecognitis* is evident in Johann Heinrich Alsted's *Philosophia digne restituta: Libros quatuor praecognitorum philosophicorum complectens* (1612), which is divided into four books titled respectively, *Archeologia, Hexiologia, Technologia*, and *Canonica*.[41] In particular, the second book, which is devoted to *Hexiologia*, that is, the doctrine of intellectual habits, makes use of Zabarella's ideas. The problem of precognitions and principles in Alsted relates directly to the habit of understanding. Understanding is, Alsted states, "contemplative habit by means of which we are inclined to assent firmly and evidently to first principles."[42] In particular, Alsted recognizes two kinds of understanding, natural or acquired. Natural understanding concerns the immediate grasping of the first, common, evident, and immediate propositions, concepts, and principles. It is characterized by the act of intellection, which knows directly and intuitively intelligible species; while acquired understanding, which is the real habit, concerns a kind of second nature that the mind attained through experience, and has to do with the formation of universals, or general principles, rather than their cognition. The process described by Aristotle in *Posterior Analytics*, II.19, is therefore twofold for early-modern Aristotelians, and encompasses both the formation and grasping of universal concepts and principles. But Alsted's originality in the history of logic, unlike Zabarella and many other contemporary Aristotelians, is his awareness of the autonomy of the science of cognitive faculties and his invention of a new science such as *hexiologia*.

In the wake of Zabarella and Alsted's ideas, in the Lutheran regions the development of facultative logic is connected with the elaboration of the doctrine of the habits and with the foundation of two new disciplines: gnostology and noology. In the gnostological tradition, the first important work is Georg Gutke's, *Habitus primorum principiorum seu Intelligentia* (1625),[43] which is a single treatment of Alsted's *Hexiologia* devoted only to "understanding," and a reelaboration of Zabarellean logic. After Gutke, in 1631, Valentin Fromme published his *Gnostologia*,[44] which exercised a powerful influence in Northern Germany, especially on Abraham Calov.[45] It is a remarkable fact that gnostological doctrines were particularly widespread, as we have seen in the previous chapters, at Königsberg University. The early reception of gnostology in Königsberg was due to Lorenz Weger, who dealt with facultative logic in his courses in the faculty of philosophy. His lectures were collected in 1630 into the volume *Prima mentis operatio*, in which he focuses in particular on the operation of apprehension, which is in his eyes the process of formation of universal concepts and principles, rather than intellection itself.[46]

However, Abraham Calov was the first to elaborate an organic system of metaphysical sciences introducing disciplines in order to investigate the understanding as the habit of principles. The sciences of the habit of principles have as subject not only the principles themselves, but also the simple terms, which are known by experience. These two sciences are *gnostologia* and *noologia*.[47]

In Calov's words, gnostology is the science that concerns the mental habit that has to do with the cognizable qua cognizable,[48] in other words the science that has to do with the mode of knowing of an object in general. The object of gnostology is the cognizable (*cognoscibile*), and deals with the mind as habit in its manner of improving knowledge according to its natural powers.[49] Calov states that the cognizable differs from the intelligible, which is "all that is," and encompasses both the somewhat (*aliquid*) and the nothing (*nihil*).[50] The cognizable has instead always a representational ground; it has objective reality,[51] while the intelligible does not: "the object is a real concept . . . an intelligible (*noema*) is in a broader sense an object, since every object that is is an intelligible, but not every intelligible is an object. In fact, all that can be understood by the understanding is an intelligible, but to the object is still required another relation (*relatio*)."[52] For the intelligible to be cognizable it must have a relation with something else, which for Calov is a relation with an object of experience, that is, with a representation in the mind, just as for Kant the mere possible to be actual and real must be experienced. Gnostology for Calov thus becomes the science that establishes first of all the origin of knowledge and the difference between sensible and intelligible cognition, between what has a representational ground and what does not, between αἰσθητός and νοηματικός. Hence Calov sketches the distinction between what is cognizable, that is, representable, and what is thinkable, which is similar to the way Kant outlines the distinction between knowing and thinking in the *Critique of Pure Reason* (B 146). What is contradictory, according to Calov, is nonbeing, which is not, however, a pure nothing. It is in the realm of thought and intelligibility, but not in the realm of the cognizable. In this way, being coincides with the cognizable and the various transcendentals of being must refer to being as a cognizable.[53] Concerning the cognizable, quoting Zabarella, Calov says that it "contains two parts: (1) the thing considered, or the material part; (2) the mode of considering, or the formal part."[54] The cognizable can be considered materially, if it concerns the being of the object itself, or formally, if it concerns the way through which it is considered in the mind. In the former case, the cognizable characterizes the objective relation to the mind (*relatio*), and in a broader sense the content of the concept of the object. In the latter case, it is what specifies the very general abstractions and makes of the being the real "first cognizable" (*primum cognitum*).[55] The being as first cognizable is not a mere concept abstracted from matter, in fact, as we have seen: it always requires a representational ground, what is called an objective reality, that is an object (*objectum*) in front of the subject (*subjectum*). In this new conceptual framework, all the transcendental affections traditionally associated with the being are referred to a cognizable, to an object of cognition in general, and this is the radical novelty introduced by Calov in ontology, one that would allow the shift of the notion of "transcendental" from metaphysics to logic.[56] According to Calov, the affections of being are very general concepts that define the transcendental being (*ens transcendentale*).[57] Affections can be either united or disjunctive.[58] Of the first group we can posit perfection (*perfectio*), unity (*unitas*), truth (*veritas*), and goodness (*bonitas*), but also time (*duratio*) and space (*ubietas*), which have no relative opposites. Disjunctive transcendentals are determined by oppositions, for instance "necessary-contingent," "cause-effect," "permanent-succeeding," and many others. It is worth noting that from the Kantian standpoint, space and time are also transcendental forms without relative opposites, while categories are characterized by their disjunctivity, which is overcome only in the third category of each group. There is therefore a striking resemblance between Calov's conception of transcendentals and Kant's transcendental forms. Kant's table of categories itself seems to be modeled on the Scholastic list of disjunctive transcendentals of being, something that has never been noticed by the scholarship in spite of the numerous researches on the topic.

But what is remarkable in Calov is that *transcendental* does not designate a mere being, but a cognizable, therefore the transcendental characterizes all essential attributes without which the cognizable would not be the object of cognition. It is but a short step to Kant. While Calov's transcendentals are attributes of an objective reality, of a thing, even if represented in the mind, Kant's transcendental forms are attributes of the mind for cognizing objects. However, it is still true for Calov that a cognizable is always a cognizable for a mind, and even if transcendentals do not pertain directly to knower, rather to the known object, they always concern that formal part of the cognizable: the mode of considering of the mind, which is called, as we shall see in the next chapter, "pure function of the mind." In no way are transcendentals "supernatural things," as Tonelli suggested, confusing them with the transcendents. We must keep in mind that, for Calov, transcendental attributes did not denote a mere being, but a cognizable, that is the transcendental attributes without which the cognizable would not be the object of knowledge. It is evident that this formulation is extremely close to the Kantian perspective and, importantly, creates a shift in transcendental philosophy from the old metaphysics to the new transcendental logic.

Calov's identification of the cognizable and its exclusion of the intelligible object in the nonbeing (*non-ens*) from the field of gnostology and ontology is polemical against the Calvinist Clemens Timpler. Timpler established that ontology dealt with "all that is intelligible as it is understandable but by the light of human natural reason."[59] Calov's critique of Timpler is analogous to Kant's criticism against Christian Wolff in the "Remark to the Amphiboly":[60]

> The highest concept with which one is accustomed to begin a transcendental philosophy is usually the division between the possible and the impossible. But since every division presupposes a concept that is to be divided, a still higher one must be given, and this is the concept of an object in general (taken problematically, leaving undecided whether it is something or nothing). (A 290/B 346)

Kant attacks the Wolffian division of possible and impossible,[61] going back to the original concept of an "object in general," which in Calov's mind corresponds to the concept of being in general, before establishing whether it is a cognizable, or a mere intelligible. Kant's table of nothing seems modeled on Calov's ideas. The first kind of nothing of the Kantian table appears to be equivalent to Calov's non-being (*non-ens*) as intelligible. In fact, Kant writes that the concept to which no intuition can be given and is without a representational ground is nothing. It is a concept without object like the *noumena*; this is similar to the way Calov defines intelligibles. This explains why for both Calov and Kant it is not possible to have a science of the intelligibles, because in some sense they are nothing. Ontology is grounded for both authors on a real being, which always has a representational ground. For both Calov and Kant, the intelligible object can be, without a representational ground, of the same kind of nothing as the being of reason (*ens rationis*), even if the two are not the same. Furthermore, both Calov and Kant deny the possibility of having a science of the intelligible object, because its knowledge goes beyond the human faculties and pertains only to God: Calov says, "it is rash to know natural things beyond nature"[62] for the same reason endorsed by Kant, that is, that speculative reason cannot "make any progress in the sphere of the supersensible" (B XX–XXI).

On the other hand, noology does not deal with the cognizable, but with the mental habit from the use of which the mind acquires the first principles of knowledge (*principia cognoscendi*).[63] Calov mentions his two direct sources: (1) Gutke's *Intelligentia sive habitus primorum principiorum*, and (2) Alsted's *Archeologia*. Calov invokes also Melanchthon's distinction of the three operations of the mind: (1) simple apprehension; (2) composition and division; and (3) discourse. Simple apprehension is studied by gnostology and concerns the way through which we know sensible and intelligible objects.

Noology studies the second operation of the mind, which consists in the union of a predicate with a subject by means of a copula in order to formulate propositions. From these propositions issue principles and axioms, which are the proper object of noology. The *prima principia cognoscendi* are "the most common and known axioms, from which every our cognition, which from nature we can have, depends."[64] For this reason *prima principia cognoscendi* are the grounds of the book of nature (*liber naturae*), as we can read it. *Principia cognoscendi* are not principles and grounds of nature itself, but they are heuristic and explanatory devices to understand and know the world. Calov states that the book of nature differs from Scripture because reason and divine revelation are different. Consequently, we can have for Calov either supernatural (*supernaturalia*) or natural (*naturalia*) principles. Natural principles are in general definitions, hypotheses, and postulates.[65] There are two fundamental natural principles of noology. The first is the law of contradiction: "it is impossible for the same thing at the same time to be and not be"; the second, derived from the first, establishes that "at the same time it is impossible for the same thing to be and to be confused with the other things."[66] The second principle is a draft of the law of identity, because it deduces from the being of a thing its essence and therefore its impossibility to be confused with another object. A human—Calov exemplifies—is a rational animal, but if we do not consider its "being," that is what makes it what it is, that is its essence, or its specific difference, it will be confused with other beasts. In other words, a being because of its particular mode of being cannot be confused with another being, since the mode of being is proper to every being.[67]

In Königsberg, gnostology and noology were further developed by Eifler, who elaborates a precise distinction between general noology and special noology, which is only barely mentioned by Calov.[68] Regarding this distinction, Eifler defended two disputes titled *Noologiam generalem succincte proponens* and *Noologiam specialem succincte complectens*, later published in 1639 in the *Collegii philosophici*: the former deals with general principles of all sciences, while the latter with principles pertaining to particular sciences. In 1636, Eifler also directed Georg Nöbe's *De functionibus intellectus humani rectificandis ac dirigendis a logica*, in which the author suggested a criticism of the cognitive faculties for a correct use of the reason in the argumentations.[69] On this topic, Eifler also published his *Habitus intelligentiae disputatio* (1651) and his *Gnostica* (1653).

Calov's ideas also were followed by Georg Meier, who published his *Gnostologia* in 1662, and by Georg Wagner, who published his *Disputatio gnostologica* in 1670. In the faculty of theology too, Melchior Zeidler was interested in studying noology, and he published his *De noologia* in 1662 to establish it as an autonomous discipline.[70] Noology rapidly became the science of the principles of thought, a propaedeutic discipline necessary for any advancement in metaphysics.

The impact of gnostology and noology is not immediately evident in Kant, even if we can find some traces in his precritical works. In particular, in *Reflection 4163* (1769–1770), Kant uses the concept of "noology" to characterize the part of logic that is propaedeutic to metaphysics:

> All sciences of pure reason are either those that consider the rules of universal cognition in general through pure reason or the particular rules of pure reason themselves. *Logica. Phaenomenologia generalis, Noologia generalis* have as their end merely the rules of universal and non-empirical cognitions that are not given through any experience. Noology applied to that which is given through experience, although not through grounds of experience, is theoretical: metaphysics; or practical: morality. (17: 440)

This *Reflection* is evidence of Kant's acknowledgment of the continuity of his transcendental philosophy as propaedeutic to metaphysics with the Königsberg Aristotelian tradition of gnostology and noology. In fact, in this fragment, Kant conceives of general noology as the science that has to do with universal laws of cognition prior to any knowledge, exactly as the Königsberg Aristotelians did, and applied noology as the science of the principles of cognition of particular disciplines. Noology can therefore be theoretical or practical.[71] This distinction, as we have just recognized, comes from the Königsberg noological tradition, in particular from Eifler. The *Reflection* may be dated to around 1769–1770, during the period when Kant was conceiving his last Latin metaphysical work, his *Inaugural Dissertation On the Form and Principles of the Sensible and the Intelligible World*.

The main topic of this work was inspired by his attempt to solve the open questions of his *Dreams of a Spirit-Seer Elucidated by Dreams of Metaphysics*, that is the connection between the sensible and intelligible world. In particular, Kant's aim was to determine whether the subjective forms of cognition were the same for the sensible and intelligible world, and if both worlds were grounded in the same principles. In doing so, Kant was forced to define the objects of sensible and intelligible knowledge, and the subjective modes of investigation. In Kantian terms, it is necessary to determine the matter and the form of knowledge. In this sense, the subject of the *Inaugural Dissertation* is the cognizable (*cognoscibile qua tale*) and the mode of conceiving (*modus considerandi*) objects. Kant seems to merge the noological part of the first principles of metaphysics with the gnostological part, as we read in § 8:

> ... the philosophy which contains the first principles of the use of the pure understanding is metaphysics. But its propaedeutic science is that science which teaches the distinction between sensitive cognition and the cognition which derives from the understanding; it is of this science that I am offering a specimen in my present dissertation. Since, then empirical principles are not found in metaphysics, the concepts met with in metaphysics are not to be sought in the senses but in the very nature of the pure understanding, and that not as innate concepts but as concepts abstracted from the laws inherent in the mind (by attending to its action on the occasion of an experience), and therefore as acquired concepts. To this genus belong possibility, existence, necessity, substance, cause etc., together with their opposites or correlates. Such concepts never enter into any sensory representations as parts, and thus they could not be abstracted from such a representation in any way at all. (2: 395)

This passage is crucial to understanding Kant's transcendental philosophy as a transformation of the Königsberg Aristotelian tradition of gnostology and noology. It is clear for Kant that the philosophy of the first principles of pure understanding is metaphysics, or at least a part of it. As we have seen, in *Reflection 4163*, philosophy that deals with the first principles of metaphysics is noology, which in the Königsberg Aristotelian tradition was a part of metaphysics, namely, the introductory part that established the foundations of metaphysical thinking. In *What Real Progress Has Metaphysics Made in Germany Since the Time of Leibniz and Wolff?* Kant characterizes the science of the concepts and principles of the understanding as ontology (20: 260). Kant specifies that ontology is only a part of metaphysics and pertains to it only in a propaedeutic function, as a hallway or vestibule of metaphysics itself. It is a part of transcendental philosophy because it contains the conditions and the first elements of every a priori knowledge. Ontology is "a resolution of knowledge into the concepts that lie a priori in the understanding, and have their use in experience" (20: 260), namely what Kant calls "analytic" in the *Critique of Pure Reason*. Kant adds that there has not been much progress in the field of ontology since the days of Aristotle (20: 260), and in my opinion this statement shows that Kant had in mind the Königsberg Aristotelian tradition rather than Wolffian metaphysics, otherwise there would have been some advancement in this discipline. Kant's variegated terminology in defining these sciences in these years of troubled attempts reflects the multiplicity and ambiguity of the Königsberg Aristotelian tradition. Indeed, "the philosophy which contains the first principles of the use of the pure understanding" (2: 395) or "the rules of universal cognitions that are not given through any experience" (17: 440), as Kant would say, is noology, and was considered by Königsberg Aristotelians like Calov as a part of ontology, as an introduction to metaphysics.[72]

In the Inaugural *Dissertation*, Kant pushes his argument further, pointing out that the subject-matter of metaphysics is not something that comes from experience, it is not an object, rather it pertains to pure understanding in its modes of knowing. Understanding knows by means of the forms that are modes of knowing (*modi cognoscendi*) objects. These forms, these *modi cognoscendi*, are not innate (*connati*) to the mind, rather they are acquired (*acquisiti*). And this, as we shall discuss in detail in the following pages, corresponds perfectly to gnostological elaborations, according to which the ways of grasping all possible objects (*modi apprehendendi quodcunque objectum*) constitute a mental habit (*habitus mentis*)—that is, they are acquired. A decade later, in the lectures on the philosophical encyclopedia, as well as in those on metaphysics, Kant returns to the topic stating that Plato was convinced that in the human mind there were traces of innate ideas, while Aristotle would teach the contrary. According to Kant, Locke followed Aristotle in supporting the view that all the concepts of the mind are acquired. Kant concludes, stating that "assuming something innate is decisively contrary to philosophy" (29: 16). This issue will be further developed, as we will see, in the *Critique of Pure Reason* and in other critical writings.

In *Reflection 4851*, dated to between 1776 and 1778, Kant divides metaphysics into general metaphysics (*metaphysica generalis*) and special metaphysics (*metaphysica specialis*), following the Protestant scholastic tradition.[73] General metaphysics deals with reason and its concepts, and coincides with transcendental philosophy, whose parts are ontology and the critique of pure reason (18: 9). In *Reflection 5130*, referring back to this division, Kant states that ontology is the science of the first elements of knowledge of the pure understanding, that is, concepts and judgments (18: 100).

In the *Critique of Pure Reason*, Kant's conception becomes more complicated. Kant calls "critique" the philosophy of pure reason that examines propaedeutically the faculty of reason in its possible a priori knowledge (A 841/B 869). It contains all the principles of knowing a priori, both sensible and intelligible. Kant adds that "an organon of pure reason would be a sum total of all those principles in accordance with which all pure a priori cognitions can be acquired and actually brought about" (A 11/B 24). An exhaustive application of such an organon would constitute for Kant "a system of pure reason" (A 11/B 25). This system, following Wolff, has four main parts: (1) ontology; (2) rational physiology; (3) rational cosmology; and (4) rational theology. Ontology corresponds to transcendental philosophy, which "considers only the understanding and reason itself in a system of all concepts and principles that are related to objects in general, without assuming objects that would be given" (A 845/B 873). The "critique" is propaedeutic to this system of pure reason, but its utility is only negative, because it serves not for the amplification but only for the purification of reason (A 11/B 25). The "critique of pure reason," as "critique," is not, according to Kant, a part of transcendental philosophy, or rather it is, but only in a propaedeutic role.

In the *Critique of Pure Reason*, therefore, what was gnostology for the Aristotelians becomes the part of transcendental philosophy that examines the a priori condition for the possibility of knowledge by understanding an object in general, that is, categories and principles.

Categories, indeed, correspond to the simple terms and concepts of gnostological tradition. In this sense, if we want to take the parallelism to its extreme, gnostology would coincide with the "Analytic of Concepts." Noology, on the other hand, in dealing with principles and axioms, would coincide with the "Analytic of Principles."

Kant's famous letter to Marcus Herz of February 21, 1772 already explained that the "analytic" was a part of metaphysics. The work, which should be titled *The Limits of Sensibility and of Reason*, would be composed in two parts, one theoretical and one practical. The theoretical part would be divided into a phenomenology, which in 1781 became transcendental aesthetic, and a metaphysics (10: 129). Most probably, in Kant's perspective, the part of metaphysics would have included not only "Analytic," but also the "Dialectic" and the "Doctrine of Method," if it is true that his purpose was to deal with the nature and the method of metaphysics (10: 129).

In Kant, it is quite evident that disciplines like gnostology and noology, which were a matter of metaphysics, gradually turn into a new kind of logic, and that metaphysics could not be anything more than a logic.

HABIT AND PHYSIOLOGY

If the nature of the structures of the mind is quite clear according to Kant's transcendental logic, then its origin is not so obvious. It is quite striking that to date Kantian scholarship has neglected to address this crucial question.[74] To understand Kant's position, it is necessary to investigate the very nature of the "a priori" in critical philosophy, and to dismantle the ideas that considered the "a priori" to be innate. This commonplace is based on false biases for at least two reasons that I shall explain in this section: (1) Kant was a fierce opponent of the doctrine of innate ideas; and (2) in his writings he characterizes the pure concepts of the understanding to be acquired, as we have already seen in the *Inaugural Dissertation*, where he outlines a theory of knowledge according to which a priori concepts are acquired from the logical laws of thought upon their application to the object of sensation.[75] Yet, one may wonder, what has all this to do with Aristotle and the Aristotelian tradition? I want to suggest that Kant's transcendental logic is based on a natural acquired logic, which is a kind of Aristotelian habit that the mind attains, like a second nature, in occasion of experience.

Aristotle deals with the problem of habit in the *Categories* in two distinct places, as a category itself and as a kind of quality.[76] Habit, Aristotle states, differs from disposition in that it is more stable and durable.[77] Dispositions, in fact, are easily removable and change quickly. But if a disposition stays long, takes root in the mind, and is hard to remove, it becomes a habit.[78] Consequently, we can say that for Aristotle all habits are dispositions, but not all dispositions are necessarily habits.[79] In *Rhetoric*, Aristotle maintains that a habit gives rise to all the actions that we do because we are used to doing them,[80] and he adds that "habit is something like nature, for the distance between 'often' and 'always' is not great, and nature belongs to the idea of 'always,' habit to that of 'often.'"[81]

The most important Aristotelian treatment of the theory of habits is in the *Nicomachean Ethics*. Aristotle characterizes five intellectual habits: (1) art; (2) science; (3) prudence; (4) wisdom; and (5) understanding.[82] Art and prudence relate respectively to production and action, whereas the habits involved in logic are science, understanding, and wisdom. For science, Aristotle means scientific knowledge, that is, the knowledge of what is known as necessary.[83] This kind of knowledge is possible only through demonstration, which must be based on true and well-known principles.[84] These principles are provided by the understanding.[85] Wisdom is both understanding and science of higher things, like causes and principles, because wisdom both knows what follows from the principles and possesses the truth about the principles.[86]

The reciprocal relations among science, understanding, and wisdom are developed by Aristotle in the final chapters of the *Posterior Analytics*, which we have already encountered as a crucial issue to understanding the genesis of facultative logic. According to Aristotle, wisdom is knowledge of true, higher, and superior things. Before knowing these things, however, we must know true things in general; that is, we must acquire scientific knowledge. Scientific knowledge is only possible through demonstration, but demonstration is based on principles, and only understanding gives assent to principles; therefore, for wisdom and scientific knowledge understanding is necessary. Thus, for Aristotle, understanding is the fundamental habit without which no science and no wisdom are possible, and the Aristotelian tradition has always recognized the importance and significance of this particular habit. We have already noted that during Antiquity and the Middle Ages, the theory of habits was strictly related to the problem of acquired or speculative understanding. But it is also true that the problem of acquired understanding has to do with a second nature which is not immediately coincident with either the habit of understanding or with science.[87] Rather, as Charles Lohr has rightly pointed out, the search for the principles of demonstration, that is, the twofold process of ἐπαγωγή and νοεῖν, was completely neglected by the Aristotelian tradition before the Italian Renaissance. It was Jacopo Zabarella who rediscovered these two moments by means of which principles are found and known.[88] It is therefore necessary to examine Zabarella's treatment of these habits and his deep impact on Königsberg Aristotelianism.

In Zabarella, the issue of habit arises essentially in response to two questions: on the one hand, to characterize the nature of logic, and, on the other hand, to determine the extent of demonstrative knowledge. Zabarella tackled the question of habit in his logical works, in particular in the *De natura logicae*, as well as in the last chapter of his commentary to *Posterior Analytics*. According to Zabarella, logic cannot be identified with any of the five intellectual habits listed by Aristotle, because it does not deal with the object either from a theoretical or from a practical standpoint. It is not science, because its objects are second notions (*notiones secundae*), which are not universal, necessary, or real.[89] It does not coincide with the habit of understanding or wisdom, because the former has to do with principles, the latter with the cognition of first causes,[90] while logic has to do only with the structure of reasoning. Neither is it an art, because it does not have the power to construct or modify its object.[91] Logic is not prudence, because prudence concerns actions, which are obviously not the object of logic.[92] Rather, the effectiveness of logic consists in serving the perfect acquisition of the other five intellectual habits. As such, it is the condition without which understanding, science, wisdom, prudence, and art are not possible. Zabarella, therefore, conceives of logic, like grammar and rhetoric, as an intellectual instrumental habit, just because it is a tool and means for all the other disciplines.[93]

Zabarella thematizes the habit of logic in connection with science, particularly in his commentary to *Posterior Analytics*. He deals in this work with the two main habits that presuppose logic, namely understanding and science. Understanding is the habit of the cognition of principles, while science is the habit of demonstration.[94] Zabarella states preliminarily that the habit of principles, as with all the other habits, is not innate, but comes from experience. However, it is a priori of every cognition according to the principles that it has acquired.[95] He explicitly states that the habit of principles is not inborn in us, but is accidental, and is acquired by experience. Principles are nonetheless considered to be a priori, and precognition for all other kinds of habit and cognition.[96] The formation of the habit of principles is described according to Aristotle. All knowledge comes from sensation, which is a kind of a power of judgment (*facultas iudicatrix*) that shows the differences among things. The method that proceeds from sensation to the acquisition of general concepts and principles is called induction.[97] Induction for Zabarella is clearly the means to acquire the habit of understanding, but it is not to be confused with the act of intellection. Induction in fact produces and makes cognizable general concepts and principles from experience, while intellection knows them in a clear and evident way. Induction is not a method for demonstrating something unknown from something already known, but rather it is the notification of the thing itself to the mind (*notificatio rei per se ipsam*). It presents and reflects sensible knowledge to the understanding and makes it intelligible. Sensible knowledge is therefore prior to any other cognition, but it is not the sole kind of knowledge: besides sensible, for Zabarella there is also intelligible or intellectual knowledge, which is the only knowledge properly speaking.[98] Thus, from Zabarella's standpoint, there is no doubt that all our cognition begins with experience, in fact our cognitive faculties are awakened by experience through the simulation of the senses, yet not all our cognitions arise from experience, since there is an essential contribution of the understanding in grounding scientific knowledge, first, in finding the first principles, and second, in making correct reasoning through demonstration. Zabarella's account of knowledge, therefore, is not very different from Kant's analysis of cognition in the "Introduction" of the *Critique of Pure Reason* (B 1).

Zabarella's theory of habits enjoyed, as we have seen, widespread success in Germany. We can count more than a dozen authors who were working on the doctrine of habits in the seventeenth century, such as Bartholomeus Keckermann, Clemens Timpler, Heinrich Nolle, Georg Gutke, Valentin Fromme, Michael Eifler, Georg Meier, Johann Geilfus, and Georg Wagner.[99]

As we saw in the previous section, however, it was Alsted who developed a first systematic theory of habits in his *Hexiologia*. Intellectual habits are defined by Alsted as that which arranges the mind in order to make cognition possible.[100] To every habit corresponds one and only one operation of the mind. Habits can be simple or mixed. Simple habits characterize an intellectual or volitional power. They are true or false. Among simple, true habits we can distinguish those that are necessary and those that are accidental. Among simple, true, and necessary habits, we can find natural habits or supernatural habits. Natural habits are either theoretical, practical, or productive. Theoretical habits (understanding, science, and wisdom), "which are inclined to assent to necessary things,"[101] concern logic. Understanding is "a contemplative habit which is inclined to assent firmly and evidently to first principles,"[102] as well as "the habit of principles, that is the intellectual power of determining the assent to firm and self-evident principles."[103] Understanding is necessary because the innate natural lumen, "which is the intellectual power itself,"[104] is not sufficient to assent to the first principles. First principles are grasped immediately, but they are not known scientifically, because they are indemonstrable and the premises of demonstration.[105] According to Alsted, the act of understanding is twofold: on the one hand, it is the apprehension of simple terms; on the other hand, it is a kind of judgment, or discriminative power, which recognizes the various things in experience with the help of sensation.[106] Instead, science is the habit that "is inclined to assent to necessary conclusions knowing the proper causes."[107] The habit of science differs from that of understanding because it concerns true and evident conclusions based on principles. Therefore the certainty of science comes from "the firm agreement with the object of the understanding without any doubt and fear."[108] Certainty can be true or apparent. Apparent certainty is when the "understanding from probable causes and an effective will, firmly adheres to the object." True certainty is when the "understanding according to the truth of things, or to solid and firm cause, or infallible authority, adheres to the object."[109] Alsted is influenced by Timpler and, unlike Aristotle, states that a science of singular things is possible.[110] According to Aristotle, science is only that which is universal and necessary, and it is not possible to provide a demonstration of singular or accidental things. Yet, Protestant philosophers, in particular Calvinists like Alsted or Keckermann, wanted to ensure the scientific character of reasoning and theological conclusions, extending the scientific validity over the universal conclusions to the singular and historical facts dependent on divine providence, attesting to the validity of the Scriptures.[111] For Alsted not only is it possible to have a science of the nonbeing and of accidental things.[112] Wisdom is the habit that "is inclined to assent to necessary conclusions, according to first and higher causes."[113] Wisdom is the habit of metaphysics,[114] and it is also characterized as a "combined habit of understanding and science, that is, the habit of principles and conclusions."[115] Therefore, wisdom exceeds understanding and science in dignity, but it cannot exist without them.

In Lutheran Königsberg, the situation is quite different. The doctrine of habits plays a fundamental role in gnostology and noology. Against Alsted, Calov states that "*Hexiologia vainly imagines itself as an autonomous discipline*. For there no necessity compels us to accept the same, since all things pertaining to the habit they ought to be explained here [in gnostology]."[116] On the contrary, "*only to gnostology can be assigned the study of the constitution and division of the habit.*"[117] Like logic for Zabarella, Calov considers gnostology at once a habit and an instrumental discipline,[118] which has to do with the habit of the mind knowing an object perfectly.[119] A habit is something that comes to natural cognitive powers,[120] a "firm quality rooted in the mind for the perfection of the cognition of the object."[121]

In his gnostology, Calov makes a sharp distinction among the various possible objects of knowledge. To the cognizable and the intelligible, which we have already mentioned, Calov adds a third component: the knowable. The knowable (*scibile* or *contemplabile*) is a particular kind of cognizable that our mind understands by means of the causes.[122] Unlike cognizing, knowing characterizes, for Calov, the contemplation of necessary being (*ens necessarium*).[123] It therefore follows that the mind performs three peculiar operations: cognizing (*cognoscere*), understanding (*intelligere*), and knowing (*scire*). *Cognoscere* means to have or to acquire a cognition; *intelligere* means to understand or conceive of the object of knowledge directly; *scire* means to know scientifically or apodictically or discursively, by means of causes. On these operations Calov grounds a new system of philosophical disciplines: (1) gnostology deals with the cognizables, which have a representational ground; (2) noology concerns the intelligibles, but only if they are principles resulting from the combination of simple terms provided by gnostology to the understanding; (3) science is concerned with necessary things, which are known by means of demonstration on the basis of the principles provided by noology; and (4) metaphysics deals not only with necessary things, but in particular with those that are first and causes.

This system of science became a standard in the Lutheran intellectual framework of the seventeenth century, especially in Königsberg. Calov's treatment of the doctrines of habits within the investigation of human cognitive faculties became common in the first half of the eighteenth century, but lost its specificity as an autonomous discipline. Christian Wolff played a key role in this development, in particular for our understanding of Kant's philosophy. He dealt with habits in his *Psychologia empirica*, which soon became the discipline of facultative logic. Wolff's treatment differs markedly from the analysis of the Aristotelian tradition: none of the five intellectual habits is examined. Nonetheless, Wolff maintains the difference between disposition and habit.

A disposition is either natural, "if it exists in the nature of the mind without any previous exercise," or acquired, "if it exists in the mind only with a previous exercise."[124] The acquired disposition is specifically called habit, therefore a disposition becomes habit through exercise. In this context, Wolff includes very meaningfully a disquisition on a posteriori and a priori knowledge. A posteriori knowledge is given by experience,[125] while a priori knowledge is possible by means of the mere inborn faculty of thinking.[126] This leads to the conclusion that what is a priori depends on the innate faculty of thinking, and what is a posteriori depends on what is acquired. However, this is not true for Wolff. In fact, if it is true that what is a posteriori is knowable by sensation (if the object is external), or by apperception (if the object is internal), it is also true that our faculty of knowing a priori characterized by the operation of reasoning (*ratiocinatio*) is a habit.[127] A priori knowledge is given by the three operations of the mind, sketched by Melanchthon, namely *notio*, *judicium*, and *discursus* (or *ratiocinatio*). But the latter is not possible without the first two operations, which in the Königsberg

Aristotelian tradition were investigated by gnostology and noology. Taken together, these three operations of the mind characterize the activity of the understanding, which is itself considered a habit. In particular, understanding is a "habit of reasoning distinctly and of connecting arguments."[128] This specificity of understanding is characterized by Wolff as "solidity" (*soliditas*). In fact, only what is solid and firm possesses the habit of demonstrating and proving. Solidity, therefore, characterizes for Wolff the main aspect of science: "science is of who is solid and possesses firm doctrine."[129] This means that the main habit of the understanding as a faculty is science.

The main object of science is for Wolff, like Calov, the knowable (*scibile*). To explain the process of acquiring solidity, Wolff refers, even if not explicitly, to the Aristotelian doctrine of *Posterior Analytics*. Sensation is not sufficient for science, in fact, "we know as much as we save in memory."[130] Memory can be latent and cannot lead to knowledge, thus reproductive imagination is necessary to bring to light things that were forgotten.[131] Once sensible experience is in the mind, by means of images, it is possible to acquire new knowledge. Furthermore, the acquisition of this new knowledge is characterized by Wolff as a habit or an art of finding (*ars inveniendi*). In the philosophical tradition originating with Cicero and later developed by Renaissance scholars in particular, the *ars inveniendi* was a special logic the aim of which was to find new knowledge and truth. In Wolff, this logic becomes "the habit of collecting true unknown things from true known things."[132] If the object is a posteriori, the habit is an *ars inveniendi veritatem a posteriori*, while if the object is a priori, the habit is an *ars inveniendi veritatem a priori*.[133] The *ars inveniendi a posteriori* is necessarily based on something that is acquired either by experience or by observation,[134] while the *ars inveniendi a priori* is given by the a priori connection of notions and propositions by means of reasoning, without being occasioned by experience.[135] Only the latter is properly speaking the *ars inveniendi*. Wolff, however, points out that also the "true" *ars inveniendi a priori* is in a broader sense acquired, because it begins from acquired notions (*ex notionibus acquisitis*), on which judgments and arguments are made.

In sum, it is possible to say that the theory of habit in Wolff pertains to the study of cognitive faculties. Wolff characterizes understanding in all its facets as a habit which in its use determines scientific knowledge. Both a posteriori and a priori knowledge require as their essential condition the acquisition of this habit, which is a real logic for the exercise of the three operations of the mind.

Wolff's treatment of habit is not only confined to facultative logic, but also to the definition of logic itself, as one might expect.[136] Logic is the "science of directing the cognitive faculties in knowing truth,"[137] but science is nothing other than the habit of demonstration.[138] Logic is therefore the habit of demonstration that directs the cognitive faculties in knowing truth. In other words, like Zabarella, logic is conceived of as a habit. In § 5, following the Aristotelians, Wolff distinguishes habit from disposition using Calov's terminology: a certain natural disposition of the mind is given in directing its operations in knowing in conformity with its rules, a function that is better carried out by the habit, if the disposition is previously exercised.[139] Mind in its nature has innate dispositions that through exercise become habits. On the conceptual pair "disposition-habit," Wolff grounds his natural logic. We can speak of natural logic when a natural disposition that can lead to a habit directs the operations of the mind, namely, the cognitive faculty, in knowing truth.[140] Natural logic can be either innate natural logic or acquired natural logic.[141] The former has to do with natural dispositions in directing the operations of the mind, while the latter deals with habits in knowing truth. From this distinction, therefore, we can say that the former deals analytically and formally with the condition of possibility of the operations of the mind, while the latter deals with how these operations are directed in knowing truth and acquiring science.[142]

In Wolff, as we have noted, the habit characterizes the nature of understanding itself, which, far from being something inborn, or given by nature, in its use and its application to experience develops natural innate dispositions, transforming them into habit. In other words, in knowing truth the habits are a priori for the direction of the operations of the mind, even if they are acquired a posteriori in the exercise of the cognitive faculties on experience. For Wolff there is no identity between the a priori cognitive structure of the mind and the nature of the mind itself. The cognitive structure of the mind is always acquired by means of its real use. However, we must bear in mind that natural logic deals only confusedly and unconsciously with these logical issues of cognition, which are explained clearly by artificial logic. The only difference between natural logic and artificial logic, with the exception of clarity and distinctness, is the fact that the former deals with the ways in which the logical structures arise, which is why the conceptual pair "disposition-habit" comes into play, while the latter deals with these structures only according to their use in compliance with particular laws.

Wolff's doctrines were widespread and systematized in Wolffian textbooks, which were the basis of Kant's philosophical formation. For instance, in his *Institutiones philosophiae rationalis*, in the preliminary chapter on the nature of philosophy, Baumeister distinguishes an objective and systematic philosophy from a subjective and habitual philosophy. Only the latter is philosophy properly speaking. It consists in the habit of investigating things according to their sufficient reasons. According to Baumeister, a habit characterizes "promptitude according to which with less time or effort, than at other times are required, the causes of things are knowable."[143] The one who has this habit is a philosopher.[144] Subjective philosophy is eminently called the habit of philosophical cognition (*habitus cognitionis philosophicae*).[145] This habit cannot pertain to every human being, but the philosopher must be taught to attain this scientific knowledge, which is proper to philosophy.[146] Scientific knowledge is also a demonstrative habit.[147] What is interesting in Baumeister's treatment, and seems absent in Wolff's philosophy, is that there is a correspondence between the subjectivity of cognition and the acquisition of the habit. Science becomes in Baumeister eminently subjective, just because it is grounded in the habit, which is singular and pertains to the knowing subject. Without habit, subjectivity would not be possible, because otherwise logic would be based simply on the nature of the human being, which is by its essence the same for every being. Baumeister's position reflects his conception of logic, so much that, what knows distinctly according to laws of understanding is defined not only as artificial logic, but also as subjective and habitual: "artificial logic considered subjectively and habitually is nothing other than a science or a habit, distinctly of arguing and of applying rules distinctly, which direct the operations of the understanding in investigating and judging truth."[148] The strict relationship between natural acquired logic and artificial logic is quite clear: "artificial logic is essentially not different from natural logic."[149]

Alexander Gottlieb Baumgarten deals with the doctrine of habits in an innovative way in his *Metaphysica*. In § 577, Baumgarten does not hesitate to call habits the higher faculties of the mind that are acquired through exercise.[150] Baumgarten distinguishes the habits acquired (*acquisiti, erworbene*) by exercise (*Uebung*) from innate natural dispositions (*connati, angebohrne, dispositiones naturales*), which do not require exercise, and from supernatural infused habits (*göttliche Fertigkeiten der Seele*).[151] But which are the lower and the higher faculties of the mind? Among the lower faculties, Baumgarten mentions memory, reminiscence, *facultas fingendi*, foresight, and judgment. These faculties are not habits but innate natural dispositions.[152] The power of judgment has a particular place, because in its higher form it is a habit,[153] for the power of judgment can be (1) sensible, or (2) intellectual. In a broader sense the power of judgment is sensible and coincides with taste, and its discipline is called imprecisely "critique."[154] This kind of power of judgment is innate, while the intellectual power of judgment is a true habit and its discipline is called "critique" in general.[155] According to Baumgarten, therefore, the judgment that pertains to aesthetic is only an innate natural disposition, while that which pertains to logic strictly speaking is a habit. Baumgarten revives the Aristotelian distinction between sensations as a discriminative power and understanding as the power of making judgments.

The problem of the nature of logic as habit, that is something acquired and not innate, is developed by Georg Friedrich Meier in his *Vernunftlehre*. Meier explains the difference between natural logic and artificial logic by means of the conceptual pair "native wit-schooled wit" (*Mutterwitz-Schulwitz*), which Kant uses in *The Blomberg Logic*. Logic as science is called artificial logic or schooled wit. Native wit, on the other hand, concerns innate, natural logic. The unconscious use of native wit leads understanding and reason to develop an acquired natural logic.[156] Between natural logic and artificial logic, as was the case for Baumeister, there is no real difference, if not in the clearer or more confused knowledge of the logical laws. Meier seems to emphasize more the former than the latter: (1) native wit and schooled wit do not contrast with each other; (2) without native wit, artificial logic is not possible; (3) without native wit, it is not possible to learn and to exercise the laws of artificial logic; (4) without schooled wit, it is possible to reason, while without native wit, it is impossible; (5) without artificial logic and with only native wit, scientific knowledge is possible; and (6) artificial logic is a completion of native wit.[157]

In § 533 of the *Auszug*, Meier summarizes his position:

native wit is called innate natural logic (*logica naturalis connata*), science is knowledge and erudite exposition of schooled wit, or artificial logic (*logica artificialis*). Indistinct knowledge of the laws of native wit and the capacity to follow them, which is attained through the mere use of native wit, is called acquired natural logic (*logica naturalis acquisita theoretica et practica*), and it is ascribable to native wit in the a broader sense.[158]

The main features of the doctrine of habits of the Wolffian school, with which Kant was acquainted, were: (1) there is an "a priori," not innate, but acquired in the form of a habit; (2) the habit concerns the *formation* of the logical structures of understanding in their use, not the actual *use* of this structure; (3) logic, which deals with the formal structures of understanding in their use by laws in knowing the truth, is subjective because it is based on the habit; (4) there is correspondence between habit and subjectivity; and (5) the habit pertains only to the higher faculties and not to the lower faculties.

Kant takes advantage of these reflections on the problem of habit and its relation to cognitive faculties at the end of the 1760s, in conjunction with the draft of the *Inaugural Dissertation*. As we have seen in § 8, after his definition of metaphysics as the science of the first principles of pure understanding, Kant writes that there are no innate concepts, but "concepts abstracted from the laws inherent in the mind (by attending to its actions on the occasion of an experience), and therefore as *acquired* concepts" (2: 395). Kant adds that these concepts are possibility, existence, necessity, substance, and cause: all concepts that in the critical period will be included in the table of categories. According to Kant, concepts are either objects of the understanding or formed by understanding, but do not constitute its nature; rather, they are its logical structure. These pure concepts of the understanding are not pure in the sense that they are abstracted from something material, but they are "originally" pure because they have nothing to do with sensation, and therefore they are a priori and not a posteriori. But still we do not know why concepts are acquired and not innate, and in which sense they are acquired. Kant explains that the pure concepts of understanding are not inborn; that is, they are not part of understanding's nature from birth, but rather, they arise "later." They are born from the exercise of understanding, from its real use in occasion of experience. Therefore, we can say that according to Kant concepts are acquired in the same way as a habit was in the Aristotelian tradition and in Wolff's philosophy. Kant specifies that these concepts must be understood as inherent—that is, acquired from the laws in the mind—reminding us unequivocally of the rules of acquired natural logic or artificial logic in the Wolffian sense. They are acquired, but epistemically they are a priori of every possible knowledge and for this reason they must be understood as if they were "innate." But Kant did not endorse innatism of any kind, be it Platonic, Leibnizian, or Crusian; hence, he chose to characterize this concept as "originarily" acquired. They derive from the natural laws of the mind, even if they are not innate, because they are rooted in its nature as potentialities that become active and developed in occasion of experience.

In the following paragraphs, Kant also seems to characterize as originarily acquired a priori the forms of sensibility, that is, space and time.[159] The first occurrence in which the forms of sensibility are said to be acquired is Kant's treatment of time. He writes that "the concept of time rests exclusively on an internal law of the mind, and is not some kind of innate intuition (*intuitus connatus*)," in fact, "the action of the mind, in coordinating what it senses, would not be elicited without the help of the senses" (2: 401). In this context, "innate intuition" means that we do not originally have the content of an intuition, since the content or the matter of knowledge is provided only by sensation. This does not mean that time is empirically acquired from experience, but in fact that the mind has the foundation of the form of intuition originarily. The thesis that the pure forms of sensibility are originarily acquired finds corroboration in Kant's statement that if space had not been "given originarily by the nature of the mind [...] then the use of geometry in natural philosophy would be far from safe" (2: 404–5). In the conclusion of the first section on the forms of the sensible world Kant still maintains that space and time are originarily acquired forms. In fact, Kant states that it is natural to ask whether space and time are innate or acquired in the sense of abstracted from sensation. He writes that the latter case has already been refuted by what has been demonstrated previously on the very possibility of geometry (2: 406). Therefore, only the former case remains, namely, that space and time are "somewhat" innate, but he argues that the former view "ought not to be that rashly admitted for it paves the way for a philosophy of the lazy (*philosophia pigrorum*)" (2: 406). Kant is refining his peculiar form of "nativism" toward what he will call the theory of "original acquisition" in the critical period.[160] Kant expounds that without any shadow of doubt both space and time are not innate, but acquired. They are acquired, but not by abstraction from the sensation of objects, but rather "from the very action of the mind, which coordinates what is sensed by it," in accordance with its permanent laws. In other words, they are originarily acquired in the mind. Sensation, Kant remarks, reawakens the action of the mind and here there is nothing innate but the law of the mind that coordinates what is sensed (2: 406), all the rest is acquired originarily or by experience. Kant's nativism here is limited to the intrinsic laws of mind, which are dependent from its very physiological nature. By nature the mind possesses some inborn features or dispositions that in the occasion of experience originarily generate space, time, and the pure concepts of the understanding. The two grounds of pure intuitions and concepts are innate, but space, time, and concepts in themselves are originarily acquired. The distinction between "innatism," such as that of Plato and Leibniz, and this peculiar form of "original acquisition" is rather blurred and sometimes led to apparently inconsistent positions. But in this phase of the generation of the critical philosophy, Kant's oscillation between innatism and the acquisition of the forms of sensibility is explainable with the fact that he aims to distance himself (1) from the innatist theories of Plato and Malebranche, who asserted that intuition was native also in its use; (2) from Leibniz's philosophy, according to which all ideas issued from the ground of the soul; and (3) from Locke's empiricism, for which space and time were acquired a posteriori by experience. Kant aimed to find his own personal way and to establish an innovative epistemology.

Kant is proposing a new model of mind, which is very close to the Aristotelian one, conceiving its main logical transcendental structure in its origin and use as a habit. My supposition is confirmed by Kant himself in his famous letter to Marcus Herz. Kant recognized in a spirit of self-criticism the inadequacy of his investigation in the *Inaugural Dissertation*, in which he was satisfied to explain only negatively the nature of intellectual representations. The same problem occurs in this letter, where he discusses the possibility of applying the model of the *intellectus archetypus*, or the *intellectus ectypus*, to human understanding (10: 130). Kant states that neither of these two options is feasible, both because understanding is not a cause of the object by means of its representations and because the object is not really a cause of the representations of understanding (10: 130). Kant is denying both pure idealism and pure realism: the subject does not produce the object, but neither is the object the only cause of the representations of the subject. The pure concepts of understanding, therefore, must not be abstracted from the impressions of the senses, neither can they be the expression of the receptivity of representation by senses: they must have their origin in the mind, but neither because they are caused by the object nor because they produce the object. Pure concepts should not be a posteriori as modifications of the mind by the objects (10: 130). Their nature is a priori of any possible experience.

In this letter, Kant outlines a brief history of how these concepts were understood by the various philosophers. The first philosopher is Plato, who conceived of a spiritual divine intuition at the root of the pure concepts of understanding (10: 131). Alongside Plato, Kant places Malebranche, who equally considered the origin of understanding as an actual and permanent intuition of God.[161] Certain moralists, and Kant was probably thinking of the "moral sense" philosophers, conceived of intuition as the basis for cognition of the original moral laws. The philosophical system based on the original intuition is called *influxus hyperphysicus*. Christian August Crusius, on the other hand, would have conceived of some laws of the power of judgment and some concepts as implanted in the soul by God, since they are innate, in such a way that they could be in harmony with the things of the world. This system is defined as *harmonia praestabilita intellectualis*, and is compared to Leibniz's standpoint (10: 131). But Kant reveals to Herz that while he was studying these innatist theories, he encountered a radically different doctrine that was more feasible for the explanation of his epistemology: it was the Aristotelian doctrine of categories, as we shall see in greater detail in the next chapter (10: 132).

The letter to Herz marks the first meaningful appearance of Aristotle in Kant's *corpus*;[162] indeed, prior to 1770 Aristotle was cursorily mentioned a scarce four times (10: 32; 2: 124; 2: 202; 2: 342), while from *The Blomberg Logic* and *The Philippi Logic* we know that between 1771 and 1772 Kant engaged closely with the Aristotelian works. In this period Kant became aware that Aristotle's doctrine of categories was able to link all the concepts of pure reason to a certain number of original elements arranged according to a few laws of understanding much better than all the other epistemological models common at the time, that is, empiricism and rationalism.

BETWEEN LOCKE AND LEIBNIZ

It is noteworthy that in these years, but also in the critical period, Aristotle is often associated with John Locke. Kant establishes a comparison between these two authors based on their common view of the origin of concepts. In particular both Aristotle and Locke were deeply involved, according to Kant, in establishing a physiology of understanding, which Kant understood as the science that deals with the origin of concepts. But Kant's analogy between Aristotle and Locke could be misleading for our purpose. Both, in fact, agree that concepts are produced a posteriori in the understanding in relation to what is given by sensation, and in this way all statements on the Latin saying *nihil est in intellectu, quod non fuerit antea in sensu* must be understood. There are many passages showing that Kant viewed Aristotle as the first theorizer of this doctrine, but saw Locke as its real systematizer: "in modern times Locke has been the follower of Aristotle and he has maintained the *conceptus acquisitus*" (28: 372), "Locke demonstrates the principles: *nihil est in intellectu, quod non fuerit antea in sensu*, which was briefly outlined by Aristotle" (28: 176). But this has certainly nothing to do with Kant's theory of original acquisition. In this framework, the physiology of the understanding is not even concerned with the Aristotelian theory of habits, but with the difference between a posteriori and a priori knowledge, for which Locke is blamed in the *Critique of Pure Reason*:

> The famous Locke, from neglect of this consideration, and because he encountered pure concepts of the understanding in experience, also derived them from this experience, and thus proceeded so **inconsistently** that he thereby dared to make attempts at cognitions that go far beyond the boundary of all experience. (B 127)

The comparison between Aristotle and Locke is made by Kant also on another level that is more interesting for our purposes, and opposes these two authors to Plato and Leibniz: "Locke follows Aristotele, Leibniz more Plato" (28: 377). The opposition between the Aristotle-Locke binomial and the Plato-Leibniz binomial is played out on the conceptual pair "acquired-innate." In the chapter "The History of Pure Reason" in the *Critique of Pure Reason*, for the first time in a printed work, Kant opposes Aristotle and Locke against Plato and Leibniz. He writes that concerning the origin of the elements of pure cognition of reason, that is, if they come from experience or if they are independent from it, Aristotle must be considered as the leader of the empiricists, Plato the leader of the noologists. In this context, "noologist" does not refer to "noology," but rather to the position that establishes the direct intellection of ideas, that is, of the intelligible. Kant adds that in recent times Locke has followed Aristotle, while Leibniz followed Plato, even if Leibniz was very far from the Platonist mystical system (A 854/B 882). This opposition in Kant's mind originates early on and has a long gestation, as the *Reflections* of the 1760s prove.

In the lectures on the philosophical encyclopedia, based on Feder's *Grudriß der philosophischen Wissenschaften*, and probably composed between 1777 and 1780, the opposition is developed very vividly. According to Kant, Plato maintained that there were inherent in the mind previous traces and that knowledge was nothing other than memories (29: 15), while Aristotle would have taught the exact opposite. Among the moderns—Kant adds—Leibniz follows Plato, even if he does not believe in spiritual intuition, but only in innate knowledge, that is, in concepts of things before knowing them. Locke, on the other hand, is Aristotle's genuine disciple, and maintains that all concepts are acquired. Kant glosses this part with a pithy statement: "something innate is definitely contrary and uncongenial to philosophy" (29: 16). This sentence recalls *The Pölitz Metaphysics*, in which Kant states that "we have not innate concepts (*notiones connatae*), rather, we acquire everything, we attain *notiones acquisitae*. The understanding acquires concepts in the extent it is exercised" (28: 542). Kant frequently juxtaposes Aristotle and Locke to Crusius, as in *Reflection 4894*, dated around 1776 and 1778. In this *Reflection*, Kant states that the *intellectualia* are not innate for Locke, while for Crusius there are innate intuitions and principles:

"Crusius deals with *conceptus connatos* or *axiomata connata per praestabilitam cognitionem*" (17: 22). Also for Plato—Kant writes—*intellectualia* are innate and immediately grasped by means of intuition, while for Aristotle they are acquired. In *Reflection 1641*, Kant maintains that Locke investigates the origin and the acquisition of the concepts of the human understanding coming from experience, while Crusius brings back to immediate intuition and instinct the laws of human reason (16: 62). In *The Volckmann Metaphysics*, datable around 1784–1785, just after the statement according to which Locke is a follower of Aristotle, Kant asserts that Leibniz deals with innate concepts, but in a perspective that differs from the mystic Platonic perspective. Crusius followed Plato in conceiving innate concepts, in particular, in establishing the criterion of truth and falsity that rests in the mind (28: 372).

In short, according to Kant, Aristotle and Locke pursued the same philosophical project, elaborating a theory of acquired concepts of the understanding, a project called the physiology of understanding. The physiology of understanding deals specifically with the origin of concepts, that is, how they are acquired. Kant is obsessed with this issue.[163] It is particularly remarkable in *Reflection 4446*, datable around 1771 and 1772, in which in characterizing Locke's perspective on acquired concepts Kant speaks of "subjective habit" (*subiective Gewöhnung*) (17: 554). Kant establishes a strict connection between the problem of acquired concepts and subjective habit in such a way that the entire discussion on innate ideas takes on a new dimension in the light of the Aristotelian doctrine of habits: concepts are not innate ideas in the mind, but they inhere to it like a habit, like a second nature. Kant adds that the study of this subjective habit concerns primarily the *physiologia intellectus*, "where the origin of concepts is explained" (17: 554).[164]

In *The Philippi Logic*, transcribed more or less in the same years of *Reflection 4446*, Kant states that Locke has investigated the derivation and the origin of the concepts and in so doing he has philosophized "subjectively." The reference to the subjective approach and to the subjective habits means that Locke was primarily concerned with the origin and the formation of the concepts in the particular mind of the subject. The physiology of mind explains how concepts arise subjectively in the mind and Kant characterizes this research as "critic," in opposition to the dogmatic perspective of the

Wolffian tradition (24: 338). Thus, at early stages of his critical philosophy, more or less in the same period when he was writing his letter to Herz, Kant included the physiology of the mind in his critical enterprise.

Kant, however, became very soon aware of the weaknesses of the physiological project and of the fact that physiology cannot be part of his transcendental philosophy, at least as physiology was understood by Locke. In fact, while Aristotle and Locke deal with the generation of general concepts *from* experience, Kant deals with the formation of concepts in the mind in *occasion* of experience, concepts that are not general ideas of particular things in the world, but universal ways of conceiving and considering that are acquired like habits. In the later *Vigilantius Metaphysics* (1794–1795) Kant explains that "Aristotle and later Locke set up a (so-called) physiology of reason because they viewed a priori cognition as something which can be acquired empirically, [. . .] they thus assumed, in view of the origin, all cognition as sensible (*nihil est*, etc., said Aristotle) and believed that the more a proposition is raised up through abstraction, the more it approaches an a priori proposition" (29: 958–959). Kant consciously picked up this physiological project, but he "elevated" (*erhoben*) it into what we can call a "transcendental physiology,"[165] where the concepts of the understanding are a priori originarily acquired in occasion of experience and not generated by experience itself. As it was conceived by Aristotle and Locke, the physiology could not fit into Kant's transcendental project, it required a completely new reconfiguration. Unfortunately, Kant never developed and systematized his ideas on the origin of the a priori forms of cognition. What we can do is to put the pieces together and follow the traces that Kant left us to reconstruct his thought as best we can.

In the critical period, Aristotle and Locke's physiology corresponds roughly to the traditional acquired, natural logic of the Wolffian tradition mentioned in the previous section. Both physiology and acquired, natural logic, in fact, seek the origin of the logical structures of understanding. This, however, does not mean that physiology is a form of logic, or that acquired, natural logic is logic properly speaking. Kant definitively expunges physiology from logic. In *The Jäsche Logic*, Kant states that Locke, like Malebranche, did not develop any logic, because his investigations were on the content of cognition and on the origin of concepts (9: 91), while logic is only about the form of cognition and the use of concepts. Also in *The Bauch Logic*, Kant supports the view that Locke deals with the origin of the pure concepts of understanding, but this does not pertain to logic.[166] In *The Dohna Logic*, like in *The Vienna Logic* (24: 796), Kant maintains that Locke speaks "of the origin of concepts, but this really does not belong to logic, but rather to metaphysics" (24: 701). In the general logic as well as in the transcendental logic, Kant seems uninterested in tackling once and for all the problem of the origin of the pure concepts of the understanding within the discipline of logic, and this is the reason why he dismisses the physiological problem; but perhaps there is more. As Paton rightly points out, in the *Critique of Pure Reason* "Kant is not concerned with the question of how experience develops [. . .] but with what is contained in experience, or with the presuppositions and conditions of experience."[167] In fact, physiology is concerned with the *quaestio facti*, while the "critique" as logic deals with the *quaestio juris*.[168] For this reason, we can also understand why Kant does not consider Locke to be a model for his own transcendental investigation: the two standpoints are completely different.[169] Locke's philosophy was highly thought of by Kant, but it was not in his estimation logic, properly speaking.[170] In fact, we know that in Kant's view no progress has been made since the times of Aristotle:

> If some moderns have thought to enlarge it by interpolating **psychological** chapters about our different cognitive powers (about imagination, wit), or **metaphysical** chapters about the origin of cognition or the different kinds of certainty in accordance with the diversity of objects (about idealism, skepticism, etc.), or **anthropological** chapters about our prejudice (about their causes and remedies), then this proceeds only from their ignorance of the peculiar nature of this science. (B VIII)

In spite of Kant's resistance to engaging directly and explicitly with the origin of pure a priori forms of cognition of the mind in his transcendental philosophy, as such an investigation would have pertained to metaphysics or psychology, it nonetheless remains a key issue in understanding his transcendental logic. In fact, since transcendental logic deals with these pure a priori forms of cognition, the problem of their genesis has some relevance in order to have a complete picture of Kant's philosophy of mind. Thus, since physiology, or natural acquired logic, is the ground of transcendental logic, in the sense that it explains the origin of the logical, transcendental structure of the mind, it is important to shed some light on Kant's view. If my reconstruction is right, we cannot maintain that in Kant there is a sharp distinction between physiology or the psychological nature of the mind and logic such that logic is no longer founded on psychology, as some scholars argue.[171] The *Reflections* of the 1760s and of the '70s show that psychology and physiology are the natural foundation of logic, even if they are not parts of it.

The question of the relation between physiology and logic is not confined to preparatory works of the *Critique of Pure Reason*, but it reemerges with vigor in the polemics with the Leibnizian Johann August Eberhard and with Kant's answer in his *On a Discovery Whereby Any New Critique of Pure Reason Is to Be Made Superfluous by an Older One* (1790).[172] The work was composed in response to Eberhard's charge, according to which Kantian thought was a bad copy of Leibnizian philosophy. Eberhard's fiercest polemics related to innatism, and the acquisition of the forms of sensibility and the concepts of understanding. Before tackling the controversy between Kant and Eberhard, however, it is advisable to understand what Leibniz's conception of innatism was, as well as Kant's understanding of it.

It is well known that Leibniz exposed his theory of innate ideas in the *Nouveaux Essais*, which were published posthumously in 1765 by Rudolf Erich Raspe, and later in the complete works edited by Ludwig Dutens in 1768. But Leibniz's influence on Kant is a matter of debate. Giorgio Tonelli, who reconstructed the complex and variegated reaction to the publication of the *Nouveaux Essais* of various intellectuals of the time, suggests a possible impact of Leibniz on Kant in the period of the "great light": "as the great upheaval in Kant's thought took place in 1769, and as this upheaval had as one of its main characteristics the rejection of sensibility as the sole source of knowledge, it is easy to infer that Kant's reading of the *Nouveaux Essais* may have been one of the elements prompting him to adopt his new solution."[173] But, Tonelli's investigation is very convincing in showing that the *Nouveaux Essais* were not understood by the majority of the intellectuals of the time, which included Eberhard himself. Therefore, "if a reading of the *Nouveaux Essais* really affected Kant's 1769 philosophical revolution, it cannot be considered as an effect of a positive collective reaction to the *Nouveaux Essais* because, for a long time after 1769, this reaction simply did *not* occur. Influence of the *Nouveaux Essais* on Kant may be explained by individual reasons only, unlike many other philosophical positions Kant made his own between 1769 and 1780."[174]

It is not the purpose of my research to assess Kant's debt to Leibniz; it is sufficient to recognize some degree of influence in the *Reflections* between 1768 and 1780, in an attempt to resolve the problem of innatism in opposition to Locke's empirical standpoint. In Leibniz, we find at least a twofold doctrine of innatism, one metaphysical and one psychological. Metaphysical innatism maintains that all our cognitions cannot be anything other than innate, whereas psychological innastism, developed in the *Nouveaux Essais*, established that the fundamental and necessary truths were innate, while contingent and derived truths were, so to speak, acquired in occasion of experience and of the exercise of the faculties of the mind. Kant was well aware of this distinction, unlike many of his contemporaries.[175]

Leibniz famously deals with the problem of innatism in the first book of the *Nouveaux Essais*, confuting Locke's empiricist position. Leibniz states that there are ideas and principles that do not belong to senses, and are inborn in the mind. Senses, however, have the function of reawakening the awareness of these ideas and principles.[176] These ideas can be called innate or primitive, because they come from inside the mind itself.[177] Innate ideas and principles are a part of natural logic, which everyone employs without consciousness, according to Leibniz. The truths of this logic belong directly to natural reason or to instinct.[178]

In two places, however, Leibniz distinguishes his innatism from Plato and Platonism.[179] Platonism maintained that all cognitions are memories, and that the inborn truths of the mind, which are innate, are a residue of previous, direct, intellectual intuitions. Even if we adopt such a position, Leibniz writes, original cognitions must be preceded by a previous state of knowledge in which they were again innate, or inborn, and so on ad infinitum.[180] In conclusion, the fact that innate knowledge, ideas, and truths are inborn in the mind does not mean that they are actually thought. They are natural dispositions and active or passive habits.

The distinction between Leibniz and the Platonists, the notion of innate ideas as virtual, unconscious dispositions and the conception of acquired ideas by experiences, are issues that were particularly clear in Kant's mind, despite his contemporaries, and he does not neglect to announce the fact to Eberhard.

In the essay *Ueber den Ursprung der menschlichen Erkenntniss*, as in *Ueber den wesentlichen Unterschied der Erkenntniss durch die Sinne und durch den Verstand*, Eberhard charges Kant with reiterating Leibniz's innatism in the characterization of the forms of sensibility.[181] In particular, Eberhard criticizes Kant not by attacking the *Critique of Pure Reason*, but by using the entry "A priori" in Carl Christian Erhard Schmid's *Wörterbuch zum leichtern Gebrauch der Kantischen Schriften*.[182] In his dictionary, Schmid presents a detailed analysis of Kant's conception of the pure forms of sensibility as if they were a development of Leibniz's position.[183] Schmid then emphasized Kant's originality compared to Locke's empiricism. In his essay, Eberhard sarcastically notes:

> The Kantian theory of a priori cognition has as its foundation the Leibnizian doctrine of innate concepts, even if Kant does not call them innate, probably he did not want to leave the opportunity that its forms of representation could be conceived in this way, since Locke refuted innatism so well. A special sophistication![184]

Kant responds to Eberhard's charges in *On a Discovery*, saying that the *Critique of Pure Reason* does not allow representations that are innate or inborn. In fact, he adds that the *Critique of Pure Reason* conceives all representations in general as acquired, be they of intuitions or the concepts of understanding. According to Kant, in fact, there is an original acquisition (*ursprüngliche Erwerbung*) "of that which previously did not yet exist at all, and so did not belong to anything prior to this act" (8: 221). It concerns (1) the form of things in space and time; and (2) the synthetic unity of the manifold in the concepts. In fact, Kant explains, the cognitive faculty derives neither of these two things from the objects, but they issue a priori from the faculty itself. In detail, Kant points out that the ground of the possibility of sensible intuition, that is the mere receptivity peculiar to the mind, is innate, while space in itself is an originarily acquired representation. Furthermore, Kant adds that categories are originarily acquired concepts and that they presuppose nothing innate save the subjective conditions of the spontaneity of thought in accordance with the unity of the transcendental apperception.[185] This theory of original acquisition corresponds quite exactly to the processes developed in the *Inaugural Dissertation*, as we have seen in the previous section, therefore Kant remained fairly consistent with this idea from the early 1770s.[186] Unfortunately, in this case as well, he does not say much more about the origin of the concepts.

From an examination of the controversy with Eberhard we can say that for Kant: (1) space and time and the categories are originarily acquired; (2) space and time have an original, innate ground in the receptivity of sensibility; (3) categories differ from derived or determinate concepts; and (4) categories have an original, innate, ground in the nature of the understanding in its spontaneous activity. The innate character of the cognitive faculty of the mind derives directly from its physical, biological, or physiological nature, while the structures are generated and differentiate themselves supervening on what nature gives to the human being at birth, like the Aristotelian habit as a second nature. Therefore Kant's logic relies mostly if not entirely on psychology, or at least on the physiological nature of the mind, in which the first elements of knowledge such as the pure intuitions and the categories are grounded.

Kant's Aristotelian model of mind, in which natural disposition are developed in habits, goes a long way toward explaining his frequent of use of the biological metaphor of preformism and epigenesis to characterize the structure of the cognitive faculty. In the eighteenth-century, in authors like Charles Bonnet and Albrecht von Haller, preformism, or "theory of evolution," was in general the theory that the individual, with all its parts, preexists in the germ cell and grows from microscopic to normal proportions during the genesis. This means that preformation concerned primarily the unfolding and the quantitative growth of preexisting parts and not the generation or the development of new organs or faculties. Epigenesis, on the other hand, which was developed originally by Aristotle, and later in the eighteenth century by Pierre Louis Moureau de Maupertius, Caspar Friedrich Wolff, and Johann Friedrich Blumenbach, is the denial of preformism, being the theory that an organism develops its organs and faculties from the successive differentiation of an originally undifferentiated structure. Beyond Kant's real understanding of these two theories, which has been heatedly debated in recent scholarship,[187] his use of the analogy between the evolution of the living being and the development of the mind in relation to epigenesis is remarkable.

John H. Zammito remarked that "there was no affirmation of epigenesis in any of Kant's writings before 1787," and the use of epigenesis in the lectures and in the *Reflections* of the 1770s is far from being proved.[188] However, given some similarities with the doctrines exposed in the *Dissertation* and in the 1772 letter to Herz,[189] we can say with a some degree of confidence that a group of *Reflections* on epigenesis belongs to the early stages of Kant's critical thought at the beginning of the 1770s, as Erich Adickes originally dated them.

All these early references to epigenesis and preformation concern the explanation of the origin and of the source of the concepts of the understanding, and they will remain paradigmatic for all successive developments in Kant's philosophy over next two decades. Kant's preference for epigenesis is dictated by his rejection of any version of the Leibnizian model of mind, in particular that of Crusius, based on preestablished harmony and innatism. In this context the recourse to epigenetic theory is only meant "to draw attention to the fact that the concepts of the understanding are acquired and not innate."[190] The concepts of the understanding are acquired in the sense that we have already emphasized above; that is, they are originarily acquired and this original acquisition is far from being an endorsement of "classical innatism," as supported by Plato and Leibniz.

A first occurrence of the categories as an epigenetic system is to be found in *Reflection 4275* (1770–1771), and it also represents the first comparison between Locke and Aristotle:

> Crusius explains the real principle of reason on the basis of the *systemate praeformationis* (from subjective *principiis*); *Locke*, on the basis of *influxu physico* like Aristotle's; *Plato* and *Malebranche*, from *intuitu intellectuali*; we, on the basis of *epigenesis* from the use of the natural laws of reason. (17: 492)

The Crusian position is characterized as preformism, in other words reason unfolds and expands original principles and laws that are already present at birth.[191] Kant's opinion on Crusius occurs also in the 1772 letter to Herz, and in *Reflection 4446* (1772), where his position was characterized as *harmonia praestabilita intellectualis* (10:

131) and *methodus cognitionis praestabilitae* (17: 554). On the other hand, Kant defines his own position as epigenesis: the natural laws of the reason present in the very psychological nature of the mind develop in occasion of experience its principles. This development is like the acquisition of a habit, which once obtained operates like a second nature. The first position is defended by Plato, the second by Locke, the third is upheld by Crusius, while the latter is Kant's theory.

The first implicit encounter of the biological metaphor in Kant's published writings in the field of epistemology is at the beginning of the *Analytics of Concepts* in the *Critique of Pure Reason*:

> I understand by the analytic of concepts [. . .] the still little investigated dissection of the capacity of the understanding itself, in order thereby to investigate the possibility of a priori concepts, seeking them out in the understanding alone, as their place of birth, and analyzing them in their pure general use; this then is the peculiar business of a transcendental philosophy. The remainder is the logical treatment of concepts in philosophy generally. We shall therefore follow the pure concepts up to their first germs [*Keime*] and dispositions [*Anlagen*] in the human understanding, in which they lie prepared [*vorbereitet*], until finally, on the occasion of experience, they are developed and through exactly the same understanding are displayed in their purity, freed from their attending empirical conditions. (A 65–66/B 90–91)

This passage was repeated without any modification in the second edition of the *Critique* in 1787, a sign that Kant was convinced of his position. A number of scholars have noted that the terminology employed by Kant has striking resonance with the biological debates of the time. Philipp R. Sloan has argued that the use of terms such as *germs* (*Keime*) and *dispositions* (*Anlagen*) has a preformationist flavor, and that Kant here was in fact supporting a weak notion of preformationism rather than epigenesis. In particular, Sloan recognizes similarities with some compelling passages taken from *Of the Different Human Races* (2: 434–5) and from the *Lectures on Anthropology* (25: 694, 700), all datable to around 1775–1777, and all confined within a restricted biological and anthropological field, which does not necessarily correspond to Kant's endorsement of the same thesis for his epistemic model of mind.[192] Further, while in 1775–1777 Kant employs *germs* and *dispositions* in a context with terms univocally characterizing preformation, like *unfolding* (*Auswickelung*) and *preformed* (*vorgebildet*) (2: 434–5), in 1781 he prefers more neutral words, usually associated with epigenesis, such as *developed* (*entwickelt*) and *prepared* (*vorbereitet*). However, if Sloan's hypothesis were correct, this would lead to the conclusion that either Kant had changed his view from his early *Reflections*, or that all the *Reflections* concerning epigenesis must be datable to after 1786. But there is another problem of some importance. In the second edition, where the above-mentioned passage is repeated, Kant famously supports in § 27 the theory of the epigenesis of the pure concepts of the understanding. In § 27, Kant states that there are only two ways to conceive a necessary agreement of experience with the concepts of its object: either experience makes possible concepts, or concepts make possible experience (B 166). Experience, however, cannot make possible concepts, because categories are a priori concepts independent from experience. Supporting their empirical origin would be a kind of equivocal generation (*generatio aequivoca*). Thus, only the system of the epigenesis of pure reason remains, that is, categories contain the grounds of the possibility of every experience (B 167). In this passage, unlike in precritical reflections, Kant deals more with the use of categories rather than their origin. At the end of the paragraph, Kant excludes a third possibility, that is, that categories are neither principles of cognition, thought spontaneously a priori, nor principles attained from experience, rather innate, *subjective* dispositions of thinking arranged by God in such a way that their use was in agreement with the laws of nature that we can find in experience. This is exactly Crusius's system, which is called a preformist system of pure reason (B 167). This cannot be the Kantian system because categories in this case would not be necessary (B 168), while for Kant categories are necessary to provide scientific knowledge. According to Kant, Crusius's dispositions are merely subjective in the sense that they are arbitrary, that is, God implanted in the each mind different dispositions, which only unfolded in the course of experience, but which remained substantially diverse for every subject. While for Kant dispositions must be objective, not arbitrary, even if they pertain to the knowing subject.[193] This is the reason why Kant rejects

Crusius's peculiar form of arbitrary, dispositional innatism. In a footnote to § 36 of the *Prolegomena*, Kant mentions explicitly Crusius as the theorizer of this third way: "Crusius alone knew of a middle way: namely that a spirit who can neither err nor deceive originally implanted these natural laws in us" (4: 319). However, Kant writes:

> since false principles are often mixed in as well—of which this man's system itself provides not a few examples—then, with the lack of sure criteria for distinguishing an authentic origin from a spurious one, the use of such a principle looks very precarious, since one can never know for sure what the spirit of truth or the father of lies may have put into us. (B 167)

Kant is manifestly endorsing an epigenetic standpoint in 1787, while in 1781 he seems to support a generic form of preformationism. This means that between 1781 and 1787 Kant changed his mind, as Zammito has suggested.[194] The problem is that in the same work, over a span of six years, he maintained two possible contrasting biological conceptions that would have reflected his model of mind remains open. This difficulty led the scholarship to question what Kant's real opinion was. We are faced with three possible solutions that are not mutually exclusive. The first solution is that in 1781, Kant was not referring to a preformationist theory, but to epigenesis, even if moderate and weakly determined.[195] There are certain clues suggesting the validity of this hypothesis. In spite of Sloan's convincing arguments, *disposition* (*Anlage*) was quite a common term in the eighteenth-century debates on Leibnizian epistemology and on his version of innatism. For instance, in dealing with innate ideas as something only virtually active, Leibniz calls them natural dispositions, or habits, or attitudes, that the 1778 German translation of the *Nouveaux Essais* renders with the terms *Anlagen* (*dispositions*) or *Gewohnheiten* (*habits*).[196] Kant recognizes the Leibnizian advancement on innatism, in particular in comparison to Plato and Crusius, stating that Leibniz "supposed certain innate predispositions of reason as existing in us, which had only the use that we, in relying on them, would find the objects themselves in agreement with these ideas" (29: 959). Leibniz's ideas from this perspective seem very similar to Kant's hypothesis of originarily acquired dispositions in occasion of experience, but still one thing was missing in Leibnizian philosophy. Strictly speaking, even if experience can solicit a natural disposition virtually present in the mind, no idea comes from outside of the mind; therefore, the problem of innatism and original acquisition becomes a cul-de-sac. The substantial difference between Kant's theory of original acquisition and Leibniz's dispositional innatism consists in the fact that from the Leibnizian standpoint both the contents and the forms of knowledge are dispositionally innate, while for Kantian philosophy only the logical forms of knowledge are originally acquired and all the matter of knowledge comes from experience. Only Kant's model of mind, distinguishing the originarily acquired forms of cognition from the empirically acquired matter of cognition, could resolve the Leibnizian view.

Furthermore, from a merely epistemological standpoint, in 1777 Johann Nikolaus Tetens posed the question of whether it was possible to establish an analogy between the recent biological discoveries about the body and the development of the soul by employing extensively this terminology. In particular, he wanted to know whether the "shaping [*Ausbildung*] of the faculties is an evolution [*Evolution*] of an already available natural disposition [*vorhandene Naturanlage*], or an epigenesis [*Epigenesis*] that creates [*hervorbringt*] new faculties for which before there was nothing more than the receptivity [*Empfänglichkeit*] to receive them."[197] Tetens is perfectly aware of the difficulty of this question, and in fact writes that if a comparison between the faculties of the soul of an adult and the first dispostions (*Anlagen*) in the soul of a child must be established, and if then we want to know whether the faculties of the adult are only developed from the dispositions of the child, or if these faculties arise subsequently from nothing, we would start an endless investigation, the solution of which is beyond the limit of experience, a limit that Kant himself notoriously does not want to surpass in his critical philosophy.[198] In fact, from experience it is hard, if not impossible, to establish whether a faculty is something already preexisting or something totally new. For example, if in children we recognize a certain form of impudicity, which disappears when they are adults, and we recognize the same form of impudicity in Tahitian women, we can conclude that the feeling of pudicity is an invisible preexisting disposition that becomes active under the action of particular impressions. At the same time, however, nothing would prevent someone else from believing this feeling is a newly generated faculty that was not previously present in the mind in occasion of those particular impressions. Experience in fact does not provide a sufficient proof for one side or the other.[199] The only possible solution would be to penetrate deeply into the human mind, but according to Tetens this is not yet possible. Tetens's attitude is thus skeptical, as he does not really know "whether the idea of the development [*Entwickelung*] of our body agrees with the idea that one has of the development of the soul."[200] Thus he aims only to advance some hypothesis and to make some remarks in particular on the system of Bonnet and Wolff, which are nevertheless quite interesting for our purpose.

First and foremost, Tetens writes that the German philosophers are all epigenetists in the case of the soul, just as the German physiologists are evolutionists in the case of the body. It is therefore perfectly possible to maintain the preformationist theory at a strictly anthropological and biological level and an epigenetic doctrine at an epistemological level.[201] This could explain Kant's apparent contradiction in the 1770s between his logical and anthropological works.

Second, since experience does not provide sufficient grounds for establishing whether a faculty unfolds from preexisting germs or is newly generated, preformationism and epigenesis can coexist perfectly; that is, some faculties can be preexisting while others can be produced in the mind on particular occasions, and given Kant's contrasting opinion on epigenesis we cannot exclude that he also endorsed different positions for various faculties.

Last, Tetens extends his reflections to all human faculties, including reason, even if reason would intrinsically characterize human nature. The case of the savages, in whom the faculty of thinking would be lacking, generates the same aporia. Is reason a natural disposition or something that supervenes? Since in the case of the savages reason does not unfold, one could conclude that reason is not original in the mind. At the same time, however, one could argue that reason is present but it needs the proper nourishment for its unfolding as the head needs the proper nourishment for its growth.

In all these unsolvable problems, Tetens believes that there is in the mind an inscrutable inborn nature (*angeborne Natur*),[202] which is a fundamental force of the soul (*Grundkraft der Seele*),[203] and on which "are grounded the mere possibilities, which are considered only as faculty *in actu primo, in potentia remota, remotiori, propriori* ecc. according to the language of the ancients."²⁰⁴ On this fundamental or original force (*Grundkraft oder Urkraft*),²⁰⁵ Tetens grounds his psychological system. In the eleventh essay, "On the Fundamental Force of the Human Soul and on the Character of Humankind," Tetens writes that this fundamental force belongs directly to the nature of the mind, using the conceptual pair "Anlage-Keim" as it appears in the *Critique of Pure Reason*. In particular, he states that this fundamental force in the soul, before the conception (*Empfängniß*) and in the embryo (*Embryon*), had the disposition (*Anlage*) to become a human being, and, therefore, "there was already present [*vorhanden*] the fundamental germ [*Grundkeim*] of feeling [*Gefühl*] and reason [*Vernunft*]."²⁰⁶ The fundamental force is specifically the disposition (*Anlage*) to become the power of sensation (*Empfindungskraft*) and the intellect (*Verstand*).²⁰⁷ In the very nature of the mind the power of sensation and intellect are mere dispositions (*bloße Anlagen*) or remote faculties (*entfernte Vermögen*), "therefore not as faculty of sensation, representation, thinking, willing, but only as the faculty to receive them."²⁰⁸ Tetens, therefore, characterizes the fundamental force as the germ (*Keim*) of the faculties, but still he has to explain what this germ (*Keim*) or disposition (*Disposition*) to acquire feeling and reason is. This is, according to Tetens, the hardest question (*größte Frage*) in psychology, to which he can only answer disjunctively: "either it is not possible to have an idea of this fundamental force, or it is possible only one."²⁰⁹ Tetens's skeptical attitude involves also his characterization of the fundamental force. Since "the force can be known by us and characterized only by the effects that it produces," it is only possible to say that this fundamental force "contains in itself the germ of the fundamental faculties [*Grundvermögen*] of feeling, of representing, and of willing."²¹⁰ Experience can teach us nothing else: "one must surrender in the face of this difficulty and must not enter into the dark depths where the fundamental force of the soul lies."²¹¹ Despite these difficulties, Tetens makes an important point. In characterizing the soul as an *entelecheia* that suffers and acts in Aristotelian terms,²¹² he recognizes in the possibility of receiving sensation (i.e., an excellent modifiability) and in thinking spontaneously the only two main innate characteristics pertaining to the fundamental force of the mind that we can know. Nothing can be said with certainty about their origin of all the other faculties of the mind, whether they are products following epigenesis or educts according to preformation. The correspondence of Tetens's ideas with Kant's thought in *On a Discovery* is quite striking. In *On a Discovery*, Kant writes that there must be a foundation (*Grund*) for the a priori production, that is, for the original acquisition of space, time, and categories in the subject, and that this foundation is innate (*angeboren*) (8: 222). He also added, as we have seen previously, that there are two innate characteristics specific to this foundation and they are the "mere peculiar receptivity [*Receptivität*] of the soul [*Gemüth*]" and the "spontaneity of thinking [*Spontaneität des Denkens*]" (8: 222–223).

It is possible to conclude, without necessarily inferring a direct indebtedness between Kant and Tetens, that the parallelism between the biological development of the body and that of the mind was particularly popular among epistemological models in the formative years of critical philosophy. One might add that a correspondence between the biological and the epistemological models was not necessary; rather, these parallelisms generated problems and aporias. An inconsistent use of technical terminology outside of biology may be sufficient explanation for the oscillations that appear in the Kantian model of the mind. The adoption of a jargon is not proof of an endorsement of one biological doctrine over another. Rather, as is often the case in Kant's philosophy, it reflects his repeated attempts to refine his ideas by looking for support, evidence, and proofs from other disciplines.

A second possible solution, supported by what we have previously shown, is that Kant maintained his own, original conception of "moderate" or "weak" epigenesis in which the boundaries with preformationism were blurred, and which differed from contemporary eighteenth-century epigenetic theories. Zammito has been quite clear on this, saying that Kant "may not have grasped clearly what he was playing with in the analogy to epigenesis," and that he has "not come to terms with the implications for his analogy between epigenesis and transcendental philosophy."[213] Kant's ambivalence toward epigenesis is evident in § 81 of the *Critique of the Power of Judgment*. In dealing with prestabilism, Kant writes that

> It considers each organic being generated from its own kind as either the educt or the product of the latter. The system of generatings as mere educts is called that of individual

> preformation or the theory of evolution; the system of generatings as products is called the system of epigenesis. The latter can also be called the system of generic preformation. (5: 423)

Kant explicitly defines epigenesis as a generic system of preformation against the more specific doctrine of individual preformation (or theory of involution or encapsulation), making it quite clear that the former is a broader, less-restricted theory compared to the latter. Epigenesis is therefore a weak kind of preformation, thus the alleged preformationist language of the first edition of the *Critique of Pure Reason* can be perfectly compatible with the endorsement of his epigenetic system of pure reason in § 27 of the second edition. However, it is questionable whether in § 81 Kant had in mind a parallelism between his biological conception and his model of mind. What is certain is that already in the years between 1776 and 1778, in *Reflection 4851*, in examining the origin of concepts, Kant employed the same biological terminology to characterize his epistemology. He points out that all concepts are either educts (*educta*) or products (*producta*). If concepts are educted, the system is called preformationism, if they are produced, the system is called epigenesis. Kant immediately rejected preformationism in favor of epigenesis. Products—he explains—issue either from the empirical, physical influx, or from the consciousness of the formal structure of sensibility and of the understanding in their relation with experience, and in this latter case they are a priori and not a posteriori. He added, moreover, that innate ideas arise from mysticism, while acquired ideas can be produced as a result of the epigenesis either a priori or a posteriori. In this sense, the study of the mind regarding acquired ideas can be physiological or critical. The critique concerns the a priori purity of the cognitive faculty and the distinction between sensibility and understanding, while physiology deals with the a posteriori origin of the concepts (18: 8). Already around the time of the publication of the first edition of the *Critique of Pure Reason*, Kant conceived his epistemic model of mind as a kind of epigenesis. The focus on the formal structure of sensibility and the understanding as the two sources of the a priori products suggests the influence of Tetens. As we have seen above, Tetens pointed out that sensibility and the faculty of thinking were the only two innate capacities of human mind, or germs (*Keime*), on which were based all the other dispositions (*Anlagen*). Tetens's reflections are included in Kant's new transcendental philosophy. Kant, however, was aware of the limits of Tetens's physiology of mind, which is characterized, on the one hand, as a theory of the evolution of concepts (*Evolution der Begriffe*), that is, as a form of epistemological preformationism, and on the other hand, as "all actions by means of which concepts are produced (*erzeugt*)," with a clear reference to epigenesis (18: 23). Kant's imprecision in characterizing Tetens's standpoint is probably due, as we have seen, to the ambivalent position taken by the latter with regard to epigenesis and preformation. In any case, be it epigenesis or preformation, Kant explicitly states that he is not concerned with "the evolution of concepts, like Tetens," because he "investigates the concepts of pure reason merely subjectively," that is, in terms of how they are acquired by the mind, in a Lockean perspective (18: 23).[214] On the contrary, in his transcendental logic, Kant aims to explain the use and not the origin of these concepts as they are employed objectively in the possible cognition in occasion of experience.

A third plausible solution of Kant's apparent contradiction is that the analogy, as Hans Ingesiep has hypothesized, was mainly an intuitive illustration according to some structural similarities between his new model of mind and the epigenetic theory, but in no way could the analogy "be construed as a claim for any compelling ontological connection between the respective philosophical and biological positions."[215] Quarfoord, too, puts "some constraints on attempts to use the development of Kant's views on generation to trace changes in his epistemological view," stressing that the position, according to which the topic of epigenesis has only an illustrative function in epistemological context, is a more plausible interpretation.[216] In general, whether we consider the analogy as something structural, or as a merely explanatory device, Kant's real understanding or misunderstanding of eighteenth-century biological theory does not affect the structure of his new logic; rather, it is evidence that he was looking for a confirmation of his epistemology in other disciplines, in this case in biology, as he did for the synthetic a priori judgments in arithmetic and geometry. What is really important is that something is produced a priori by epigenesis.

Scholars were not always in agreement on the nature of these products. Some supported the view that epigenesis reflects the power of the mind to form materials into objective experience, organized by categories,[217] others that the epigenetic products are "objects of knowledge,"[218] or that they are "non-empirical, metaphysical knowledge of possible experience."[219] If my reconstruction is correct, the most reliable interpretation, in particular in relation to the generation of the categories, is advanced by Hermann J. De Vleeschauwer.[220] Following his analysis, epigenesis concerns the original acquisition of the categories "in the sense of a genuine production of a priori forms out of an underlying ground or faculty," which does not already contain them analytically.[221] The production of these a priori forms would be "occasioned by experience." But this would have led to a misleading assimilation of the epigenesis to "the illegitimate concept of an equivocal generation of a priori forms out of an a posteriori material,"[222] which Kant explicitly rejects. The real question now is, therefore, how the a priori forms are originarily acquired in the occasion of experience without being caused by experience, that is, without falsely empiricizing the transcendental deduction of the categories.

A shrewd answer may be found in early reflections on the generation of concepts, such as *Reflection 3930* (1769), in which Kant makes it clear that:

> Some concepts are abstracted from sensations, others merely from the laws of the understanding for comparing, combining, or separating abstracted concepts. The origin of the latter is in the understanding; of the former, in the senses. All concepts of the latter sort are called pure concepts of the understanding, *conceptus intellectus puri*. We can of course set these activities of the understanding in motion only when occasioned to do so by sensible impressions and can become aware of certain concepts of the general relations of abstracted ideas in accordance with the laws of the understanding; and thus Locke's rule that no idea becomes clear in us without sensible impression is valid here as well; the *notiones rationales*, however, arise no doubt by means of sensations, and can also only be thought of in application to the ideas abstracted from them, but they do not lie in them and are not abstracted from them. [. . .]

> The philosophy of the concepts of the *intellectus puri* is metaphysics. [. . .] The concepts of existence (reality), possibility, necessity, ground, unity and multiplicity, whole and part (everything, nothing), of the composite and the simple, space, time, alteration, motion, substance and accident, force and action, and everything that belongs to ontology proper, are related to the rest of metaphysics [. . .]. (17: 352)

This precritical *Reflection*, before the discovery of the Aristotelian categories, seems to suggest that a priori concepts are acquired from the laws of understanding in its activity of comparing, combining, and separating. In fact, the result of these activities is the pure concept of the understanding (*conceptus intellectus puri*). But these three activities in *The Jäsche Logic* seem to supersede the logical origin of common concepts, that is, of representations common to several objects (*conceptus communis*) (9: 94). One can doubt that in this tentative, precritical reflection Kant was thinking of the pure concepts of understanding as categories, especially since in *The Blomberg Logic* abstract concepts refer only to a posteriori concepts that are educted (*ektypa*) (24: 253), while we know that categories are produced. In other reflections, such as *Reflection 3988* (1769), or *Reflection 4172* (1769-1770), Kant states that the pure concepts of understanding issue from the inner laws of the mind or reason in occasion of experience (17: 378, 443). In *Reflection 409* (1772-1779), Kant states that the pure transcendental concepts of understanding are mere abstract concepts of reflection (15: 166).[223] What seems clear from these *Reflections* is that for Kant categories issue from the use of the natural powers of understanding in the occasion of experience. Of course, comparing, combining, separating, and abstracting are all activities of understanding, but not in the occasion of a possible experience. In fact, in order to compare, combine, separate, and abstract, the content of the concept must already be given, and one or more representations must already be present to the mind. These operations of understanding concern merely its logical use, not its real or transcendental use. Thus, according to my reconstruction of the problem of habit in Kant, categories concern the transcendental or real use of the understanding, when the understanding has to do with the manifold of the content of experience given by sensibility.

Only in this case, understanding is occasioned by a possible experience. A passage from *Metaphysics L₁* is particularly important in understanding Kant's position:

> Even the concepts of the understanding, although they are not drawn from the senses, do arise on the occasion of experience; e.g., no one would have the concept of cause and effect if he had not perceived causes through experience . . . Accordingly the senses do constitute to this extent the ground of all cognitions, although not all cognitions have their origin in them. [. . .] But how do they come into the understanding? One must not assume them as innate and inborn, for that brings all investigation to a close, and is very unphilosophical. [. . .] But concepts have arisen through the understanding, according to its nature, on the occasion of experience; for on the occasion of experience and the senses the understanding forms concepts which are not from the senses but rather drawn from the reflection on the senses. *Locke* was badly mistaken here in that he believed *all* concepts to be drawn from experience; for he did draw them from the reflection which is applied to the objects of senses. Thus with respect to matter all arise from the senses; with respect to form from the understanding, but they are not inborn in understanding, but rather come about through reflection on the occasion of experience. We practice this action of reflection as soon as we have impressions of the senses. This reflection becomes familiar to us by *habit* so that we do not notice that we reflect. (28: 233–4) (emphasis added).

Kant clearly states that the pure concepts of understanding are not drawn from the senses, but they arise in the understanding in the occasion of experience. The fact that Kant is referring to categories is clear from his example of the concepts of understanding, "cause and effect," which in the *Critique of Pure Reason* is the second category of relation. It is clear, however, that every cognition begins with sensation, in other words, sensation always comes before intellectual knowledge. But this does not mean that sensation is the only source of cognition, as we well know. So the real question is how do pure concepts come into the mind? They are not innate; we have already explained this. They arise, Kant reiterates, in the occasion of experience, but in this case, he adds, "from the reflection on the senses," as in *Reflection 409*. What does Kant mean by reflection? Clearly he is not thinking of the Lockean conception of reflection, which is applied to sensible objects, otherwise the concepts of the understanding would be produced by a *generatio aequivoca*. In order to explain his notion of reflection, Kant argues that what is important is not the matter of cognition, which always comes from sensation, but the form of cognition, which is not innate, but issues "on the occasion of experience," when we have impressions from the senses. The form of cognition, which is the structure of the pure concepts of understanding, comes from the action of reflection on the occasion of experience, but not from reflecting on experience, which is, as we shall see, a different matter. This reflection, Kant adds very meaningfully, becomes familiar by habit, so much so that when we reflect we are not aware of what we are doing, just because this reflection is a kind of second nature that acts spontaneously in the acquisition of the form of cognition. In this passage, Kant openly declares that the concepts of the understanding are acquired through a process of reflection like a habit, and the reference to habit refers us directly to the Aristotelian tradition. In this case, reflection must not be understood as a kind of meditation on something, or as logical reflection in the sense of "a mere comparison, for in its case there is complete abstraction from the cognitive power to which the given representations belong, and they are thus to be treated the same as far as their seat in the mind is concerned" (A 262–3/B 318–9). This reflection is not as Kant defines it in *The Jäsche Logic*, namely, as the logical act through which a posteriori concepts are generated "as to how various representations can be conceived in one consciousness" (9: 94). Rather, reflection is

> the state of mind in which we *first* prepare ourselves to find out the *subjective conditions* under which we can arrive at concepts. It is the consciousness of the relation of given representations to our various sources of cognition, through which alone their relation among themselves can be correctly determined. (A 260/B 317) (emphasis added)

Reflection, according to Kant, determines the relation between sensibility and understanding, which means how understanding works on occasion of experience, that is, when the concepts are originarily acquired. What is more, Kant characterizes this relation as a subjective condition under which we arrive at concepts, that is how, as individual subjects, we acquire concepts, that is, categories. In particular, he calls "transcendental reflection":

> The action through which I make the comparison of representations in general with the cognitive power in which they are situated, and through which I distinguish whether they are to be compared to one another as belonging to the pure understanding or to pure intuition. (A 261/B 317)

This means that nothing other than reflection recognizes the various places and the several steps in the acquisition of knowledge from sensation to understanding, and it identifies to which faculty a particular representation pertains. And we know that through this reflection understanding acquires its pure a priori concepts like a habit. But this process of reflection is similar to what Aristotle describes in the famous passage of *Posterior Analytics* II.19, where the Stagirite explains the acquisition of the habit of understanding. In fact, from sensation, through memory, many experiences and the formation of images, according to Aristotle, we transform sensible knowledge into intellectual knowledge. This passage establishes the relation between these two forms of knowledge. The transition from sensation through imagination up to the understanding is, for Aristotle, a kind of reflection, where reflection is the process of internalization of the sensible object in order to make out of it intelligible cognition. It is no coincidence, therefore, that early-modern Aristotelians like Zabarella and Calov refer to this process of reflection as "notification," just because it explains the passage from the sensible through the intelligible, in other words, how sensible cognition becomes intelligible.

We find a parallel of the Aristotelian text in the passage of *Metaphysics* L_1 that we mentioned earlier. On occasion of experience, the sensible object induces the work of the understanding, which is the faculty for judging, since all actions of the understanding can be traced back to judgments (A 69/B 94). But, Kant explains, "through the senses only singular judgments arise; thus through them we do not receive the concept of cause and effect" (28: 235). So how do we explain the formation of the categories? Like Aristotle, Kant presents this process as a transition from sensation to understanding by means of the imagination, in this period called formative power (*bildende Kraft*). Kant explicitly asks "how do the pure concepts of the understanding enter the head?," in other words, how are categories acquired? He answers:

> we have cognitions of objects of intuition by virtue of the formative power, which is between the understanding and sensibility. If the formative power is *in abstracto*, then it is the understanding. The conditions and actions of the formative power, taken *in abstracto*, are pure concepts of the understanding and categories of the understanding. (28: 239)

This is indeed an obscure passage, in which imagination taken *in abstracto* seems to be the understanding, but of course these two faculties are different for Kant. To make it clear, Kant exemplifies the origin of the pure concept of the understanding of "substance and accident." It comes from imagination, or formative power, in the following manner:

> The formative power must have something permanent underlying it, besides the manifold that alters, for were there nothing at the foundation of the formative power, then it also could change nothing. Now the permanent is the pure concept of substance, and the manifold of accident. (28: 239)

According to Kant, the category of substance can be acquired only if the mind can recognize something permanent not only in what changes after many experiences, but also and foremost after all the accidents are removed. We must distinguish the substance as a "category" from the "schema of substance," otherwise there would be a vicious circle, since for Kant the substance seems necessary in order to recognize something permanent. As James van Cleve has rightly pointed out, "Kant defines substance as that which can exist only as subject, never as predicate (see B149 and B288). Here, of course, the terms 'subject' and 'predicate' mark an ontological distinction between kinds of entity, [. . .] so we might (in first approximation) restate his definition by saying that a subjectance is a bearer of properties that cannot itself be borne by anything. This is the perennial definition of substance, to be found in Aristotle."[224] This is the only real definition of the category of substance in Kant, and it does not involve a temporal dimension. "Permanent" here means something that remains after all the accidents are removed. Once having produced the category of definition of something, one can apply the "schema of substance" of the category of substance, which involves the temporal dimension, since it is "the persistence of the real in time, i.e. the representation of the real as a substratum of empirical time-determination in general, which therefore endures while everything else changes" (A 144/B 183). *Mutatis mutandis*, this is what Aristotle says in *Posterior Analytics* II.19,[225] when he states that although sense-perception is common to all animals, in some the sense-impression comes to persist; whereas those animals in which this persistence does not come about have either no knowledge at all outside the act of perceiving, or no knowledge of objects of which no impression persists, while in those animals that perceive and retain sense-impressions, out of the persistence of such sense-impressions generate a common notion of what persists in the imagination and in the intellect. For instance, in seeing many individuals, the mind retains and discovers something persistent, which is the common notion of human beings, which is the permanent underlying the manifold of humans taken into consideration. Beyond all the accidents of Socrates and Callias, such as the snub nose or the color of the eyes, which may mutate, the substance that remains and that cannot be predicated of anything else is that they are both humans.

In Kant, this process of transition of cognition from sensibility to understanding through imagination, is a kind of reflection, so much that "understanding a priori is thus the faculty for reflecting" and not only the faculty of concepts, of judgments, and of rules (28: 240). Kant also adds that parallel to the understanding as the faculty of concepts is sensibility as faculty of intuition. The parallelism is possible according to Kant because both sensibility and understanding deal with "original forms" (*ursprüngliche Formen*), where "original forms" means "originarily acquired." Kant distinguishes sensibility and understanding because the former consists only in forms, while the latter is also the faculty of rules. Both sensibility and understanding, however, have a common root in the consciousness, which is the necessary condition of all cognitions (28: 240), as Kant had already stated in *Reflections 4851*.

In conclusion, according to Kant, the pure a priori forms of cognition, that is, space, time, and categories, are originally acquired like an Aristotelian habit. This acquisition does not prevent them from operating a priori of all possible empirical knowledge since they are structures like a second nature. This second nature rests on the ground of the very first, intimate, innate nature of the mind, which is properly speaking the fundamental germ and source off all possible dispositions that may develop in occasion of experience generating the intuitions of sensibility and the pure concepts of the understanding. This system of production of the a priori forms of cognitions is what Kant calls epigenesis, and constitutes the core of his "transcendental physiology," which is the basis of his transcendental logic.

2

TRANSCENDENTAL LOGIC

MATTER AND FORM

We saw in the previous chapter that facultative logic deals mainly with the cognitive structures of the mind and their origin. In this chapter, we will see how these cognitive structures and forms work, examining Kant's transcendental logic in particular in order to find the Aristotelian conceptions behind his doctrines. We have already recognized the importance for Kant's epistemology and facultative logic of the conceptual pair "matter and form" of cognition. I will now go on to show its importance for transcendental logic. I will not consider the role played by this distinction in general logic, according to which matter is the content of a logical inference and form is its figure and structure, a distinction that is present in Kant, as in the Wolffian and Aristotelian traditions.[1] Rather, I will consider the conceptual pair in his epistemological program.

The "matter and form" distinction was first introduced by Kant in his facultative logic in the *Inaugural Dissertation*, by way of characterizing two fundamental elements of cognition that were to become central issues in the critical period and reappeared at crucial points later on, such as in the "General Remarks on Transcendental Aesthetic" and the "Introduction: Idea of a Transcendental Logic" in the *Critique of Pure Reason*. Matter concerns the a posteriori content of cognition given by sensation, while the form is the pure and a priori structure of the mind through which it is possible to cognize objects. Scholars have neglected the importance of this conceptual pair, reducing it to the distinction between sensation and concepts, which results only in a leveling of Kant's thought without explaining why Kant uses a different terminology, nor accounting for its originality in the elaboration of his theory of knowledge.

The big issue is that the conceptual pair is absent, or at least marginal, in the Wolffian tradition. It is mentioned only once in Wolff's *Philosophia rationalis*,[2] and it is not present in Baumgarten's *Acroasis Logica*, in Meier's *Auszug aus der Vernunftlehre*, and in Feder's *Logik und Metaphysik*, the logical textbooks, in other words, read or used by Kant.[3] Matter and form seem to be two new, or hitherto unexplored, concepts in the eighteenth-century logical framework, though they appear to acquire a new momentum with Kant's philosophy. Such a picture is tendentious, however, if we consider the other important philosophical tradition in Königsberg, namely Aristotelianism, where this conceptual pair is at the heart of epistemology.

Königsberg Aristotelianism, as we have seen, makes a significant use of the concepts of matter and form to characterize the basic elements of cognition. The sources are Aristotle's *Metaphysics* and *On the Soul*. In the first book of *Metaphysics*, Aristotle states that sensation generates experience, and with experience we attain knowledge of particulars.[4] Knowledge of particulars, however, is not a universal and scientific knowledge: it is only probable because it is based on a limited number of cases. Scientific knowledge, therefore, does not concern sensation, because by means of it we know only matter, and matter is not necessary, rather, it is a mere accident. Sensations make us know particulars, but not the reason or the causes of things.[5] Scientific knowledge concerns the form that makes us know the universal, that is "what is" a thing.[6] This treatment of the distinction between matter and form, between particular and universal, occurs many times in Aristotelian writings. The opposition between particular and universal knowledge is present also in Wolffian logic, but not in the sense that Kant uses the conceptual pair.

The Aristotelian issue concerns the way through which we know the form. In *On the Soul*, Aristotle explains that the affections of matter affect the senses and are transformed by the imagination into images and by the understanding into intelligible forms. There is a process of notification of knowledge from matter to form that I have characterized as a form of reflection. Yet neither is this how the distinction appears in Kant. There is in Aristotle a radically different understanding of these two concepts compared to Kant. Form always pertains to the known object; it is the formal cause. Although it is epistemologically an explanatory and heuristic device for the mind, in actuality form pertains to the thing; in other words it is not something that can exist without its corresponding matter. Everything is composed of matter and form, the knowledge of which, if we have cognition of a thing, always concerns the thing and not the knowing subject.

In *Nicomachean Ethics* I.7, 1098 a 25–35, however, Aristotle uses the distinction in the Kantian sense: "[. . .] we must not look for equal exactness in all fields of study, but only such as belongs to the subject matter of each, and in such a degree as is appropriate to the particular line of investigation." This passage is directly reminiscent of *Metaphysics* II.3, 995 a 15–30, where Aristotle states that it is necessary to be trained in "how" (πος) every knowledge must be investigated, and it is absurd to seek simultaneously the knowledge and the method of obtaining it (τρόπος ἐπιστήμης). Τρόπος ἐπιστήμης is a central concept in Aristotle's epistemology. Most of the time, τρόπος means manner, method, but also direction, way, disposition, attitude, and, in this specific case, from one who knows to what is known. For Aristotle, τρόπος ἐπιστήμης is the point of view, the perspective that one takes in investigating. For instance, one should not take a rigorous τρόπος ἐπιστήμης as a material object, as one should do for mathematics, because matter is accidental and therefore it does not demand scientific knowledge. Every subject-matter requires a particular method or mode of investigation. This is particularly clear from Aristotle's words: "[. . .] a carpenter and a geometrician both try to find a right angle, but in different ways; the former is content with that approximation to it which satisfies the purpose of his work; the latter, being a student of truth, seeks to find its essence or essential attributes."[7] Both carpenter and geometrician have the same matter of cognition, that is, the right angle, but they investigate and consider it differently, that is, with divergent intentions, and this is the idea that establishes the many standpoints of the various knowing subjects. The differences of the point of view depend on the various habits that have been acquired by the knowing subjects.

It is mainly from this passage that the Aristotelian tradition has elaborated a theory of subjectivity of cognition. The first to assess the conceptual pair "matter and form" of cognition, as we have seen, was Zabarella, with the distinction of subject-matter (*res considerata*) and mode of considering (*modus considerandi*).[8] Zabarella's distinction became quite popular during the first half of the seventeenth century in authors such as Alsted and Calov.[9] But what is striking is a significant terminological shift: while Zabarella spoke of a "subject" (*subjectum*) that "has two parts, one material and it is called matter; while the other is form, and it is called mode of considering,"[10] Calov dealt with an object (*objectum*) that has two parts, that is subject matter and mode of considering, showing a new kind of sensitivity. Calov adds that beings are the material object, while the form is our possibility of knowing them (*scibilitas*).[11] The form, Calov states, is a pure function of the mind (*pura mentis functio*),[12] which means that our mode of considering (*modus considerandi*) is a pure function of conceiving, knowing, and signifying from different standpoints the matter (*res considerata*). It is pure because it abstracts from the matter, that is from the *res considerata*. It is no giant leap to Kantian intuitions and categories such as pure forms without matter.

Calov's theories are standard for Königsberg Aristotelians like Melchior Zeidler, Andreas Hedio, and Paul Rabe up to the first decades of the eighteenth century. But the distinction occurs many times also in Leibniz's philosophy, which represents a turning point in the understanding of the conceptual pair.[13] It assumes different meanings in various contexts. Normally speaking, instead of a mode of considering (*modus considerandi*), Leibniz prefers to use the expression mode of conceiving (*modus concipiendi*).[14] Probably the most meaningful occurrence of *modus considerandi* is in the short treatise *Primae veritates*. Dealing with the principles of indiscernibles, "there cannot be in nature two singular things, differing only numerically," Leibniz establishes the distinction between matter and mode of considering:

> In that context things are considered only in a certain respect, not in every mode—as, for example, when we consider shapes alone, ignoring the matter that has the shape. And so it is justifiable to consider two perfectly alike triangles in geometry, even though two perfectly alike triangular material things are not found anywhere.[15]

According to Leibniz, form and matter constitute two different aspects of the same thing. When things are not conceived in every mode, or not completely (*omnimode*), rather according to a particular *modus considerandi*, it is possible to find in nature two things equal to each other. If we consider a triangle only for its form or figure, it is always possible to find a similar triangle. But if we consider also its material aspect, it is impossible to find another identical triangle. In nature, therefore, in a very Aristotelian way, what distinguishes the various beings is properly matter. If we consider two things only from the logical standpoint, namely for their form, these can be considered identical. The form is therefore definitely the mode of conceiving, considering, knowing, dealing, and determining the object of cognition. Leibniz adds significantly: "space, time, extension and motion are not things, but modes of considering grounded [in things]."[16] In this sense, space and time, with extension and motion, are forms through which the objects are determined in a very particular way: they are modes of accessing a portion of reality. The modes of considering never provide an exhaustive knowledge of the object in its totality, in its essentiality according to a complete determination. They provide a partial knowledge of objects from their particular standpoint, as the objects appear to the knowing subject, rather as they are in truth. This is particularly striking, as we will see, in relation to Kant's conception of space and time, which are forms of intuition for sensing and cognizing, which provide the mind the appearance of the object. In order to have a perfect knowledge of the objects as they are, according to Leibniz, a process of clarification and distinction is required, which transforms the confused knowledge of things as they appear to us according to specific *modi considerandi*, and gives a complete intelligible notion of the objects as they are.

We find the conceptual pair matter and form in many Eclectic philosophers like Crusius and Knutzen.[17] In particular, Kant's teacher, in his *Elementa philosophiae rationalis*, retains the Aristotelian distinction between matter and form as material cause and formal cause, elaborating a distinction between material object (*objectum materiale*), formal object (*objectum formale*) and mode of cognizing (*modus cognoscendi*). He states that the material object is every possible indeterminate thing, the formal object is the real cause of the thing,[18] while the mode of cognizing is how we acquire knowledge of the formal object from the material object.[19]

As we have seen, in Kant, the first significant occurrence of the pair matter and form is in the *Inaugural Dissertation*. In § 4 Kant states:

> In a representation of sense there is, first of all, something which you might call the *matter*, namely, the *sensation*, and there is also something which may be called the *form*, the *configuration* namely of sensible things which arises according as the various things which affect the senses are co-ordinated by a certain natural law. (2: 392)

This means that each representation has a material part, which comes from sensation, and a formal part, which is the mode through which representations are coordinated in the mind by means of a natural law (2: 393). Kant adds that the matter of representation induces belief in the presence of a sensible object, while the form of the representation testifies to an inherent law of the mind, which coordinates the sensuous percepts from the presence of the objects. In fact, according to Kant, objects do not strike the sense by means of the form, but through matter. Form would be that which allows unification in one single representation of the sense-affecting objects. It is a stable and innate law or species (2: 393). In § 5, Kant concludes by stating that sensuous knowledge, which is not sensible knowledge, concerns matter, while form pertains to that kind of knowledge that is possible also without any object.

With the *Inaugural Dissertation*, Kant became full professor of logic and metaphysics at Königsberg, where for the rest of his life he taught courses of logic on Meier's *Auszug* and Feder's *Logik und Metaphysik*. No textbook, as mentioned previously, presents any specific discussion on the matter and form of cognition, the importance of which is established by Kant's personal additions to these manuals. *Reflection 1694* clearly illustrates the role of the distinction between matter and form. As knowledge in general of the object, philosophy for Kant is primarily a science of the laws of understanding and reason, and as such it is called logic. Logic is an analytic of the understanding, it examines its functions, but before beginning the analysis it is necessary to introduce—Kant states—the distinction between matter and form. Matter is the object (*Objekt*), while form is the subject (*Gegenstand*) of logic (16: 85). Knowledge of matter in general concerns representation, and therefore it always involves experience (16: 85–86). Knowledge of form, on the other hand, has the consciousness as condition and presupposition. Kant remarks that the form is either intuition or concept, and therefore cognizing formally means to know by intuition (*formaliter cognitio est intuitus*) or by concept (*formaliter cognitio est conceptus*) (16: 86). The former is sensible knowledge and is intuitive, while the latter is intelligible knowledge and is mainly discursive (by judgment). Distinguishing the forms of sensible knowledge from the forms of intelligible knowledge, Kant breaks with the Leibnizian tradition according to which there was continuity between sensible and intelligible knowledge: they differed only in terms of clarity and distinctness, but the *modi considerandi* were of the same quality. In the "On the Amphiboly of the Concepts of Reflections," Kant writes that Leibniz considers "the appearances for things in themselves, thus for *intelligibilia* [...] although on account of the confusion of their representations he labelled them with the name of phenomena" (A 264/B 320). For Kant there is a real difference between the forms of sensible knowledge and those of intelligible knowledge, and it is in this distinction that the very possibility of his transcendental idealism is grounded. Kant adds also that the form of intelligible knowledge as concept is the true thinking, and logic, in this case general logic, deals with thinking. So this is the reason why the subject of general logic is the mere form. Logic differs from all the other disciplines because it deals only with forms and not with the content, as already established by Zabarella: "logic abstracts from all real or objective difference of cognition, it can occupy itself as little with the matter of judgments as with the content of concepts" (9: 101).

In *Reflection 1698*, Kant mentions explicitly the Aristotelian distinction between matter and form, writing that "*materia*: object; *forma: modus cognoscendi*," and that logic does not deal with matter, but only with the form (16: 87). Kant identifies matter with the object, with the real existing thing, and the form with the mode of cognizing (*modus cognoscendi*). In *Reflection 1586*, Kant adds that the *modus cognoscendi* is scientific (16: 26). Kant takes the formulation of the Aristotelian distinction elaborated by Zabarella explicitly, neglecting Knutzen's division between the formal object (*obiectum formale*) and the mode of cognizing (*modus cognoscendi*). If it is true that Kant identifies form with the *modus cognoscendi*, it is also true that in *Reflection 1694* he characterizes two different *modi cognoscendi*, one sensible and one intelligible. There are therefore sensible forms and intelligible forms that abstract from matter and are the subject of his transcendental philosophy.

All these precritical reflections are re-elaborated in the *Critique of Pure Reason*. In § 1, he states, "I call that in the appearance which corresponds to sensation its **matter**, but that which allows the manifold of appearance to be intuited as ordered in certain relations I call the **form** of appearance" (A 20/B 34). Kant refers here quite explicitly to § 4 of his *Inaugural Dissertation*. It is extremely significant that Kant in the first edition of the *Critique* employs the terms *ordered* (*geordnet*) and *intuited* (*angeschauet*). Form is thus what allows an intuition. Kant then explains in which sense the form is a priori to matter:

> Since that within which the sensations can alone be ordered and placed in a certain form cannot itself be in turn sensation, the matter of all appearance is only given to us a posteriori, but its form must all lie ready for it in the mind a priori, and can therefore be considered separately from all sensation. (A 20/B 35)

In this way, Kant shows that what orders and allows intuition of the matter of the object cannot be derived from matter itself or from the object, but must be a priori in the mind, and is the form. Moreover, Kant argues that "pure" is all that in which we do not find anything related to matter, exactly as Calov conceived form as a *pura mentis functio*. The pure form of sensible intuition, by means of which all the manifold is intuited in a particular order, is therefore in the mind, and it is properly called "pure intuition." Pure intuitions are the forms of sensation, the *modi cognoscendi* of the sensible object. Specifically, Kant states that just as there are forms of sensibility, that is, pure intuitions, there are also pure forms of the understanding:

> If I separate from the representation of a body that which the understanding thinks about it, such as substance, force, divisibility, etc., as well as that which belongs to sensation, such as impenetrability, hardness, color, etc., something from this empirical intuition is still left for me, namely extension and form. (A 21/B 35)

Extension and form (*Gestalt*) thus pertain to pure intuition, which takes place "even without an actual object of the senses or sensation, as a mere form of sensibility in the mind" (A 21/B 35). "Transcendental Aesthetic" concerns exactly the forms of sensibility, namely the *modi cognoscendi* of the object considered from its sensible aspect.

At the end of § 1, Kant announces that the only *modi cognoscendi* of transcendental aesthetic are space and time (A 22/B 36). In this passage, Kant's conception of space and time, between objective reality and transcendental ideality, was influenced in a clear and distinct way by Leonhard Euler's Newtonian perspective and by Leibniz's standpoint. Indeed, Leibniz was the first to state in the short treatise on *Primae veritates*, as we have seen, that space and time are *modi considerandi* of an object. They provide only a phenomenal knowledge of the object, because they reveal only some, not all, perspectives on the object. The doctrine of space and time as pure forms of sensibility is not originally Kantian, but with some differences, it has a Leibnizian matrix. Kant himself reveals his debt to Leibniz in the *Metaphysical Foundations of Natural Science*, writing that "a great man" made us aware more than anyone else of "the well-founded reminder *that space belongs only to the appearance of outer things*" (4: 507).[20] It is true, however, that Leibniz adds also motion to space and time as the *modi considerandi* of sensibility. But Kant is careful to contrast this opinion, stating that "the concept of motion (as alteration of place), is only possible through and in the representation of time" (A 32/B 48). Against Leibniz he maintains that

> That transcendental aesthetic cannot contain more than these two elements, namely space and time, is clear from the fact that all other concepts belonging to sensibility, even that of motion, which unites both elements presuppose something empirical. (A 41/B 58)

Motion in fact presupposes something empirical, in other words the perception of a movable. Only in experience as an empirical datum, therefore, can there be motion; in space considered as pure form, nothing is movable. In the same way, alteration cannot be an a priori form, "for time itself does not alter, but only something that is within time. For this there is required the perception of some existence and the succession of its determinations, thus experience" (A 41/B 58). Kant denies that motion and alteration are forms like *modi cognoscendi*, designed to save the objective reality of space and time, as Euler did, by means of the indisputable law of inertia, which pertains in particular to motion. The law of inertia establishes that a body will stay at rest or stay in motion unless acted upon by a net external force.[21] This mechanical law is so self-evident and certain that, according to Euler, it is impossible to refute.[22] Thus for Euler the law of inertia is grounded in space and time, which alone accounts for their objective reality, as opposed to the Leibnizian claim that makes of them fictional ideas.[23]

If Leibniz gave Kant sufficient reason to consider space and time as *modi cognoscendi*, that is as evidence for their transcendental ideality, Euler proved their objective reality on the basis of the incontrovertibility of mechanical laws.[24] In this context, the distinction between matter and form breaks with the "Transcendental Aesthetic." Kant in fact states that space and time are nothing other than forms of sensibility, that is subjective conditions, points of view (*Standpunkte*) of the mind on experience (A 26/B 42). He points out that the forms have reality in relation to the object, that is an objective validity, but at the same time are ideal in relation to the objects that reason considers in themselves without matter (A 27/B 43). Kant makes it clear that these forms are not forms of the object in themselves, and he adds that in themselves objects are not knowable (A 30/B 45). The form must not be sought in the object, but in the subject to which the object appears, even if it pertains really and necessarily only to the appearance of the object (A 38/B 55). In this way, Kant maintains the Aristotelian and Leibnizian conception, distinguishing the form as a *modus considerandi*, from the form as essence, which is never knowable.

Taking his cue from Johann Heinrich Lambert and Moses Mendelssohn's criticism of his *Inaugural Dissertation*, Kant revisits and attempts to address Euler's objection to Leibniz in order to resolve the various controversies, fomented primarily by the Newtonians, on the ideality and reality of the pure forms of sensibility.[25] The objection states that:

> alterations are real (this is proved by the change of our own representations, even if one would deny all outer appearances

together with their alterations). Now alterations are possible only in time, therefore time is something real. (A 36–37/B 53)

The answer to this charge is not difficult for Kant, who states that time is beyond any doubt something real, that is, the real form of inner intuition. Time as form has

> subjective reality in regard to inner experience, i.e., I really have the representation of time and of my determinations in it. It is therefore to be regarded really not as object but as a way of representing myself as object. (A 37/B 53–54)

Time is characterized as a mode of representing (*Vorstellungsart*), that is a *modus repraesentationis* or *considerandi*, employing quite evidently an Aristotelian terminology.

Against this objection, Kant maintains that he has established for the first time the real and objective nature of time. Newtonians, who demonstrate the existence of time from external experience, were always confronted by idealism, because external senses can prove deceptive with regard to outer objects, while "the reality of the object of our inner sense (of myself and my state) is immediately clear" (A 38/B 55). This is possible for Kant only by distinguishing the matter and form of cognition; indeed, the Newtonians

> did not consider that both [space and time], without their reality as representations being disputed, nevertheless belong only to appearance, which always has two sides, one where the object is considered in itself [. . .] the other where the form of the intuition of this object is considered. (A 38/B 55)

Kant also takes into consideration the criticism of certain metaphysicians of nature, the Leibnizians, who hold that space and time were relations of contiguity and succession among appearances (A 40/B 57). According to Kant, they cannot explain the validity and the apodictic certainty of a priori mathematical doctrines in regard to real things. If space and time are nothing other than a product of the imagination derived by abstraction from the relations of experience, they will always be a posteriori and incapable of providing a certain and necessary ground for mathematical doctrines. With this charge, Kant repeats exactly Euler's objection to Leibnizians in his *Réflexions sur l'espace et le tems* (1748).[26]

Both positions, the Leibnizian and the Newtonian, have their advantages and disadvantages, but according to Kant only his transcendental idealism, which conceives space and time as two original forms of sensibility abstracted from matter, can overcome all difficulties (A 41/B 58). In the "General Remarks on Transcendental Aesthetic," Kant confirms that space and time are pure form of sensibility, while sensation in general provides matter (A 42/B 59–60). The form is knowable only a priori, before any real perception, while matter concerns a posteriori knowledge, that is empirical intuition (A 42/B 60).

In *On a Recently Prominent Tone of Superiority in Philosophy*, Kant points out the difference between the form of sensibility and that of the understanding in relation to matter:

> In form resides the essence of the matter (*forma dat esse rei*, as the schoolmen said), so far as this is to be known by reason. If this matter be an object of the senses, then it is the form of things in intuition (as appearances), and even pure mathematics is nothing else but a form-theory of pure *intuition*; just as metaphysics, *qua* pure philosophy, founds its knowledge at the highest level on *forms of thought*, under which every object (matter of knowledge) may thereafter be subsumed. (8: 404)

In the "Transcendental Aesthetic," Kant emphasized the intuitive nature of space and time, distinguishing them from the discursive forms of the understanding. This directly recalls *Reflection 1694*, where the formal way of cognition of sensibility was intuition, while the formal way of cognition of the understanding was concept. It is this substantial difference between the forms of sensibility and of the understanding that led Kant to reassess the distinction between matter and form in the "Idea of a Transcendental Logic" (A 50–51/B 74–75). The pure concepts of the understanding are the forms, namely, the *modi cognoscendi* of the understanding regarding any possible object. The distinction comes into play in answer to the question "What is truth?" Logical truth can never be for Kant the agreement of a cognition with its object, because logic abstracts from matter and, as we have seen, deals with mere forms. Therefore, if "we have called the content of a cognition its matter, one must therefore say that no general sign of the truth of the matter of cognition can be demanded, because it is self-contradictory" (A 59/B 85). The sign of truth must be found in the universal and necessary laws of understanding according to the form with the exclusion of any content (A 59/B 83–84). This criterion of truth has its validity within general logic, while in transcendental logic the mere form of cognition, "however well it may agree with logical laws, is far from sufficing to constitute the material (objective) truth of the cognition" (A 60/B 85). This means that mere form is not enough to formulate judgments on objects: matter is always required as content of experience. The main task of transcendental logic is therefore to explain the relation of matter and form of cognition. Kant returns to these ideas in the "Introduction" of *The Jäsche Logic*. In answer to the question "What is truth?," it is necessary to distinguish every cognition that pertains to matter, which refers to the object, to what concerns the mere form, which is the condition without which a knowledge would be impossible. Kant resolves the original problem into two different more specific questions: "(1) is there a universal material, and (2) is there a universal formal criterion of truth?" (9: 50). The answer to the first question is that a universal material criterion of truth is impossible because contradictory. In fact, for a criterion to be universal, that is universally valid for all objects, it must abstract from the differences of the various objects, that is, from their matter. But that is not all: a universal material criterion should refer to the matter from which it should be abstracted for determining whether a cognition is in accordance with that specific object. It is absurd therefore for Kant "to demand a universal material criterion of truth, which should abstract and at the same time not abstract from all difference among objects" (9: 51).

Instead, formal truth consists in the agreement of cognition with itself, abstracting from all the objects and from all the differences among them. Agreement between the object and the universal condition is no longer required. The universal formal criteria of truth are therefore "universal logical marks of the agreement of cognition with itself or—what is one and the same—with the universal laws of the understanding and of reason" (9: 51).

Kant's reflections on the distinction between matter and form in the *Critique of Pure Reason* are further developed after 1781. In the chapter "On Matter and Form" of his *Lectures on Metaphysics*, Kant resumes the ideas explored in "On the Amphiboly of Concepts of Reflection" of the first *Critique*, where matter was conceived as a determinable and form as a determination (A 261/B 318). Kant's source is without doubt Baumgarten. Kant argues that

> this difference between matter and form lies already in the nature of our reason. *Matter* is given (*datum*), what is given, thus the *stuff*. —But *form* is how these givens (*data*) are posited, the manner in which the manifold stands in connection. We see matter and form in all parts. [. . .] In our soul the sensations are matter; but all our concepts and judgments are the form. Matter in the *physical* sense is the substrate (*substratum*) of extended objects, the possibility of bodies. But in the *transcendental* sense every given (*datum*) is matter, but the form [is] the relation of the given (*dati*). (28: 575)

Kant characterizes two kinds of matter, physical and transcendental. In the physical sense, which does not concern logic, matter is the substance of which everything is constituted. In the transcendental sense, matter is every possible object of knowledge. Introducing his conception of "transcendental matter," Kant establishes a distinction with a "transcendental form" as follows:

> Transcendental matter is the thing that is determinable (*determinabile*); but transcendental form the determination, or the act of determining (*actus determinandi*). Transcendental matter is the reality or the given (*datum*) for all things. But the limitation of reality constitutes transcendental form. All realities of things lie as if in infinite matter, where one then separates some realities for a thing, which is the form. Matter is distinguished into matter out of which (*materia ex qua*), in which (*in qua*), and around which (*circa quam*). —Matter out of which (*materia ex qua*) is the thing itself which is determinable (*determinabile*), a thing which

is already determined. Matter around which (*materia circa quam*) means matter in the act itself of determination (*in ipso determinationis actu*), e.g., the text of a sermon is not matter out of which (*materia ex qua*), but rather around which something else moves about (*circa quam aliquis versatur*)—Matter in which (*materia in qua*) means the subject of inherence. Matter around which (*materia circa quam*) properly means the thoughts by which a matter is given form. E.g., the plan of a building is matter around which (*materia circa quam*), but the stone, wood, etc., are the matter out of which (*materia ex qua*). (28: 575)

Kant concludes by stating that all these differences between *materia ex qua*, *materia circa quam* and *materia in qua* are very fine, and that what is at least really important is the distinction between matter and form: matter is given in an indeterminate way and must be determined by the forms, which are intuitions and the pure concepts of understanding.

In *The Jäsche Logic* we find the final version of Kant's distinction of matter and form of cognition in connection with his transcendental philosophy. Kant writes that every cognition refers both to the object and to the subject. In general, this distinction corresponds to that of matter and form, and in fact Kant emphasizes that "in every cognition we must distinguish *matter*, i.e., the object, and form, i.e., the way (*Art*) *in which* we cognize the object" (9: 33). Kant gives the famous example of the savage who, upon seeing from afar a house without having cognition of it, has the same representation (*materia*) as a man who knows what a house is. The house, that is matter, is the same for both men, while the *modus considerandi*, that is the form, is different. As far as it concerns the form, the former has only a mere intuition (*bloße Anschauung*), while the latter has an intuition with concepts. The difference of the form of cognition consists in consciousness, because without consciousness we have only obscure representations, while with consciousness we have clear representations. Logic, Kant states, deals only with clear representations and how they agree or are in accordance with their logical form. In logic, no cognition is added concerning matter, but we have a different consideration of the object through the form (9: 35).

In conclusion, the distinction between the matter and form of cognition plays a crucial role in Kant's facultative and transcendental logic. It comes from the Aristotelian tradition and characterizes, on the one hand, the known object and, on the other hand, the subjective modes of cognition of the mind. This distinction was elaborated by sixteenth- and seventeenth-century Aristotelians like Zabarella in terms of *res considerata* and *modus considerandi*. With gnostology and noology, the *modus considerandi* assumes particular significance in a broader epistemological theory; in particular, in defining the act of cognizing, which depends on the specific habits of the mind that characterize the differences of the various *modi considerandi*. Within this tradition, the distinction "matter and form" corresponds to the distinction between "objective and subjective."

In Leibniz, the *modus considerandi* becomes one of the various modes for cognizing the object, but it provides only a partial knowledge from just certain points of view. The *modi considerandi* thus concern the phenomena, namely what appears, and not the noumena. These *modi considerandi* are in particular space, time, extension, and motion.

Kant takes up the Aristotelian distinction, probably through the mediation of Leibniz, and elaborates it in a complete new way in his transcendental philosophy. Matter and form become two central concepts to understanding Kant's transcendental idealism, in particular, transcendental aesthetic and logic. Matter represents the object in itself, which exists independently from the knowing subject. Form, on the other hand, concerns only the structures through which the mind knows. But, unlike Leibniz, Kant introduces a distinction between the forms of sensibility and those of understanding. The forms of sensibility are space and time, while those of understanding are the pure concepts, or categories. According to Kant, the forms are totally a priori, and describe the ways in which the objects appear to the subject, in other words, that without which the subject could not have experience. In this sense, Kant develops the Aristotelian distinction to elaborate a new theory of a priori epistemic subjectivity that opens the way to transcendental idealism.

SYLLOGISTIC AND COMBINATORICS BEFORE KANT

In order to arrive at such a sophisticated theory, Kant immersed himself in all the major logical doctrines then available, including

Aristotle's, which was at that time still alive in Königsberg, as we have seen, but otherwise practically forgotten. For a long time, and with good reason, Aristotelian logic was associated with the doctrine of syllogism. After the Renaissance, however, syllogism was superseded in its alleged primacy as a scientific argument by other heuristic tools, one of the most important of which was *ars combinatoria*. As tools for investigating the truth, syllogism and *ars combinatoria* are not in fact in opposition to one another; indeed syllogism was itself mostly conceived of as a particular case of *ars combinatoria*, to which it had to be returned. Issues and aspects of syllogistic and combinatorics are present at various points in Kant's precritical writings, and are important keys to understanding the development of Kantian thought, in particular in relation to categories as cognitive forms of understanding.

Despite the importance of the role of syllogistic and combinatorics in Kant's precritical philosophy, scholars have practically neglected this topic.[27] In this section, I will show Kant's main sources for syllogistic and combinatorics, examining their impact on the precritical works and showing how, from the failure of the project of a *scientia universalis*, the doctrine of the categories was born with the same scopes and objectives.

Syllogism is, following Aristotle's definition, "an argument in which, certain things being laid down, something other than these necessarily comes about through them."[28] Aristotelian syllogism is composed of three terms connected two-by-two in three simple propositions based on the relation of subject and predicate. It is constituted by two propositions known as premises, from which a third proposition necessarily derives, which is the conclusion. Premises must have in common one term, which reconnects the two other extreme terms in the conclusion. The basic structure of syllogism follows the schema, "if A is predicated of every B and B is predicated of every C, then it follows that A is predicated of every C."[29] Given this general argumentative structure, it is possible to say that Aristotle abstracts from every content, and uses simple variables to derive conclusions. This use of the variables alone makes Aristotle the founder of formal logic, even if he was not probably aware of their application.[30] Being based only on the formal structure of reasoning, the truth of the premises is not important for the correctness of the inference, and for this reason we can have for Aristotle various kinds of correct syllogism according to the validity and certainty of the premises. If the premises are true and certain, we have a demonstration; if the premises are only probable, we have a dialectical argumentation; if the premises are false or deceiving, we have a rhetorical inference.

Aristotelian syllogistic was founded on three principles to which the Scholastics add a fourth. The first principle is the law of contradiction, which is the necessary foundation for saying something with a meaning. The other two principles are the *dictum de omni* and *dictum de nullo*. In general for Aristotle, the predicate, which is predicated universally of the subject, is predicated universally also of its parts, and, vice versa, if it is not predicated of the subject, it is not predicated of its parts:

> And we say that one term is predicated of all of another, whenever nothing can be found of which the other term cannot be asserted; "to be predicated of none" must be understood in the same way. [. . .] If A is predicated of every B, and B of every C, A must be predicated of every C: we have already explained what we mean by predicated of every. Similarly also, if A is predicated of no B, and B of every C, it is necessary that A will belong to no C.[31]

Medieval philosophers gave a different elaboration of the *dictum de omni et nullo*, stating that two things that are identical to a third are identical to each other, and two things, of which one is identical to a third and different to the other, are different. Such a principle was called *principium identitatis et discrepantiae*.

Alongside syllogistic, which encompassed a large part of medieval logical *curricula*, the fourteenth century saw the rise of *ars combinatoria*, thanks in particular to the works of Ramon Llull. Llull's explicit purpose was to find "an alphabet for creating the figures and combining the principles and the rules with the aim of finding truth."[32] This alphabet was possible according to Llull because "by means of a letter, which has a lot of meanings, the understanding is more general in receiving more meanings and in constituting science."[33] *Ars combinatoria* would thus consist in a synthetic process that discovers new truths by means of the connections of objects or various symbols. In particular, Llull aimed to determine all the relations among concepts and propositions that could demonstrate scientific and religious truths.

Both syllogistic and combinatorics had mixed fortunes during the Renaissance. As a merely deductive science, unable to find new truths, syllogism faced some fierce opponents in logicians such as Pierre de la Ramée and Francis Bacon, who preferred an *ars inveniendi*, for which, according to the former, logic should not be abstracted from its content, and for the latter, it had to be based mainly on induction. In combinatorics, the logical investigation was mixed with memotechnics and magical issues, as in Giordano Bruno's *De compendiosa architectura lulliana* and Alsted's *ars combinatoria*.[34]

In early-modern German philosophy the problem of combinatorics was strictly related to those of ontology and the formation of concepts through abstraction. In Aristotelian and Scholastic philosophy, abstraction was the main issue on which the concept of "being" was based. Suffice it to recall that the term *ontology* occurred in Goclenius's *Lexicon philosophicum* only in the entry "abstractio."[35] In this sense, it is easy to understand that the problem of concepts was not only the logical-epistemological question of their formation from particulars—the Aristotelian problem of induction (Goclenius, for instance, mentions Jacopo Zabarella's theory of induction)—it was also ontological, its purpose being to determine pure universal concepts that could be predicated of all things as constitutive of the things in themselves, that is, the transcendental concept of being. This is the reason why ontology dealt with the *ens in abstractissima ratione*. This very abstract concept of being was nonetheless only a kind of abstract universal concept that was incapable of providing the basis of a truly descriptive theory of reality, as the philosophers of the German Enlightenment sought: in fact, the concept of being designates all and nothing at the same time, it is too abstract to have any reality, and indeed it could be seen as coinciding with the notion of the merely "possible." They viewed the Aristotelian-scholastic analysis as naive, and turned their attention to the works of Gottfried Wilhelm Leibniz and John Locke.

Leibniz was appreciated especially for his attempt to establish a general science with the *ars characteristica universalis*, which could explain the whole of reality by means of universal primary concepts. These universal concepts, however, were not only explanatory concepts. Indeed, the problem of the *inventarium* of simple terms of logic had a metaphysical significance as well, that is, the universal concepts determined the ontological structure of reality.

In Leibniz's logical works, for the very first time, syllogistic merged systematically with combinatorics.[36] Leibniz's standpoint is crucial to understanding Kant's early philosophy. Leibniz spent most of his life studying logic, and in particular combinatorics. A number of writings are devoted to this issue, but only a few of them were published when he was alive, and thus his thought was little known. The most important work for its seminal and programmatic value is the *Dissertatio de arte combinatoria*, in which Leibniz searched for a new art of thinking, a logic of invention that could describe the entire world. In a letter to Rudolf Christian Wagner, Leibniz was quite clear on this point: "for logic or art of thinking I mean the art of using the understanding, therefore not only of judging what is established, but also finding what is concealed."[37] In this passage, Leibniz shows his Pythagorean and Platonic legacy, and combinatorics becomes the tool for unveiling the most intimate and secret structure of the world, a magical key to disclose all mysteries. Leibniz's Pythagorism is evident in his statement that "there is an old saying that God made everything in accordance with weight, measure, and number. [. . .] From the time of Pythagoras, people have been persuaded that enormous mysteries lie hidden in numbers."[38] Leibniz believes that Pythagoras brought this opinion to Greece from the Orient, and that Plato himself went to Egypt to learn the secrets of mathematics.[39] From this arcane art, men slipped into futile superstitions and made a sort of vulgar Cabbala. This was not the end of the Pythagorean project, however, as it was revived by Ramon Llull, Heinrich Cornelius Agrippa von Nettesheim, Pedro Gregoire, Giordano Bruno, Johann Heinrich Alsted, and Athanasius Kircher, all of whom were unable nonetheless to establish a real science.[40] Leibniz mentions also Jakob Böhme, who believed he had discovered an Adamitic or "nature-language" (*Natur-Sprache*), whereby to discover marvelous things through numbers. But all previous attempts to find this universal language, by means of which notions and things are aptly ordered, were in vain according to Leibniz. Indeed, none of them made any serious attempt to elaborate a language, which contains the art of finding (*ars inveniendi*) and the art of judging (*ars iudicandi*). Leibniz expresses his astonishment at the fact that three great minds such as Aristotle, Joachim Jungius, and Descartes did not attempt such an endeavor.[41] For Leibniz, only after having established an *ars characteristica universalis* can mankind discover a new organ with which to improve the power of the mind.[42]

Leibniz conceived *ars characteristica* and *combinatoria* as a tool for the improvement of knowledge. This tool—he writes in *De organo sive arte magna cogitandi*—corresponds to an alphabet of human thoughts, and is "the catalogue of those concepts that are conceivable in themselves and from the composition of which all the other ideas are derived."[43] For concepts conceived in themselves, Leibniz means those first concepts that do not imply the concept of something other in order to be understood, in other words, those terms that are conceivable a priori. The task of analysis is to perfectly resolve all ideas in those first concepts, and where this is not completely possible, it is nonetheless useful to employ definitions to trace complex ideas back to the simple ones.[44] Leibniz's aim was a complete analysis of the "human thoughts in a sort of an alphabet of primitive notions,"[45] establishing the table of predicaments on which, by means of calculations, it is possible to apply combinatorics. In fact, "every human reasoning is made by means of signs and characters" and "all human thoughts can be resolved in few thoughts, which must be considered [. . .] and from which it is possible to form the characters of the derived notions."[46] This leads to the idea of a universal science which allows a complete and exhaustive description of the world from first concepts. If it could exist, "an exact language [. . .] through which notions can be traced back to a sort of alphabet of human thoughts, all conclusions that derive from the given notions could be discovered by means of a sort of calculation,"[47] like in mathematics. This true language would be like the Cabala of mystic words, or an arithmetic of Pythagorean numbers,[48] but unlike those attempts, this language would be possible in such a way that:

> henceforth, whenever controversies arise, there will be no need of more disputation than what occurs between two philosophers or calculators. It will be sufficient to pick up their pens, sit down at the desks and say to each other (and if they wish also to a friend called for help): let us calculate.[49]

Leibniz's universal science should include not only syllogistic, but also mathematics itself. On this point, Leibniz is very clear: "arithmetic is a science completely subordinated to the combinatorics, that is to the science of formulas in general."[50]

Leibniz's project relies on: (1) the possibility of solving all concepts in a precise number of the simplest concepts, which are not further resolvable; (2) the possibility of an *ars characteristica* in which the fundamental concepts are marked by a symbolic character; and (3) the possibility to determine, by means of calculations similar to those of mathematics, the relations among characters and among the concepts signified by them.[51]

From Leibniz's perspective the universal primitive concepts of the *ars characteristica combinatoria* were not only heuristic instruments for explaining reality in all its complexity; they were also products of the analytic power of the mind, which can move from concrete particulars to general abstract concepts, but they were also the constituent blocks of reality. As such, primitive concepts are not knowable through the demonstrative science of logic, but only through an intuition, which pertains only to God. Thus for Leibniz universal concepts are the result of an act of abstraction of the mind, which nonetheless obeys some objective constraint, and even if the mind does not grasp any similarity among things, conceptualization can always be performed by some other mind, or by God himself, and finally the act of God is anything but arbitrary, having an ontological correlate in things. Universal concepts determine the ideal structure of reality; they are knowable as an abstraction of the mind, but they are also concrete elements of reality, which can be grasped immediately only by a divine intuition. Leibniz's general science is therefore not only considered a structure and object of the human mind, it rests also on the assumption that it mirrors, if only partially, the ontological structure of reality. In Leibniz's conception of philosophy, the logical aspect and the metaphysical aspect are strictly related, because "there is a rigorous parallelism between the doctrine of the monad as a spiritual microcosm that produces from its essence all its contents and representations, and the logical thesis that the subject contains in itself its own predicates."[52] This kind of parallelism confers on universal concepts both an ideal and a real existence.

A completely different standpoint was upheld by the logic of British empiricism. This school combined a broad Aristotelian perspective with a nominalistic theory of universals, which was typical of the medieval logic still widespread in the logical textbooks of Oxford and Cambridge. There are three general claims of British empiricism concerning the problem of universals: (1) universals exist only in the mind, and not in nature; (2) names refer directly only to concepts and not to real existing things; and (3) universals refer to particular concepts of the mind, that is, they are concepts of concepts.

Hobbes was one of the first to defend this thesis, according to which the universal "is never the name of anything existent in nature, nor an idea or phantasm formed in the mind, but always the name of some word or name."[53] So that when a "man" is said to be universal, it is not to be understood that any man was or can be universal, but only that "man" is a universal name common to many things: a "man" in itself does not exist in nature, even if there is a concept in the mind correspondent to a "possible" existing thing in nature to which the universal name "man" can be referred by means of the concept itself. Universal concepts are nothing more than a product of the imagination, which is the reason why concepts bring to mind sometimes one thing, sometimes another. If universal concepts refer to mental concepts, then, according to Hobbes, these in turn can refer either to a concrete thing or to its cause that is produced by the mind. In the first case, we deal with concrete concepts, for example, a body, and in the second case with abstract concepts, for example, corporeity. For "concrete," he means the name of anything existing in nature. Abstract concepts always denote the cause or the essence of concrete concepts and never the things themselves, so they are concepts of concepts, like the universals. But abstract concepts are not always universal, because the concrete concept "Lentulus" has as its abstract concept "Lentulity," which is not a universal.[54] But every universal is an abstract concept and in this way it is possible to resolve the problem of universal concepts by reducing them to abstract concepts and looking for whether they refer to particular things or not. In this way, universal concepts are never the constituent blocks of reality, but rather an heuristic instrument to explain it.

Hobbes's standpoint was further developed by John Locke, whose views were widespread in Germany throughout the eighteenth century. Locke clearly sustains that everything that exists is particular, therefore, general and universal concepts are not concerned with the real existence of things, but rather "are the inventions and creatures of the understanding, made by it for its own use, and concerns only signs, whether words or ideas."[55] Universal concepts are the products of the power of the mind, which can "abstract its ideas and so they become essences, general essences, whereby the sorts of things are distinguished."[56] Locke agrees with Hobbes that universal concepts are the result of abstraction, but not all abstract concepts are universal. Indeed, all simple ideas have abstract as well as concrete concepts: "the one whereof is (to speak the language of grammarians) the substantive, the other an adjective; as whiteness, white, sweetness, sweet."[57]

Besides this distinction, Locke mentions a particular kind of basic and original idea, in other words, abstract concepts that are applicable to everything, such as extension, solidity, mobility, perceptivity, motivity, existence, duration, and number. These are primitive ideas of the mind to which all the others can be reduced and are the universal constituent blocks of knowledge characterizing the act of cognition. They pertain only to the power of the mind in its activity to provide a possible description of the world correspondent to reality, but they do not pertain to reality itself. In opposition to the Leibnizian standpoint, Locke reduces all investigation of universals to the possibility of the mind knowing and experiencing the world with a particular heuristic and explanatory strategy, leaving aside the ontological aspects. However, from the conjunction of the logical-ontological Leibnizian standpoint with the epistemological Lockean perspective, new eclectic philosophical positions emerged in Germany between 1730 and 1760 with philosophers such as Alexander Gottlieb Baumgarten and Christian August Crusius, to name only the most prominent.

Besides Locke and Leibniz's views of the universal concepts, the German debate was determined by Johann Jakob Brucker's reconstruction of the problem in his *Historia philosophica doctrinae de ideis* of 1723. Brucker offers a brief but exhaustive overview of the different positions on the problem of universal concepts from Scholastic philosophy up to British Empiricism. Brucker shows a particular preference for nominalistic philosophers, especially Locke, whose doctrines are carefully examined in the third section of his work on the problem of concepts in modern philosophers. Brucker emphasizes the logical-epistemological reduction of universal concepts from being the constituent essence of substances to the final result of the first operation of the mind (apprehension). Brucker describes the shift from an ontological realistic standpoint, which is found also in Leibniz, to a heuristic logical nominalistic perspective on the universals. In fact, according to Brucker, following the Lockean paradigm, the universal concept must not be confused with its cause; the latter is something that really exists, while the former is what pertains only to the mind.[58] A particular person, such as Socrates or Plato, is the cause of the generation of the universal concept. This position leads to the problem that in this way what the mind really knows—its object—is just a concept or composition of concepts rather than the substance or ontological structure of the world that causes them. What is really and most knowable for the mind is only the universal as an abstract concept, while the mind is wholly ignorant of that to which the concept refers, even if the substance in itself is the first object of knowledge.

In Brucker, it is evident that the problem of universal concepts consists in the dialectic between abstract and concrete concepts, and this would set a pattern for subsequent philosophers. In general, the expression "abstract concept" (or *in abstracto*) denotes a universal concept which has been abstracted by the mind from reality and has no relation to it: it exists only in the mind, not in nature. "Concrete concept" (or *in concreto*), on the other hand, is a universal with a particular relation to reality as its constituent feature: even if it exists in the mind, it can be found in nature in the various particular things.

The problem of the combinatorial project and eighteenth-century metaphysics was to reconcile somehow abstract concepts with concrete concepts in order to find a perfect correspondence between the logical and the ontological aspects of reality and to determine the structure of reality precisely. In the *Schulmetaphysik*, Baumgarten reclaimed the opposition between abstract and concrete concepts in relation to the problem of universals in his *Metaphysica*. In § 149 he writes:

> A universal being is either seen in a more determined being, which is to say an inferior being, i.e. a being in which more determinations are posited than in itself, or it is not (§ 10). In the prior case, it is seen concretely, in the latter, abstractly. The former is the physical universal (in many, in a fact); the latter is the logical universal (after many, after the fact).[59]

According to Baumgarten, the universal is always conceived in relation to the singular, which is contained in it in the sense that a singular is always described by its respective universal. There are two kinds of universal concepts: the *universale in concreto* and the *universale in abstracto*. *Universale in concreto* is also defined as *universale physicum*, which means that the universal really exists in nature and can pertain to many things, even if it "is" singular in the things. In fact, *universale in concreto* realizes itself in the singular, and like the Aristotelian form inheres in the matter. The *universale in concreto* does not exist independently from the thing in which it is. However, it is possible to conceive of it independently from the thing, and in this case the universal is *universale in abstracto*, which can be grasped only after the consideration of many things and which has objective reality only as a product of the mind. What really exists in nature is only the *universale in concreto*, which refers to a particular thing in reality, even if it expresses a universal nature. *Universale in concreto* and *universale in abstracto* differ only in their consideration as something that pertains directly either to reality or only to the mind.

Baumgarten explains his view better from an epistemological perspective in the *Acroasis logica*, in the section titled *Noetica seu de conceptibus*, which clearly shows a Lockean heritage. According to Baumgarten, the object of a concept can be either an "*ens singulare seu individuum*" or "*universale, hoc est, pluribus commune.*"[60] He labels the "*conceptus singularis seu individui*" as an "idea," while the "*conceptus communis, seu eiusdem in pluribus*," that is, the universal, is a "*notio.*"[61] All the concepts are either ideas (singular) or notions (universal). Notions, however, always follow ideas, because the latter deal with singular things while the former with a number of things considered together. Mind strives for universal notions that can collect singular ideas under one concept, because these universal concepts "promote the extension and the rationality of knowledge, and therefore are helpful."[62] If the objective universal is what cognition is looking for, even though it follows singular ideas, it cannot exist independently from singular things, even if they are not singular. The problem is therefore the relation between the singular and the universal. According to Baumgarten, everything that actually exists is singular and individual, and so what the mind actually knows is an idea and never a notion: we know Socrates, Plato, and Aristotle, but never the universal "human being." Since particulars are known by sensation, the idea comes from sensation and is "*conceptus per sensum*," which is called intuition.[63] However, the notion, that is, the universal, is not a "*conceptus per sensationem*," but formed by abstraction (*Absonderung*).[64] For instance, we know "human being" from Socrates, Plato, and Aristotle, but we know it as "rational animal" only by abstraction and specification. "*Conceptus per abstractionem*" is called "*abstractus*." All universals are notions, notions are abstract concepts, ergo, universals are abstract concepts. Concepts like "Lentulity," which are abstract but not universal, are not considered by Baumgarten because they are useless for knowledge, and they say nothing more than the singular idea. Baumgarten, therefore, equates universals with abstract concepts and singular concepts with concrete concepts. The abstraction from sensation to universals is also a process of clarification and illumination (*Aufklärung*), which is possible only through a process of analysis or resolution (*anatomia*), by which the concepts become clearer and more distinct. When a concept cannot be solved, it is called "*conceptus irresolubilis*" or "*simplex*."[65] These insoluble concepts are for Baumgarten the building blocks of knowledge, by means of which all reality can be explained. However, they do not pertain to reality itself, because no ideas correspond to them, but they concern only the explanatory power of the mind.

Baumgarten's view of the origin and formation of universals was widespread during the German Enlightenment, as Samuel Christian Hollmann's *Philosophia rationalis* testifies. According to Hollmann, all that exist are singular and individual things (*res singulares et individua*); these differ from other things not in a physical sense but in a logical sense, according to their determinations. The mental object of a singular thing is an idea, like in Baumgarten. When the mind abstracts from the various determinations, and finds determinations in common with other things, it grasps a universal concept. The singular thing, that is, the idea, is always logically subordinate to the universal concept, although no universal can be formed without particular ideas. From the epistemological standpoint, ideas are prior to universal concepts, which would be mere names without references to the things. Furthermore, universal concepts are obscure in themselves, and the more abstract they are, the more obscure. Universal concepts that are less abstract and therefore less general are clearer, and they permit cognition of particulars. About their existence, Hollmann explicitly agrees with Aristotle's view that universals are nothing outside the mind but achieve their reality only in relation to concrete things. Being a product of a specific mind, universal concepts are always arbitrary: they can differ from person to person according the activity of abstraction of each mind. Ideas, on the other hand, are not arbitrary but necessary, because they come from reality.[66] The relation between abstract concepts and ideas or concrete concepts is ontologically oriented in favor of the ideas, which only have a real existence in nature, while it is logically solved in favor of universals, which involve the activity of the "pure understanding," namely an understanding that has to do only with pure abstract forms and not with concrete knowledge.[67]

Christian August Crusius went further than Baumgarten in his exploration of the relation between abstract and concrete concepts, making this distinction one of the central claims of his *Weg zur Gewissheit*. The distinction rests on the proper operation of the judgment, which is abstraction.[68] Abstraction always begins from individual things. From these, the mind discards the peculiarities of each, looking for a common nature and forming in this way the universal concept. Crusius calls this kind of abstraction *abstractio latitudinis*, or specifically logical abstraction, which is one of the various kinds of abstraction, alongside *abstractio externa*, *abstractio metaphysica*, *abstractio mathematica*, and *abstractio physica*.[69] In every kind of abstraction there is a concept, which is abstract as a result, and a concept, which is abstracted. In Hobbes's terms, the latter is called *concretum*, or the object of the abstraction, while the former with respect to the *concretum* is called *abstractum*.[70] Furthermore, in relation to the content of the abstraction, concepts can be either concrete and irresolvable or abstract and resolvable. In the former case, a concrete or irresolvable concept is a general concept, which can be considered in two ways: first, as a union of manifold parts or properties, like the concept of society; second, as an example according to which it is possible to know many things, even if not clearly, like the universal of beauty looking at Michelangelo's paintings as a canon for the evaluation of all beautiful things.[71] In this sense, a concrete concept is not the object of abstraction; rather, it is a general concept that can be given in reality to comprehend and collect the manifold within it. A concrete concept is, therefore, a real universal, which manifests itself in reality and denotes a singular entity, which, however, gathers together manifold elements that are within it.

A concrete concept is an irresolvable concept, either because not yet resolved, or because it is completely irresolvable by the human understanding (*notio indissolubiliter concreta*).[72] A distinct conception of a concept, on the other hand, is possible only for the resolvable abstract universal. A distinct cognition of abstract universals is a property of mathematical knowledge, while the cognition of concrete universals pertains to physical, philosophical, and ethical knowledge.

From Baumgarten, Hollmann, and Crusius's theorizations, it is quite evident that Leibniz's admonition of a "general science [. . .] of the thinkable in general as such" remained buried inside the old cabinets of the Hannover library and had very little circulation in the subsequent decades.[73] For instance, the young Wolff's hostility toward syllogistic, which he studied during his youth, is well known: "syllogism is rejected as useless not only for finding but also for examining truth."[74] Leibniz openly criticizes Wolff's antisyllogistic position: "about your corollaries, I would not say in an absolute way that syllogism is not a tool for finding truth."[75] The weight of Leibniz's criticism must have been extreme if Wolff, in *Ratio praelectionum*, altered his view, stating that syllogism was a tool for finding truth.[76] About the problem concerning combinatorics, Wolff confines his treatment to just a few paragraphs of the *Psychologia empirica*, showing scarce interest for the topic.[77] Combinatorics is characterized as the "art that teaches how to find useful signs and the way of combining them according to a particular law."[78] The author mentions that combinatorics was conceived by Leibniz as a *speciosa generalis*. It was based on the calculation, that is on the recombination of irresolvable notions which led to the formation of derived concepts. It was in particular the tool of arithmetic and syllogistic. Wolff nonetheless recognizes that the discovery of combinatorics is very difficult,[79] and in many places he states that this art is a *desideratum* that is hard to achieve.[80]

In the *Philosophia rationalis*, Wolff's examination of syllogistic covers 272 paragraphs. In spite of this extensive exposition, it is hard to find any original points in Wolff's treatment. Only the doctrine of prosyllogism and episyllogism seems to have exerted some influence on Kant,[81] probably through Meier's *Auszug aus der Vernunftlehre*.[82] In "On Transcendental Ideas," one of the few passages in which Kant deals with syllogism in the critical writings, he states:

> Reason, considered as the faculty of a certain logical form of cognition, is the faculty of inferring, i.e. of judging mediately [. . .] The given judgment is the universal rule (major premise,

maior). The subsumption of the condition of another possible judgment under the condition of the rule is the minor premise (*minor*). The actual judgment that expresses the assertion of the in the subsumed case is the conclusion (*conclusio*) [...] Now every series whose exponent (whether that of the categorical or the hypothetical judgment) is given may be continued; hence the very same action of reason leads to a *ratiocinatio polysyllogistica*, which is a series of inferences, that can be continued to an indeterminate extent either on the side of the conditions (*per prosyllogismos*) or on the side of the conditioned (*per episyllogismos*). (B 387)

Kant's passage refers explicitly to Wolff's conceptuality of "episyllogism" and "prosyllogism," but also to the *ratiocinatio polysillogistica*, which according to Wolff is a "series of syllogisms connected to each other."[83] Kant's appropriation of Wolff's doctrine of syllogism is very superficial, and I do not think it was influential in his early understanding of syllogism and combinatorics.

In the precritical period, probably one of the most important sources for combinatorics for Kant was the Bernoullis' studies on mathematical logic. Kant possessed in his private library a copy of Jakob Bernoulli's *Ars conjecturandi*.[84] Jakob Bernoulli is mentioned at least twice in Kant's writings, the first time in *The Blomberg Logic*, where he is named as the inventor of the rule of mathematical calculation of the logic of probability (24: 38), the second in *On the Discovery*, in the controversy with Johann August Eberhard. Jakob Bernoulli, with his brother Johann, published in 1685 a short treatise titled *Parallelismus ratiocinii logici et algebrici*. In this work, the Bernoullis, who were not acquainted with Leibniz's ideas on combinatorics and mathematics, showed the parallelism between the mathematical language and logical language, with the aim of reducing the latter to the former: an enterprise destined to fail. The conceptual background behind the Bernoullis's conception was Descartes and Pascal's mathematism,[85] although their ideas were steeped in Port-Royal logic.[86]

The parallelism between logic and mathematics is on three levels: (1) when ideas are composed of multiple things, this happens by conjunction, while in mathematics two quantities are composed by addition; (2) when from the concept of a more complex idea we remove the concept of a less complex idea, the difference of the former idea should remain, such as when from a major quantity we substract a minor quantity, the difference between them should remain; and (3) when the convenience or identity of two ideas is discovered in the mind, or their inconvenience or diversity, they are affirmed or denied in a reciprocal way by means of the particles "is" or "is not" in a judgment (*enunciatio*), like when between two quantities we perceive equality or inequality, they are connected with signs such as "=, >, <."

These analogies between logic and mathematics led to a fourth more important conclusion, that is, the identification of the *principium identitatis et discrepantiae* with the mathematical rule of proportion:

> Syllogistic reasoning is based on, or its foundation is, the rule of *de omni et de nullo*, that is the rule of proportion, that is axioms of mathematical reasoning: "two things that are equal to a third one, are equal to each other." A thing that is major or minor than one of two equals, is major or minor to the other equal too, that is if a = b, and c = b, therefore a = c.[87]

The short writing ends with mention of Nicolas Malebranche's words, "mathematics is the true logic," which is useful in finding the truth and extending the mind's cognition.[88] It is clear, therefore, that, for the Bernoullis, mathematics is the true logic to which syllogistic should aspire.

Another possible Kantian source for combinatorics is Johann Andreas Segner.[89] Kant's private library contained both the *Einleitung in die Natur-Lehre*[90] and the *Astronomische Vorlesungen: Eine deutliche Anweisung zur gründlichen Kenntnis des Himmels*.[91] Segner is often mentioned by Kant in support of the Kantian argument of synthetic a priori judgments of mathematics (B 15) for his mathematical works, in particular, for his "Arithmetic," which is probably the *Elementa arithmeticae et geometriae* (1739) or the *Anfangsgründe der Arithmetick* (1764). The most interesting work for our reconstruction is *Specimen logicae universaliter demonstratae* (1740). The aim of this work is to establish a formal, symbolic system for syllogistic:[92] "Our purpose is nothing else than general and easy laws of formation and resolution of syllogisms, through which we build them."[93] In so doing, Segner is following the Wolffian tradition of geometrical exposition,[94] but he includes also elements of the Eclecticism.[95] Segner's logic is characterized in particular by a use of the symbols aimed at supplying the inadequacy of the natural language when it tries to express exactly the relations among ideas.[96] Another characteristic of Segner's logic is the parallelism between mathematics and logic, like the Bernoullis, specifically in the identity of the principle of the *dictum de omni et nullo*, which is never fully thematized in the work,[97] and of the proportionality: "(categorical) syllogism is a reasoning for which given the relations of two ideas to a third idea, one understands the relation between the former two. Therefore, if $A = B$, and $B = C$ then $A = C$."[98] Given these general characteristics, Segner's logic is the study of the ideas and of their relations. The basic relation is that of inclusion or containment: "of two ideas A and B, A is involved or contained in B, if posited a posteriori B, then A is posited a priori."[99] On this relation, all other kinds of relation depend: opposition, agreement, identity, diversity, subordination, coordination, and infinite opposition.[100]

The peculiar aspect of Segner's logic is its theory and classification of judgments. Judgment (*iudicium*) "is the relation that intercedes between two ideas in a mental representation; and proposition is this relation expressed by words."[101] The original element of Segner's logic is the classification of judgments according to their levels of determination. A judgment is perfectly determined when the relation between two ideas is precisely characterized according to the *species infima*, following the law of inclusion.[102] A judgment is indeterminate if it represents the most general relation between two ideas.[103] All judgments that represent all the other kinds of relation between two ideas are imperfectly determined.[104]

Segner's work did not enjoy much success among his contemporaries, if not in the debate on combinatorics and logic instigated by Gottfried Ploucquet.[105] Ploucquet's writings had a wide circulation during his life, as August Friedrich Bök's collection of his work published in 1766 with some critical essays by the most authoritative logicians of the time testifies.[106] In the *Methodus calculandi in logicis inventa*, Ploucquet defines the logical calculation as the "method of determining the unknown things from known things according to constant laws."[107] Despite this plain definition, which recalls the

Aristotelian definition of syllogism, Ploucquet is sure that "from various objects, different methods arise," therefore, "the calculations vary infinitely, or so much as the kinds of things themselves vary."[108] The infinity of calculations is evident by the different method used for geometrical quantity, forces, degrees, or mere logical or physical things. The variety of the calculations is quite clear in mathematics, where "the variations in simple arithmetic do not correspond to variations in geometry."[109] Establishing various methods, in particular distinguishing also geometry from arithmetic, Ploucquet undermines the foundations of the possibility of a universal science, such as the Leibnizian *ars characteristica*. In fact, he establishes that: (1) not all the things can be taught through universal calculation; (2) if universal calculation could exist, it would express the first principles of ontology, in which, however, there is no use for calculation; (3) if a universal calculation were possible, it would be necessary to know all things first; (4) calculation is always a posteriori of knowledge, thus consideration of things in their material aspect comes first, and not the formal aspect, as it should be; and (5) a universal calculation could pertain only to an immortal being.[110]

The impracticality of a general *ars characteristica combinatoria universalis* is due, according to Ploucquet, to the impossibility of completely reducing concrete concepts to universal abstract concepts. In fact, if there are as many calculations as there are things, namely concrete concepts, then the mind must consider all the concrete concepts in the calculation, a task that is impossible to realize for its limited powers. The *ars characteristica combinatoria* is based on abstract concepts that cannot provide an exhaustive explanation of reality.

Ploucquet develops his theory of universal concept in a short essay titled *Von dem Ursprung der allgemeinen und abgezogenen Begriffe*, which reveals admirably his Aristotelian and Lockean legacy. Universal concepts are the outcomes of the abstraction of the common properties of many objects, even if strictly speaking they do not exist in nature because any operation of mind is always singular, and being singular the object of the operation must also be singular, because otherwise a different operation to make singular concepts universal would become necessary, but also because in this case the first operation would be based on a singular, and so on, ad infinitum. In this case, the universal concept is a "singular" but indeterminate and general concept. Since the universal concept is an indeterminate concept, it cannot be the specific object of the operation of the mind that denotes something in reality. Therefore, according to Ploucquet, it is possible to deal properly only with concrete concepts, not with abstract concepts: the former has an epistemological-psychological validity, while the latter has a merely logical validity that does not describe the whole of reality exhaustively.[111]

Ploucquet's investigation is strictly psychological. He neglects the possibility of universals in a strict sense, because every operation of the mind is a single act that cannot be called universal. In addition, every object that is conceived *in abstracto* and not *in concreto* becomes a nonobject. Nonetheless, the mind demands universal concepts because in its analysis of reality it focuses its attention on the impression of similarity and almost completely neglects the diversity among things. Thus, the mind repeats the concept of a given particular until it assumes a universal validity for manifold concepts. Therefore, a universal concept is nothing other than frequent repetition of the same "singular" concept of which the mind had prior experience. Further, in addition to the actual diversity of particular objects, the psychological processes of the individual mind also deny the validity of universal concepts. In fact, for instance, if the mind could see clearly what happens in all other minds regarding a certain concept of a number, it would know that the modifications of the affections in one mind differ from those of another mind, when they are actually representing that number. Despite his criticism of the validity of universal concepts, Ploucquet argues that the rules, definitions, and divisions of reasoning and other logical elements have only a heuristic value and no ontological consistency. Science proceeds by using formal universality in its arguments, and this is the only reason for accepting the use of universals. In conclusion, "Ploucquet accepts universals with regard to their *Bedeutung*, but rejects them as regards their *Sinn*, because they are psychologically individual images with a representative function."[112] In Ploucquet, therefore, universal concepts are mere names by which it is possible to describe and explain reality, but they are not its constituent elements, as they are for Leibniz.

Ploucquet's calculation does not aspire to universal science, rather, it aspires to an actual application to syllogistic.[113] Like Segner, Ploucquet maintains that the idea is the true object of the understanding and the building block of logic. Judgment is a comparison between two ideas: the first idea in the operation of comparison is called subject, while the second idea is called predicate. In comparing them, if the subject and the predicate are conceived as identical, we have an affirmation; while if they are conceived as different, we have a negation. The peculiar aspect of Ploucquet's logic is that "affirmative judgment conceived by mind is not the understanding of two things, but of only one,"[114] "all affirmative judgments are reducible to one idea."[115] An affirmation, therefore, is nothing other than the expression of one thing by different signs, and in fact every predicate inheres specifically and determinately to the subject, and it is in the mind as one single notion. The distinction between subject and predicate in affirmative judgment is merely explicative, that is, it is conceived with the aim of communicating to others the concepts of the mind, so much that some scholars believed, according to Ploucquet, that symbolic logic was a necessary tool for linguistic communication. In other words, calculation would no longer be a descriptive and heuristic tool of reality; rather, it is what allows the intersubjectivity of knowledge beyond natural languages.

Ploucquet's position was appreciated, although criticized in some of its parts, by Johann Heinrich Lambert. Although Lambert was convinced, like Ploucquet, that there are many symbologies and kinds of calculations of which syllogistic is only one case, he develops his conception in at least two aspects. The first reason is well explained by Lambert in his correspondence with Holland: Ploucquet's method is not "a language neither an art of signs, but only an abbreviation."[116] Ploucquet's approach was considered almost useless for the description of reality, rather it was useful only to communicate in a brief and easy way what has yet to be demonstrated. A second reason for disagreement between Lambert and Ploucquet is the ontological approach of the former in comparison to the latter. For Lambert, truth could be described through logic, and this description was not merely heuristic, but also outlines the foundations of reality itself. In carrying out this project, Lambert, in his *De universaliori calculi idea disquisitio*, endorsed Leibniz's model reducing quantity to quality: it is necessary to find "a method that deals with qualities, or truths, or ideas of things in the same manner with which algebra deals with quantities," in such a way that we can make calculation of qualities, truths, and ideas.[117] Formulating this "actual" *ars characteristica*, which is not merely logical, in such a way that it can characterize the ontological constitution of reality requires the simplest concepts and their relations to be sought. The aptness of the description relies on the resolution of the simplest concepts and of their composition through their relations.[118] Also in the *Versuch einer Zeichenkunst der Vernunftlehre*, Lambert focuses on the problem of concepts as qualities and their relations, but with the emphasis on characteristic marks. A characteristic mark is the element that allows one thing to be represented and distinguished from another. The concept is what is composed of characteristic marks and the representation of a thing in thought.[119] A concept is either simplest or irresolvable when it is constituted by few characteristic marks that are not further resolvable.[120] Given these premises, the combination is not among concepts, but among characteristic marks of concepts. Among these characteristic marks, a particular place is taken by relation, which is the characteristic mark through which a concept is known or determined by another concept.[121]

In Lambert, the problem of fundamental, simplest, irresolvable concepts and their relations is traceable back to the essay *Criterium Veritatis* (1761). Every truth, according to Lambert, is grounded in fundamental concepts (*Grundbegriffe*) and derived concepts (*Lehrbegriffe*). Fundamental concepts are those whose possibility and correctness is immediately understood as soon as they are represented. They are based on inner sensation (*sensus internus*)[122] and have an immediate characteristic mark of truth. In this truth, the truth of derived concepts is based. Conversely, the correctness of the concepts of the first principles of the mind and of every science relies on both the simplest and derived concepts. Theorems, on the other hand, based their correctness on both concepts and principles. In particular, they follow the law of contradiction and they are demonstrated by the doctrine of syllogism. Such a doctrine is the mediated characteristic mark of their truth.[123] Every scientific knowledge is therefore based for Lambert on syllogism, like for Aristotle. However, unlike Aristotle, Lambert follows Locke in finding in the simplest concepts the constituent blocks of reality. Lambert's theory of fundamental concepts as the basis of every truth is in fact a methodological rigorization of Locke's philosophy, which structured all knowledge on simplest ideas coming from sensation and reflection. In fact, the constituent elements of Lambert's *ars characteristica combinatoria* are not essences or numbers as in Leibniz,[124] but come from the primitive contents of experience, which are immediately accepted as absolutely true and valid.

In the *Neues Organon* Lambert explains how the mind achieves these fundamental primitive concepts. Lambert is clear in stating that to understand a thing means to have a representation of it by a concept.[125] A thing is easily distinguishable from other things if they have nothing in common or, if it is absolutely different from the others, which is the same thing. However, in a comparison between two or more things, a common and similar characteristic mark is more recognizable than diversities. In this way the mind represents to itself the common characteristic mark rather than the individual characteristic mark proper to a particular thing. The operation of the mind that enables this consideration is called abstraction. If the mind abstracts the common characteristic marks from the individual ones, it forms an abstract universal.[126] In the realm of experience, the abstract universals, which are common to many things, that is, the fundamental concepts, are existence, unity, solidity, extension, duration, and succession.

These are the universals that describe the whole of reality; on one hand, they are grasped from the experience as *universales in concreto*, on the other hand, being the subject of logic, they are *universales in abstracto*. Lambert explains that they really inhere in things *in concreto*—not as such, but as a property or characteristic of a thing. Solidity does not exist by itself in nature—in fact it is an abstract universal—but it always exists as a solid thing, that is, as property of a body. Therefore these universals have no independent reality apart from real existing things, even if their existence for Lambert is indubitable. They have only a mental reality insofar as they are the universals through which the mind has the particular concept of a thing, that is, can achieve a scientific knowledge of it. However, according to Lambert, "the conceptual elements, of which is constituted the a priori truth or our knowledge, reflect the actual structure of the world."[127] This is an original undisputed position, which leads Lambert to the construction of architectonic science in which universals are the constituent blocks of reality.

The examination of these fundamental concepts was completed by Lambert only in 1771, with his *Anlage zur Architectonic*, in which, however, he does not achieve his purpose of developing an *ars characteristica combinatoria*, just as it is not achieved in the *Neues Organon*. In the *Architectonic*, Lambert gives a rhapsodical exposition of fundamental concepts, such as consciousness, existence, unity, duration, succession, will, extension, motion, and force. His own philosopher's stone remains undiscovered, however, despite the fact that he, more than anyone else, made every possible effort to get closer to the solution, approaching the original perspectives of Leibniz.

Another important source for Kant's early thought is Joachim Georg Darjes. Darjes's influence on Kant's philosophy is confined to the 1750s and 1760s (1: 390; 1: 398; 28: 54); indeed, we do not find his name in Kant's later works (24: 482; 24: 777). Darjes's logic, mainly presented in his *Introductio in artem inveniendi* (1742) and his *Via ad veritatem* (1764), and in their German translations, is aimed, like Segner and Lambert, at discovering a rigorous symbolic systematization of syllogistic. Even if in his youth Darjes maintained a sharp distinction between logic and the *ars characteristica combinatoria* in favor of the more scientific character of the latter,[128] in the mature works he establishes a parallelism between these two sciences following the models of the Bernoullis. The *ars characteristica combinatoria* is a science that "teaches the way of finding the determinations of things by means of a continuous substitution of equivalent signs," and this substitution is "called calculation by philosophers."[129] For Darjes it is necessary to establish the signs at the very outset, and then to deal with how they are combined and substituted. Logic, too, like the *ars characteristica combinatoria*, is formed by signs that composed in an optimal manner can express all things in a determinate way, but while the signs of combinatorics are general (and most of the times are symbols), those of logic are mere terms. Darjes establishes three general rules that identify logic with *ars combinatoria*, and which are very similar to those of mathematics: (1) searching for a simplest, primitive, irresolvable term and associating it with a sign; (2) establishing connections among primitive terms; and (3) composing derived terms from primitive terms.[130] Given this parallelism, logic consists mainly of a combination of ideas. The combination of two ideas is called judgment,[131] while the combination and the deduction of judgment is a reasoning, which in symbolic logic is properly called syllogism.[132] Darjes's combinatorics thus becomes a symbolic representation of syllogistic, which aspires for its precision and truth to the calculation of mathematics.

The last source for understanding Kant's philosophy is Johann Caspar Sulzer. His *Facies nova doctrinae syllogisticae* (1755) is the only book of Aristotelian logic cataloged in Kant's own library.[133] Unlike the other works of the time, Sulzer's logic is based on the theory of classes, which is nothing other than an exposition by sets of the Porphyrian tree. Even the law of contradiction is expressed using classes: "it is impossible that the same thing is and is not in the same determinate class."[134] The basic element of the theory of classes is the concept or idea.[135] Everything that sensation observes in nature is singular, and a singular thing is always distinguished by means of a characteristic mark from another singular thing, and is called individual.[136] If the various singular things are similar for some characteristic marks, they can refer to the same class. The class of first order, in relation to which singular things convene, characterizes the species.[137] If two classes of the first order convene, we have a class of second order which characterizes the kind.[138] If also the classes of the second order convene, then we have the class of the highest kind. All of these classes convene in the end with the class of the highest kind, which is being.[139] The determination of these classes convenes in the definition of the concept.

Once having established what a concept is, it is possible to connect two or more concepts by means of a judgment in a proposition. Judgment for Sulzer, as it will be in Kant, characterizes both the operation of combination and the proposition as the result of that combination.[140] A proposition is constituted by three terms: (1) subject; (2) predicate; and (3) a copula to link subject and predicate.[141] If two combined concepts convene, then we have an affirmation, otherwise a negation. Sulzer's logic therefore deals mainly with the categorical proposition, which affirms and denies the predicate to the subject. The relations established by the copula are four: (1) between the thing and its essential characteristic marks; (2) ascending from the individual to the species and to the kind; (3) descending from the kind to the species up to the individual; and (4) between the thing and its accidental characteristic marks.[142] The various relations are determined also by the quantity of the proposition, which can be universal, particular or singular. All these kinds of proposition can also be either affirmative or negative. On such kinds of propositions that determine specific classes, it is possible to apply the classical operations of opposition, conversion, and equipollence.

Syllogism is a particular kind of judgment in which the first term, the subject, and the last term, the predicate, are connected by means of a middle term.[143] The foundation of affirmative syllogism is *dictum de omni*, while that of negative syllogism is *dictum de nullo*. Sulzer then determines the various possible combinations of syllogistic figures in an algebraic way, establishing a parallelism between logical calculation and mathematical calculation, according to the Bernoullis and Segner, but using a theory of classes.[144]

In general, all pre-Kantian attempts at combinatorics have established the impossibility of a universal science, and they have applied its laws for the study of formal logic, in particular syllogistic. Some authors have searched for a parallelism between syllogistic and mathematics, considering the latter to be more useful. Other authors have emphasized the communicative or the ontological aspect of the combinatorics. There was no general agreement on this universal science, and it did not have a definitive elaboration, but its study was considered extremely fruitful, as we can read from Lambert's words: "even if a universal characteristic could pertain to the same group of things to which pertain the squaring of the circle and the philosopher's stone, nonetheless it could lead to other findings."[145] But one might ask, what do all these conceptions on syllogistic and combinatorics have to do with Kant?

SYLLOGISTIC AND COMBINATORICS IN KANT

Kant's precritical logical works are conceptually determined by these various attempts in combinatorics and syllogistic. On combinatorics, Kant makes only cursory references, even if they are very meaningful, while on syllogistic he devotes an entire academic program, *The False Subtlety of the Four Syllogistic Figures* (1762). The first, and probably the most important reflection on combinatorics of the precritical period is in the *New Elucidation*, which deserves quoting in full:

> Here we have a sample—a trifling one, it is true, but not one which is wholly to be despised—of the art of combining signs, for the simplest terms, which we have employed in elucidating these principles, scarcely differ from signs at

all. I shall take this opportunity to express my opinion of this art. After Leibniz had advertised the merits of his discovery, men of learning all complained that it had been buried along with the great man himself. I confess that the great man's pronouncements on the matter put me in mind of the will of the father in one of Aesop's fables. On the very point of dying, he revealed to his children that he had hidden a treasure somewhere in his field, but before he could indicate the place he suddenly expired. This induced the sons assiduously to turn up the field and work it over by digging it up, until, their hopes disappointed, they nonetheless found themselves certainly enriched by the fertility of their field. I suspect, at any rate, that this will be the only fruit, to be sure, which an examination of that celebrated art will yield, should there be anyone prepared to devote themselves to the execution of this task. But, if I may be permitted to say plainly what the situation is, I fear that the suspicion, somewhere expressed by the penetrating Boerhaave in his *Chemistry* concerning the most celebrated practitioners of the art of alchemy, may have been the fate of that incomparable man. Boerhaave, namely, suspects that the alchemists, having solved many remarkable mysteries, eventually came to suppose that there would no longer be anything which was not in their power, provided only that they put their hands to it. By a certain precipitate anticipation, they talked of those things as achieved which they inferred might, indeed, must happen provided only that they addressed their minds to the realisation of these things. For my own part, I do not deny that, once one has arrived at absolutely first principles, a certain use of the art of signs may be legitimate, for one has the opportunity there of employing the concepts and consequently the simplest terms, as well, as signs. However, when compound cognition is to be expressed by means of signs, all the mind's perspicacity finds itself suddenly stranded, so to speak, on a reef, and impeded by difficulties, from which it is unable to extricate itself. I even find that one philosopher of great renown, the celebrated Darjes, has attempted to elucidate the principle of contradiction by means of signs, representing the affirmative concept by the sign "+A" and the negative concept by the sign "–A," which yields the equation "+A – A = 0." (1: 389–90)

Simplest terms employed in the formulation of logical principles are not different, according to Kant, to the signs employed by combinatorics; nonetheless he decries its futility, even if he had a great respect for Leibniz's attempt. The only result to which it could lead is tilling the soil of logic so that it can one day be a fertile ground on which to grow lush fruits. On this topic, Kant's opinion is not different from that of Lambert, according to whom, even if combinatorics was not a realizable endeavor, it would nonetheless have served to open up new paths of investigation; and—I think—this is the case of Kant's transcendental logic. But to return to Kant's text, combinatorics is compared to the art of the alchemists, who attempted vainly to unveil all the arcane secrets of nature. In particular, Kant criticizes the position of Darjes, whom he charges with falling into a circular argument when he sought to demonstrate the law of contradiction, having already presupposed it in establishing a priori the signs of combinatorics. In this short passage, Kant admits that the combinatorics might have some use where the first absolute principles have already been discovered. In fact, the simplest concepts and terms can be used as signs, but he criticizes the opportunity to express by signs complex knowledge, and this because even infinite combinations of simple terms fail to give a comprehensive description of reality. This conception returns in the *Inquiry Concerning the Distinctness of the Principles of Natural Theology and Morality*, where he understands the utility of the combination, but only after finding all first, simplest, irresolvable concepts:

> Metaphysics has a long way to go yet before it can proceed synthetically. It will only be when analysis has helped us towards concepts which are understood distinctly and in detail that it will be possible for synthesis to subsume compound cognitions under the simplest cognition, as happens in mathematics. (2: 290)

Kant conceives here, as in Leibniz, combination as a kind of synthesis, which must be preceded by a complete analysis. As will be made clear, for Kant a complete analysis of what is given from experience is impossible, therefore the task of finding the first, simplest and irresolvable concepts is never-ending. In mathematics, the use of combinatorics is possible because the concepts are arbitrary and invented by the mind, and we know a priori all the characteristic marks, but for given concepts this is not possible, because, in a very Lockean way, we cannot dig into the essence of things and know all their characteristic marks.

Kant's considerations on syllogistic are very different from those on combinatorics. *The False Subtlety* represents Kant's first logical writings, and—I believe—is a coherent development of logical doctrines barely touched upon in the *New Elucidation*.[146] Unlike the *New Elucidation*, however, Kant has to do directly with the foundation of general logic. Kant at the very beginning defines "to judge," which means "to compare something as a characteristic mark with a thing" (2: 47). This definition seems to come directly from the tradition of combinatorics, as in fact both Segner and Ploucquet deal with a judgment as a comparison between characteristic marks.

Kant then states that the thing itself is the subject, while the characteristic mark is properly the predicate. Every comparison between the subject and the predicate is expressed by the copula *is* or *are*, which when used *simpliciter* designates the predicate as a characteristic mark of the subject, while when used with the sign of negation, it signifies that the predicate is a characteristic mark opposed to the subject. In the first case, when the characteristic mark pertains to the subject, the judgment is affirmative, when the characteristic mark is opposed to the subject, the judgment is negative (2: 47). In this regard, Kant is completely faithful to the conceptual elaborations of his contemporaries.

The characteristic mark is a mark of the subject only in affirmative judgments; therefore, the predicate is always considered as a characteristic mark of a thing in general. In fact, that which is properly called characteristic mark pertains to the subject and is not merely a predicate of it. There is, therefore, according to Kant, a necessary connection in the affirmative judgment between the characteristic mark and the subject, which, however, is impossible in negative judgment. Therefore, the characteristic mark is in general a predicate of a thing, and only if it pertains truly to the subject is it really a "mark." Kant constructs his entire logic on this notion of "characteristic mark." He adds that that which is a characteristic mark of a characteristic mark of a thing is called mediate characteristic mark of the thing (2: 47). It is mediate because only by means of the characteristic mark that pertains directly to the thing does it pertain indirectly to the same thing. From this conception, Kant elaborates his idea of syllogism as a judgment expressed by a mediate characteristic mark. More in general, an inference is the comparison of a characteristic mark with a thing by means of a mediate characteristic mark. The mediate characteristic mark in the syllogism is properly called middle (*terminus medius*), like in the Aristotelian tradition.

The reduction of syllogism to judgment, as we have shown, was carried out in Johann Caspar Sulzer's work, which is probably Kant's source. But the idea was indeed quite common in authors such as Willem Jacob 's Gravesande and Johann Georg Sulzer, who were not primarily concerned with syllogistic. There is little chance of Kant having ever read Gravesande, but it is quite probable that he read Johann Georg Sulzer, who in his *Analyse de la raison* states that:

> There are many analogies between the act of judging and that of reasoning. In the judgment either two ideas are compared in such a way that they convene to the same subject or they are repugnant and incompatible with the subject. In reasoning, two propositions are compared and either in such way that there is a relation between them expressed by a third proposition, or it is impossible to find a relation and a third proposition. [. . .] reasoning is the result of the same dispositions that concur in judgment.[147]

Instead, the syllogism conceived as the comparison of two characteristic marks by means of mediate characteristic mark is quite common in combinatorics, in particular in Segner, where he deals with ideas instead of characteristic marks, which is however synonymous:

> If given three ideas, the relation of the first to the second and of the second to the third is known, and from this known relation we conclude the relation of the first to third—we are reasoning, and the operation of the mind is called reasoning or syllogism.[148]

Given this definition of "characteristic mark," "judgment," and "syllogism," Kant looks for the supreme rules of all syllogism. The first rule of affirmative syllogisms establishes that "a characteristic mark of a characteristic mark is a characteristic mark of the thing itself (*nota notae est etiam nota rei ipsius*)," while the second rule of negative syllogisms states that that "which contradicts the characteristic mark of a thing, contradicts the thing itself (*repugnans notae repugnat rei ipsi*)" (2: 49). These two rules are "the universal and ultimate ground" of every inference, and summarize the rule of the *dictum de omni et nullo*. Such elaboration of the *dictum* is no doubt original, but Kant employs it in its treatment of combinatorics, as for instance, in the above mentioned passage of the *New Elucidation*. As in *The False Subtlety*, Kant states that the first principles of truth are two: one for affirmation and one for negation. The first principle states that "whatever is, is," while the second principle establishes that "whatever is not, is not" (1: 389). There are also two ways for finding truth according to the relation between the subject and the predicate. The first method is direct and based on the rule:

> Whenever an identity between the concepts of the subject and the predicate is discovered, the proposition is true. Expressed in the most general terms, as is befitting a first principle, the principle runs: *whatever is, is, and whatever is not, is not.* (1: 389)

This rule is nothing more than an explanation of the *dictum de omni*. The second method, on the other hand, is indirect because it derives from the reduction to the first method and corresponds to the rule *dictum de nullo*:

> (1) everything of which the opposite is false is true; that is to say: everything of which the opposite is negated must be asserted; (2) everything of which the opposite is true is false. From the first of these two propositions affirmative propositions follow, and from the second there follow negative propositions. If you express the first proposition in the simplest terms you will have: *whatever is not not, is* (for the opposite is expressed by the little word '*not*,' and its cancellation is likewise expressed by the little word '*not*'). You will formulate the second proposition in the following manner: *whatever is not, is not* (for here again the expression of the opposite is effected by the little word '*not*,' and the expression

of its falsity or cancellation is similarly affected by the same little word). Now if, as the law of signs demands, you examine the sense of the signs contained in the first proposition, then, since the little word 'not' indicates that the other is to be cancelled, when both have been eliminated you will end up with the proposition: *whatever is, is*. (1: 389)

Once having established the two fundamental rules of syllogism, which were elaborated, as we have just seen, in the *New Elucidation*, Kant states the existence of two kinds of syllogism, employing an innovative terminology for the time. There is pure syllogism (*ratiocinium purum*), which is based only on the *dictum de omni et nullo*, while there is hybrid syllogism (*ratiocinium hybridum*), which requires more than three judgments connected among them.

The four syllogistic figures are grounded in three rules, which are traceable back to the rule of the *dictum de omni et nullo*. The first figure is directly based on the *dictum* (2: 51). The second figure is based on the rule according to which "whatever is contradicted by the characteristic mark of a thing contradicts the thing itself" (2: 52). The third rule establishes that "that which belongs to or contradicts a thing, also belongs to or contradicts some of the things which are subsumed under another characteristic mark of this thing" (2: 53). The fourth figure, on the other hand, because of its unnatural character, does not follow any of these rules.

The problem of the unnaturalness of some argumentative and inferential structures is the polemical target of § 5 of *The False Sublety*. According to Kant, all four syllogistic figures can conclude directly, but the second, the third, and the fourth determine the final conclusions with a turn of phrase and by means of interpolated inferences. These three figures are almost useless because they complicate the reasonings which they are seeking to simplify. The secret art of syllogistic is nothing more for Kant than a "venerable rust of antiquity," a relic without any heuristic value. Kant's criticism of the false subtlety of the four syllogistic figures is not of course original, but it was deeply rooted in Eclectic logicians such as Thomasius. According to Thomasius, syllogisms do not lead to the discovery of truth, but they can point the way to avoiding falsity.[149] As far as the futility of logical subtleties is concerned, Thomasius bluntly states that "*a pure bare logician is a pure bare donkey.*"[150] The reduction of all syllogistic figures to the first one and the pointlessness of the others is evident for Thomasius,[151] and indeed only the first figure infers directly and with necessity to the conclusions in a clear and distinct way.[152]

The "Concluding Reflection" of *The False Subtlety* is no doubt the most significant part of the work. What is interesting in this section is Kant's attitude toward the syllogistic and combinatorial tradition that he maintained also in the critical writings. Kant states that a distinct concept is conceivable only through a judgment, whereas a complete concept is conceivable through a syllogism. In fact, to acquire a distinct concept, it is necessary to recognize something as a characteristic mark of a thing, but this is just what Kant has called at the beginning of his work a judgment. For instance, Kant writes, "in order to have a distinct concept of body, I clearly represent to myself impenetrability as a characteristic mark of it. This representation, however, is nothing other than the thought: *a body is impenetrable*" (2: 58). In this sense, Kant elaborates a theory of identity, which was already clear in the *New Elucidation*, for which the subject and the predicate, as a characteristic mark of the subject, coincide in one single concept. Kant, therefore, is in this sense very close to Ploucquet, who maintained that an affirmative judgment is nothing more than the articulated expression of one single concept in which there is identity between the subject and the predicate. Unlike Ploucquet, Kant adds that the judgment is not properly speaking the distinct concept itself, rather, like Johann Caspar Sulzer, the act of judging, that is the operation of finding a distinct concept, because only the representation after this operation is truly distinct. While for Ploucquet the judgment was the *expression* of a distinct concept, for Kant it was the *act* of a distinct concept. For this reason Kant denounces the error of modern logic: "it discusses distinct and complete concepts before it discusses judgments and syllogisms, although the former are only possible in virtue of the latter" (2: 59). This is a pivotal issue for the understanding of Kant's transcendental logic, which has been completely neglected by the scholarship. In this short writing, Kant had already elaborated the idea according to which the first, simplest, and distinct concepts had to derive from the various acts of judging, as he did twenty years later in the *Critique of Pure Reason*, deducing the table of categories from the table of judgments: we can understand distinct concepts only by starting from the acts of judging, that is the natural power of the mind to conceive a positive or negative connection between a subject and a predicate.

In the last few pages, we have emphasized certain aspects that seem to suggest that the Kantian project of the doctrine of categories is connected in some way with the failure of the project of syllogistic and combinatorics. Categories as first and pure concepts of the understanding would amount to nothing more than Kant's transformation of those irresolvable, simplest concepts of combinatorics, which combined could give a complete and scientific description of reality. The search for these concepts was for Kant destined inevitably to fail, because a complete analysis of the givens of experience was impossible. In which sense, then, can categories function as the first, simplest, and irresolvable concepts of combinatorics? Kant himself reveals it in his mature writings and letters. In a passage of *The Hechsel Logic*, datable around 1782, the year after the publication of the *Critique of Pure Reason*, Kant states:

> Someone believes that logic is a heuristic, that is an art of discovery, that is a tool of knowledge with which one makes new discoveries: in this sense algebra is a heuristic; but logic cannot be an heuristic because it abstracts from every content of knowledge.[153]

From these words, we can argue that logic cannot be a heuristic because its fundamental concepts abstract from the matter of cognition and deal simply with form: as is properly the case of categories in his "Transcendental Logic." Now we can understand why irresolvable, first, and simplest concepts of combinatorics were destined to fail: they claimed to be descriptive of reality according to matter, not simply according to the form. But thanks to Kant's discovery of Aristotelian categories, not as the highest kinds of being, which would be traceable back and similar to the first, irresolvable concepts, but as forms of cognition, that is *modi considerandi*, it was possible to lay the foundations of transcendental logic, therefore of a "formal combinatorics." In a letter Johann Schultz, dated August 26, 1783, Kant is very clear in stating that his categories as pure forms of cognition could constitute a formal combinatorics:

> You suggest that each third category might well be derived from the preceding two—an entirely correct opinion and one

at which you arrived all by yourself, for my own statement of this property of categories (*Prolegomena* § 39, Remark I) could easily be overlooked. This and other properties of the table of categories that I mentioned seem to me to contain the material for possibly significant invention, one that I am however unable to pursue and that will require a mathematical mind like yours, the construction of an *ars characteristica combinatoria*. (10: 351)[154]

It is possible, therefore, for Kant to establish a combinatorics of all ancestral and derivative concepts of the understanding, as he also suggests in the *Critique of Pure Reason* (A 81/B 107), only if they are conceived not as the building blocks of reality itself, but as the structure through which it is possible to know the reality as an object. In another letter to Jakob Sigismund Beck, dated September 27, 1791, Kant expresses the wish that from its table of categories an *ars combinatoria* may be found:

[. . .] the history of the world and of philosophy are tied up with this enterprise, and I am hopeful that, even if this investigation does not shed new light on mathematics, the latter may, inversely, by considering its methods and heuristic principles together with the entailed requirements and desiderata, come upon new discoveries for the critique and survey of pure reason. And the *Critique*'s new way of presenting abstract concepts may itself yield something analogous to Leibniz's *ars universalis characteristica combinatoria*. For the table of categories and the table of ideas (under which the cosmological ideas disclose something similar to impossible roots [in mathematics]) are after all enumerated and as well defined in regard to all possible uses that reason can make of them as mathematics could ask, so that we can see to what extent they at least clarify if not extend our knowledge. (11: 294)[155]

The passage has its origin in the *Reflection 4937*, dated 1776–78, where for the first and only time Kant connects syllogistic, combinatorics, and the table of categories:

> It is of the utmost importance to make of rational science technique. Logicians tried in vain to make this with their syllogistic as a fabric. The inventor of the algorithm had success only concerning quantities. Should not the same apply to the critique of pure reason, not for the extension, but for the clarification of knowledge? By means of the technical method it is possible to characterize for each concept its function, or better to express the functions in themselves and in opposition to each other. (18: 34)

It is evident that Kant conceives the *Critique of Pure Reason* as the result and completion of that universal science—the *ars universalis characteristica combinatoria*—which aims to extend our cognition by means of research into the first, simplest, and irresolvable concepts, but erroneously looking at the content and the matter of cognition, while instead this technique should be applied to the form of cognition. Kant tried to sketch this technique in his *Critique of Pure Reason*, only after his discovery of the potentialities of the Aristotelian categories, no longer conceived of as the highest kinds of being, but as forms or ways of considering as the Königsberg Aristotelian tradition, following Zabarella, Pace, and Rabe understood them.

This was his real awakening from a dogmatic slumber. Kant's great light and new model of mind have to do more with his discovery of the Aristotelian categories than to Hume's influence. As Kant famously writes in the "Preface" of the *Prolegomena*, "I openly confess, the suggestion of David Hume was the very thing, which many years ago first interrupted my dogmatic slumber, and gave my investigations in the field of speculative philosophy quite a new direction" (4: 260). This has always been a key passage for Kantian scholarship, to the point that some authors, like Alois Riehl, write "without Hume no Kant."[156] This passage on Hume has defined our picture of Kant's philosophical development as strictly related to the problem of causality and to that of the antinomies,[157] as may be evinced also from the 1798 letter to Christian Garve in which Kant confesses that the problem of the antinomies was the real inspiration for his inquiry (12: 256–58).[158] In order to understand Kant's statement it is necessary to read all the passages of the *Prolegomena*, where he writes that Hume does not solve "the whole of his problem, but a part, which by itself can give us no information" (4: 260). Kant is well aware of the deficiency of Hume's analysis and remarks that "the concept of the connection of cause and effect was by no means the only idea by which the understanding thinks the connection of things a priori, but rather that metaphysics consists of many other a priori concepts of this kind" (4: 260). Thus Kant emphasizes the existence of numerous concepts of the same kind as that of causality, on which the entire system of speculative philosophy would be based. Kant's aim is thus to establish "whether Hume's objection could not be put into a general form," that is to find a solution to Hume's problem "not merely in a particular case, but with respect to the whole faculty of pure reason" (4: 260). As he writes:

> I sought to ascertain their number, and when I had satisfactorily succeeded in this by starting from a single principle, I proceeded to the deduction of these concepts, which I was now certain were not deduced from experience, as Hume had apprehended, but sprang from the pure understanding. (4: 260)

From these words it is quite evident that Kant refers neither to the problem of causality in itself, nor to that of antinomies, but, as we have seen, to that of the categories and their deduction. Therefore, how is it possible to speak of a Humean influence? In my opinion, Hume suggested to Kant that the concept of causality is not an ontological or metaphysical concept that pertains to reality, as we have seen the various combinatorial attempts maintained,[159] but rather it is a concept of the understanding through which it is possible to know the world. If Kant, when he refers to Hume, thinks, as I suggest, to the categories, it is possible to determine that the *terminus ad quem* of the Humean influence was 1771, or the first months of 1772, that is, before the famous letter to Marcus Herz of February 21, 1772, with which Kant began his critical enterprise.

As we have already noted, he mentions the doctrine of the categories for the first time in this letter. It is from 1771 onward that Kant began to deal with categories, as *Reflection 4276* shows, where he lists the ten Aristotelian categories and defines them "as the operations of the understanding in relation to things, through which an object in general can be thought or placed in the mind" (17: 493). In *Reflection 2137*, dated 1772, Kant writes that "the very possibility of knowledge" depends on "the categories of the subject" (16: 248). A series of *Reflections*, from *4449* to *4457*, dated around 1772, has as its main topic the categories, and presents close analogies to the letter to Herz. If, as I argue, the awakening from the dogmatic slumber coincides with the discovery of the Aristotelian doctrine of the categories, it is necessary to understand why earlier attempts by Kant to find the table of the concepts of understanding failed, in other words to understand what problems the Aristotelian categories solved.

There is precious information to be gleaned from the passage on the awakening from the dogmatic slumber where Kant seems to suggest that the concepts of the pure understanding, the categories, are the *modi considerandi* or *cognoscendi*, that is, the forms of cognition of reality, and not constitutive elements of it. Kant did not reach this level of refinement regarding the concepts of the understanding in the 1770 *Dissertatio*, which is widely considered "as a work of little importance" or as "irrelevant" (10: 96–99). In the letter to Herz, Kant explicitly states that the *Dissertatio* "lacked something essential," (10: 130) that is the determination of the basis on which the relation between representation and the object lies. Moreover, Kant adds that

> In my dissertation I was content to explain the nature of intellectual representations in a merely negative way, namely, to state that they were not modifications of the soul brought about by the object. However, I silently passed over the further question of how a representation that refers to an object without being in any way affected by it can be possible. (10: 130–31)

Evidently, by 1770 Kant had not yet found the solution to this crucial problem, a solution he found subsequently, between 1771 and 1772, in the Aristotelian categories:

> as I was searching in such ways for the sources of intellectual knowledge, without which one cannot determine the nature and limits of metaphysics, I divided this science into its naturally distinct parts, and I sought to reduce transcendental philosophy (that is to say, all the concepts belonging to completely pure reason) to a certain number of categories, but not like Aristotle, who, in his ten predicaments, place them

side by side as he found them in a purely change juxtaposition. On the contrary, I arranged them according to the way they classify themselves by their own nature, following a few fundamental laws of the understanding. (10: 132)

Clearly, between the publication of the *Dissertatio* and February 1772, Kant found in the Aristotelian doctrine of the categories that essential aspect that he was looking for to solve the problem of the relation between sensation and understanding.[160] Its nondetermination led, in fact, not only to the exchange of their use, that is, to the amphiboly, but also to the antinomies without any preliminary critique of the limits of the cognitive faculties: the result was the conception of the pure concepts of the understanding as categories capable of determining or constructing an objective knowledge of the world, without being a constitutive part of it. Once Kant found in Aristotle the possible solution to his problem, he began to reevaluate the lesson of the Aristotelian tradition and to conceive his doctrine of the categories.

But before investigating in detail Kant's doctrine of categories and his Aristotelian legacy, there are at least two important issues in Kant's mature thought which are worth examining in relation to combinatorics and syllogistic, namely, (1) the problem of the determination of judgments in relation to categories; and (2) the problem of transcendental Topics.

On the problem of the determination of judgments, in the chapter "Transition to the Transcendental Deduction of the Categories," Kant states that what the meaning of the categories is still remains to be established:

> They are concepts of an object in general, by means of which its intuition is regarded as **determined** with regard to one of the **logical functions** for judgments. Thus, the function of the **categorical** judgment was that of the relationship of the subject to the predicate, e.g., "All bodies are divisible." Yet in regard to the merely logical use of the understanding it would remain undetermined which of these two concepts will be given the function of the subject and which will be given that of the predicate. For one can also say: "Something divisible is a body." Through the category of substance,

however, if I bring the concept of a body under it, it is determined that its empirical intuition in experience must always be considered as a subject, never as mere predicate; and likewise with all the other categories. (B 128–29)

In this context, Segner's conception of the various kinds of determination of judgments seems to have exerted some influence on the Kantian perspective. Kant states that judging means to establish a relation between a subject and a predicate. If the relation between the subject and the predicate, that is between two ideas in Segner's words, is well established and grounded according, for instance, to a relation of subordination, such as the connection between kind and species is, we have a determinate judgment. If this relation between the subject and the predicate is not well established, the judgment is indeterminate and the two terms of judgment are convertible. Thus it may be seen why in Kant all analytic judgments are indeterminate, because the two terms are exchangeable. This can lead us to the misleading conclusion that for Kant all synthetic judgments are determinate judgments, and that, therefore, there are no imperfectly determinate judgments in Kant, unlike in Segner. But this is not true. Seung-Kee Lee has shown definitively that there are imperfectly determinate judgments, such as the judgments of perception (*Wahrnehmungsurteile*).[161] In § 18 of the *Prolegomena*, Kant establishes that all judgments of experience (*Erfahrungsurteile*) are empirical because they have their grounds in perception. But not all empirical judgments are judgments of experience, because the latter also require, in addition to sensible intuition, pure concepts of the understanding (4: 297). Kant adds that judgments of experience are objective, while judgments of perceptions are only subjective. Subjective judgments of perceptions are not perfectly determinate, because they require the concepts of the understanding for a perfect determination, but nonetheless they are not completely indeterminate, as they establish a relation between the thinker and the object of perception (4: 298). Kant's analytic judgments seem to correspond to Segner's indeterminate judgments, the judgments of perception to imperfectly determinate judgments, and judgments of experience to perfectly determinate judgments. This is a remarkable parallelism that reinforces the belief that the Kantian doctrine of categories rises from the ruins of combinatorics.

The problem of a transcendental Topics in Kant is more complex, and involves some aspects of his systematic thought. Also in this case, it is probably worthwhile to deal with Kant's immediate antecedents. In one of his posthumous fragments, in reference to Meier, Lambert characterizes the architectonic as a logical Topics which would be the set of all "universal concepts under which the connection of the various truths in general is represented."[162] The most important example of logical Topics in history is, for Lambert, "the ten categories of Aristotle: *substantia, quantitas, qualitas, relatio, actio, passio, locus, tempus, situs, modus possidendi.*"[163] Logical Topics, unlike architectonic, not only lists all the fundamental concepts, but also explains their different ways of connection. Furthermore, Lambert adds that logical places (*loci logici*), that is, categories, "are mainly intentions (*Absichten*) by means of which an object can be considered."[164] The analogy between Lambert's conception of categories as standpoints or intentions for considering things and Kant's idea of categories is quite striking, almost as if Kant knew Lambert's reflections.[165] We can find an analogy between Kant and Lambert also at the end of the chapter "On the Pure Concepts of the Understanding or Categories." Kant states that a complete lexicon of pure reason, in other words, an exhaustive list of all the concepts of the understanding, is not only possible, but even easy to produce (A 83/B 109). The reference to a "complete lexicon" is an implicit allusion to Lambert's architectonic project to find all the basic concepts of cognition and reality. Kant also specifies that the headings (*Fächer*) already exist, and that it is merely a question of filling them out. In filling out these empty headings, a systematic Topics (*systematische Topik*) of all concepts would necessarily assign to each concept its proper place, while easily identifying any places that remain empty. According to Kant, a systematic Topics also has the function of assigning all the concepts, both pure and derived, to their respective places in the understanding, as Lambert attempted with his architectonic. In the "Remark to the Amphiboly of the Concepts of Reflection," Kant returns to the issue of a transcendental Topics. He writes that the position assigned to a concept either in sensibility or in pure understanding is properly called transcendental place, with a clear reference to the *loci* of the Aristotelian tradition. In the same way, the doctrine, which determines the positions and the rules of the various concepts, is called transcendental Topics (A 268/B 324). The transcendental Topics does not deal with every concept and every title under which the many cognitions belong as a logical place. In fact, this was the task of the logical Topics of Aristotle, from which only subtleties and illusions resulted (A 269/B 325). Therefore Kant, although taking his lead from the Aristotelian concept, departs in substance from the Stagirite in conceiving the transcendental Topics in a different way. In fact, the transcendental Topics contains only four titles or rules of comparison and distinction. Unlike categories, these titles do not exhibit the known object, but only the comparison of the representations, which precedes the concepts of things. This comparison, which distinguishes all the concepts, requires a preliminary reflection that could determine the place to which the various representations belong. The concepts, in fact, can be logically compared, but without referring to the place to which their objects pertain. This is not, however, possible in the real use of the understanding, in which concepts are always referred to as objects: a transcendental, a priori reflection is necessary (A 269/B 325). Without this transcendental Topics, the mind would fall into Leibniz's error of confusing the places of the various concepts, conceiving only a difference of degree from sensations to concepts of the understanding, and not also a difference of position and quality (A 270/B 326). If we examine Kant's rules of the reflection of the transcendental Topics in the chapter "On the Amphiboly of the Concepts of Reflections," we can see that they are nothing other than the rules established by the tradition of syllogistic and combinatorics: (1) identity and difference; (2) agreement and opposition; (3) inner and outer; and (4) determinable and determination (A 261/B 317).

Also in the same fragments, Kant faces the problem of a transcendental Topics in connection with its Aristotelian origin. The genesis of the doctrine of a transcendental Topics appears late, probably by the end of the 1770s at least. The first reference is in *The Pölitz Logic*. Here, Kant states that it is necessary to rethink Aristotle's Topics, which is a useful tool because when someone wants to reflect on a thing, it is necessary first to know to what science it pertains. The Topics shows the main headings in which the objects of knowledge acquire their specific place. According to Kant, these headings are properly speaking the *loci*, while the Topics is the partition of all the themes (*Thematen*) according to rules (*regelmäßige Einteilung*) of a science under which every cognition receives its proper place. Such a

Topics, which is not merely an enumeration of the themes that pertain to it, is the only real guide to reflection in scientific knowledge. The place can also be characterized by means of the determination of knowledge in a possible system, and therefore it is called *locus scientificus*, while the art that shows the place of the various cognitions in a possible system is properly the Topics (24: 596–97).

In *The Busolt Logic*, Kant reexamines the Aristotelian Topics. Aristotle's Topics becomes nothing other than a list of all headings and themes under which the object can be considered, in other words how a thing can be considered from different standpoints. Here Kant explains the difference of the various *loci*. The *locus topicus* is an alleged heading of logic under which an object can be considered. In this way, things can be considered (1) according to their kind or their specific difference, (2) through distinction or confusion, (3) as principles or consequences, or (4) as axioms or theorems. A *locus grammaticus*, on the other hand, is that through which an object can be considered according to its definition. The *locus logicus*, since it concerns only the form, is also called general mode, and it differs from the *locus communis* that concerns more specifically common and general principles (24: 681). In *The Dohna Logic*, Kant characterizes once again the Topics as the science that designates how the logical place must be determined. Kant states that the Topics is the art of bringing concepts under some other fundamental concepts (24: 778), referring unequivocally to § 10 of *Critique of Pure Reason*, calling these fundamental concepts headings (*Fächer*).

It should be clear by now that when Kant dealt with the concepts and their relations, he had in mind the Aristotelian syllogistic tradition and the combinatorics. It is from the ashes and failures of these projects that Kant's doctrines of categories advanced.

CATEGORIES AND JUDGMENTS

Kant's doctrine of categories is probably one of the most controversial in his entire philosophical corpus, especially for its connections with the table of judgments and the theory of schematism. Many scholars have seen in Kant's doctrine of categories an absolute novelty introduced in open opposition to Aristotle's logic,[166] probably following Kant's misleading verdict according to which the Stagirite "had no principle, he rounded them [concepts] up as he stumbled on them, and first got up a list of ten of them, which he called **categories** (predicaments)" (A 81/B 107). Indeed, such judgment was quite common among Eclectic logicians, for instance Thomasius stated that "categories are not grounded in the truth of things, but they are arbitrary classes depending on the powers of imagination," while Hollmann wrote that "we proscribe the very confused Aristotelian doctrine of the ten predicaments."[167] Kant's negative judgment on the Aristotelian categories therefore probably depends on the general criticism around this doctrine.

Scholars have often overlooked the Aristotelian derivation of Kant's doctrine of categories. Strikingly, the only monographic study on Aristotle and Kant did not even mention the problem of the categories,[168] and some other works examine only extrinsically the relationship between these the two doctrines.[169] Thomas K. Seung states that the Kantian conception of categories is incompatible with Aristotle's logic, and that the Kantian table of judgments differs from the Aristotelian one, but he wisely recognized that the idea of a schema of the categories is not Kant's original invention, but rather it is an important element of Aristotle's doctrine of categories.[170] Tonelli is more careful in investigating Kant's possible sources, tracing his categories back to the fundamental and irresolvable concepts of authors such as Crusius, Tetens, and Lambert, but he peremptorily states that Kant's categories most certainly cannot be traced back to the Aristotelian categories.[171] There is no doubt, however, that whoever understands this doctrine possesses a key to the understanding and evaluation of Kant's entire work.

In this section I aim to show that Kant's conception of categories has its roots in the Aristotelian tradition. Aristotle's doctrine of categories is highly problematic, so much so in fact that it can be interpreted in three different ways. First, there is the grammatical interpretation according to which the categories were found following the analysis and resolution of linguistic propositions. Then, we have the ontological interpretation according to which categories are the highest kinds of being. Finally, we have the logical interpretation, according to which categories come from the resolution of logical judgments. The problem of these various interpretations is that "the opening chapter of the *Categories* fails to reveal whether it is introducing a grammatical, a logical, or a metaphysical treatise."[172] I find this problem totally misleading since this question acquires value only if we are looking for a deduction of the Aristotelian categories, like in Kant, but this concern was totally alien to Aristotle. It is more fruitful to understand the various meanings and uses of the categories in the Aristotelian writings. In general, categories in Aristotle are: (1) what can be said without any combination; (2) schemes of predication; and (3) kinds of predicates.

The first perspective, that is category as what can be said without any combination, is developed in the second chapter of the *Categories*. Aristotle states that "of things that are said, some involve combination while others are said without combination."[173] The combination (συνπλοκή) determines a relation between a subject and a predicate. For instance, combined things are "man runs" or "man wins." In general, the combination subject-predicate is summarizable in the proposition "*s* pertains to *p*," where "to pertain" is the translation of the Greek verb "καταγορεύω," that is, "to tell," "to announce," "to denounce." A combination exists only when a predicate pertains to a subject, and in this connection a proposition takes place which can be either true or false.[174] Every proposition in this sense is not only a linguistic expression, but also a logical judgment that expresses truth or falsity. In *On the Soul* III.8, 432 a 10–15, Aristotle states that assertion and negation are different from the synthesis of imagination, and in fact what is true or false involves a combination of thoughts (νοήματα), while the synthesis of imagination is a kind of reflection of sensuous contents, except in that they contain no matter. Aristotle means that the combination of logical judgments occurs only in the understanding, while the synthesis between sensation and thoughts occurs through images thanks to imagination. The conception of truth and falsity as a result of imagination is radically different from that of logical judgments. The former designates the notification of sensations in the understanding through images, and the error can be merely psychological, that is, in the malfunction of mirroring the object by the faculties of the mind. We can call this conception "psychological agreement" of the cognition with its object. The latter is rather a wrong attribution of a predicate to a subject, and it is merely in the understanding. This conception can be called "logical truth," or truth properly speaking.[175] Of the things said without combination, on the other hand, there is no truth or falsity, and they are specifically the categories or predicaments. Therefore, from the standpoint of the *Categories*, the predicaments are concepts derived from the resolution of combined things, namely a proposition.

Aristotle, however, deals with categories also according to their schema of predication. According to this perspective, the concept of "category" cannot be conceived if not in the combination, that is the predicative relation. Categories are always conceived as things said without combination, but they are understood in their logical function regarding a possible connection. Categories as a schema of predication involve the possibility of inferring or subordinating a lower predicate to a higher one. The translation of "category" with "predicament" would be in this sense very appropriate. This conception occurs already in the *Categories* in the concept of the "schema of predication" of the first category, the substance, to which all other categories must be referred. Aristotle develops his theory of "schema" in *Metaphysics* V.7, 1017 a 7–8, where he states that "things are said to be (1) in an accidental sense, (2) by their own nature." He adds that "those things are said in their own right to be that are indicated by the schema of predication; for the senses of 'being' are just as many as these schemes."[176] A thing said to be in its own right thus concerns the properties that inhere necessarily to the subject of predication. Such kinds of things are "man is living," or "man is walking," which inhere necessarily to the human being. Things are also said to be in an accidental sense, such as the "man is musical." In some sense, we can say that categories as a schema of predication express a universal and objective reality of the subject, while being as accident expresses a mere particular and contingent aspect of the subject. Of accidental being there is no science, the accident in fact is a pure name that says nothing essential regarding the concept of the subject. The accidental aspect of predication depends solely on matter, because in the form everything is essential and necessary.[177] If the predicate attributed to the subject is combined with it, it is the being as truth; if the predicate attributed to the subject is separated from it, it is the being as falsity. The combination or separation of the being as truth and false is not real, but it is purely mental. Categories as schemes of predication are always "being as truth," and not only have a nominal and fictional realty in the mind, but also express the predicates that inhere universally and necessarily to the subject, that is, they provide an objective reality to what is said. Therefore, for Aristotle the categories as schemes of predication express problematically both the logical and the ontological aspects of the subject, and this is the reason why the doctrine of categories pertains to both logic and ontology.

Kant's indebtedness to the Aristotelian conception of the categories is quite clear in the *Reflection 4276*, dated around 1770–71, in which Kant outlines his doctrine:

> Pure sensibility. Pure Reason. Mixed.
> *ubi, quando*
> *transcendentalis philosophia*
> Aesthetics is the philosophy on sensibility, or of knowledge or of feeling.
> *Logica vel generalis vel speciatim transscendentalis.*
> Categories are the universal acts of reason, through which we think an object in general (for instance, for representations, appearance). *Aristoteles*
> 3. categories. *Thesis, synthesis, hypothesis.**
>   *coordinatio subordinatio*
> (in mere categorical judgment, like in the other three ways of judging)
> *Praedicamenta. Thesis: Possibile, actuale, necessarium cum oppositis.*
> *Praedicamenta. Synthesis: Quantitas.*
> 10 categories *Aristoteles. Pythagoras.* 1. *Substantia, Accidens,* 2. *qualitas,* 3. *quantitas,* 4. *relatio,* 5. *actio,* 6. *passio,* 7. *quando,* 8. *ubi,* 9. *situs,* 10. *habitus.*
> *postpraedicamenta: oppositum, prius, simul, motus, habere.*
> * The acts of the understanding are either in relation to concepts, where they are given in relation to each other through the understanding if the concepts and the ground of their comparison are given through the sense;
> or in relation to things, when the understanding thinks an object in general and its relations. Both standpoints differ only because in the former case representations are posed, while in the second case things are posed through representations. (17: 492–93)

In this fragment, Kant characterizes categories as the universal functions through which it is possible to know an object in general, and he associates this conception with Aristotle, a fact that scholars have completely overlooked. It is also quite striking since in this *Reflection* we find the list of the ten predicaments and the explanations of their functions. Kant points out that these functions are thesis, synthesis, and hypothesis, which Béatrice Longuenesse correctly traces back to the various roles of the categories within the judgment, and they correspond respectively to the copula, to combination according to subordination or coordination, and to modality.[178] But Kant also adds a final remark in which he makes it clear that the categories can be understood in relation to the understanding alone or to the object. According to the understanding alone, concepts have no real meaning, which is given only by schematism, while according to the object, categories are the conditions of possibility of every cognition. These two standpoints are different but complementary: the former provides the conditions of thinking and the logical use of categories, while the latter provides the conditions for cognizing and the transcendental use of the categories. If the dating of this *Reflection* is correct, we might argue that Kant had already conceived his doctrines of the categories at the beginning of the 1770s. However, all subsequent fragments from 1771 to 1778, as well as the correspondence, show that for a decade Kant focused his efforts on finding a solution to the question of the categories, which he found only with the *Critique of Pure Reason*, where he declares that he possesses the "definitions" of categories (A 82/B 108), as the 1783 letter to Christian Garve also testifies (10: 339).

Kant gives a full exposition of the doctrine of the categories in the controversial § 10 "On the Pure Concepts of the Understanding or Categories" of the *Critique of Pure Reason*. Here, the table of categories is deduced from the table of judgments, and this deduction is called metaphysical. The completeness and systematic nature of the table of categories, which according to Kant was lacking in Aristotle, thus depends directly on the completeness of the table of judgments.[179] This is not the place to question whether the table of judgments is complete or not. It is more important to focus on Kant's words: "if we abstract from all content of a judgment in general, and attend only to the mere form of the understanding in it, we find that the function of thinking in that can be brought under four titles, each of which contains under itself three moments" (A 70/B 95). If we abstract from any reference to the content of knowledge, the reflection on the table of judgments pertains to general logic or to the logical use of the understanding, which is only broadly speaking transcendental concerning the condition of thinking, but it does not pertain to transcendental logic. Kant is quite clear on this point: "general logic abstracts [. . .] from all content of cognition, i.e. from any relation of it to the object, and considers only logical form in relation of cognitions to one another, i.e., the form of thinking in general" (A 55/B 79).[180] General logic, however, by Kant's own admission, had made no advancement since Aristotle's times (B 8). We can, therefore, argue that if the table of judgments concerns general logic and general logic relies on Aristotle's discoveries, then the table of judgments must be understood within the tradition of Aristotelian logic.[181]

In *On Interpretation*, Aristotle classifies eight different kinds of judgments grouped in four classes. The first distinction concerns affirmative and negative judgments,[182] the second distinction regards simple or composite judgments,[183] the third distinction concerns particular or universal judgments,[184] while the fourth distinction concerns possible and necessary judgments.[185] It is not hard to recognize the analogies between Aristotle's judgments, conceived in various ways within the Aristotelian tradition, and Kant's table of judgments, the sole difference being that in the latter there is a third term, which is, by Kant's own admission, his own addition (A 70/B 96). This integration is essential because, as Brandt points out,[186] the judgments that Kant confines to general logic are not epistemic judgments, that is judgments that lead to knowledge, and therefore it is necessary to introduce a third kind of judgment for each class for the transition from general logic to transcendental logic. Since epistemic judgments extend our knowledge, in other words they concern also the matter and not only the form of cognition, Kant's table of judgments "does not stand in the tradition of the doctrine of judgments of Aristotle's *On Interpretation*, but rather in the tradition of Aristotle's *Analytics*," namely, within the doctrine of finding scientific knowledge.[187]

We have already emphasized that the metaphysical deduction of categories proceeds from the tables of judgments. Thus, we can correctly say that Kant begins his transcendental investigation from a composed element as a judgment, and by means of resolution he finds the simple element of the category. Proceeding from judgments, rather than simple concepts, is no doubt one of the most original aspects of Kantian logic. Kant was well aware of the revolutionary import of his metaphysical deduction in the field of logic since *The False Subtlety*. In this work, as we have seen in the previous section, Kant states that "a *distinct* concept is only possible by means of a *judgment*" (2: 58), and he adds that "the distinctness of a concept does not consist in the fact that that which is a characteristic mark of the thing is clearly represented, but rather in the fact that is recognised a characteristic mark of the thing" (2: 59). In fact, to differentiate things from and to recognize the difference between them is not the same for Kant: "the latter is only possible by means of judgments" (2: 60). To differentiate logically means for Kant to recognize that a thing A is not B, and this is always a negative judgment, that is, an act of determination.[188] Distinct concepts can, therefore, proceed only from a judgment, and if we transfer this idea to transcendental logic we can easily see that every category can be deduced only from a judgment. Not judgment as proposition, but rather as the action by means of which the category is found. It is quite clear that for Kant categories come from the acts of judging, and judging is a kind of faculty that cannot be derived from some other faculty, and is rather an original and fundamental faculty on which the higher faculties of cognition in their entirety are based (2: 60), as we have seen in the previous chapter. In this sense we can understand that Kant's transcendental logic is grounded in the facultative logic of this act of judging, which reflects the table of judgments of general logic.

We can also recognize traces of this precritical conception in the *Critique of Pure Reason* when he states that categories without any reference to a given object in a judgment merely have a logical significance, which does not determine any particular meaning (A 147/B 186). In themselves, categories have no significance, if not within a judgment. It is noteworthy, however, that in § 10 the relation between category and judgment is inverted, that is, judgments seem to be based on categories: the function that gives unity to the representations in a judgment is possible only through categories, which refer a priori to objects expressed by means of the judgment in its logical form. Thus, if it is true that categories have significance and are deducible only from judgments, it is also true that only through categories is the unity and connection of judgments possible. This for Kant means nothing other than that there are as many categories as there are judgments, or ways to express the object a priori.

In his table of categories, Kant confesses that he is on the path laid out by Aristotle, even if his conclusions are different. Categories are the only means through which it is possible to understand the manifold of intuition and to think of it as an object. They are twelve and are grouped into four classes: (1) quantity; (2) quality; (3) relation; and (4) modality. This partition, Kant states, "is systematically generated from a common principle, namely the faculty for judging (which is the same as the faculty for thinking), and has not arisen rhapsodically from a haphazard search for pure concepts" (A 81/B 107). As we have seen from *The False Subtlety*, categories are deduced from the faculty for judging, which is the same as the faculty of thinking, the only difference being in the relation that the mind does or does not have with the object. If the table of categories did not derive from the table of judgments, its completeness and necessity would not be guaranteed. The faculty for judging presents these acts only, no more, no less, because, as we have shown, the faculty in itself is innate and its operations are determined by nature. But why there are those specific operations and not others, it is not possible to know.

According to Kant, Aristotle had the merit of having sought for categories, but, as we have seen, since he had no principle of deduction, he rounded them up as he stumbled on them (A 81/B 107). Kant does not list in this case Aristotle's categories, but he criticizes the fact that among them there are several *modi* of pure sensibility, such as *quando*, *ubi*, *situs*, *prius*, and *simul*, and an empirical one, that is *motus*. These particular *modi* do not belong to the ancestral list of the primary concepts of understanding; in fact, some primary concepts are missing, while there are derivative concepts such as *actio* and *passio*.[189]

In the "Deduction of the Pure Concepts of the Understanding" Kant is concerned with the ground of the unity of the categories in the various judgments. All sensible intuitions for Kant come under categories, which are the sole conditions through which the manifold of intuitions can be grasped in the unity of the experience of the subject. Categories refer to the object independently from its actual presence or existence. In fact, similarly to Aristotle, categories for Kant can be with or without the combination of the manifold of the experience, and can be referred to an actual object or to a possible object in general. Without the combination with sensible intuitions, however, categories are mere "**forms of thought**, through which no determinate object is yet cognized" (B 150). They are general classes according to which it is possible to cognize the manifold of intuition, but without this manifold its function is to provide mere indeterminate judgments concerning an object in general. This twofold conception of categories, with or without the actual reference to the object, generates two different kinds of synthesis. The first kind of synthesis combines the sensible intuitions to the categories and it is called figurative synthesis or *synthesis speciosa*. The second kind of synthesis conceives of categories in relation to a possible intuition, that is, in relation to an object in general, and it is called combination of the understanding or *synthesis intellectualis* (B 151). Both are transcendental in the sense that they are the very ground of the possibility of a priori cognition, but the former concerns the transcendental use of the categories, the latter only their logical use. Figurative synthesis, which deals with the combination between sensation and categories, is also called "**transcendental synthesis of the imagination**," and it works by transforming sensations into intellectual knowledge through images (B 151). This "intellectualization" of the sensations by means of categories has nothing to do with truth or falsity, as it is just a notification of knowledge. Meanwhile, intellectual synthesis, unlike figurative synthesis, works only in the understanding without images, and establishes the criterion of truth. It is clear that for Kant truth cannot consist in the agreement of a cognition with its object, in other words, what we have called "psychological agreement." Since the general criterion of truth "would be that which was valid of all cognitions without any distinction among their objects," and since this criterion abstracts from all content of cognition, that is from the relation to its object, it would be "completely impossible and absurd to ask for a mark of the truth of this content," if truth concerns precisely this content from which we should abstract (A 58–59/B 83). There is not a mark of truth for the matter or content of a cognition, "because it is self-contradictory." Rather, setting aside all content, truth concerns the mere form of cognition, that is the "general and necessary rules of the understanding" (A 59/B 84). What is false, therefore, is what contradicts these general rules of thinking without any relation to the object, in other words, truth and falsity concern only the combination of the intellectual synthesis, which abstracts from the content and the matter of experience. This is merely a "logical truth," that is the "negative condition of all truth," and it concerns merely the agreement of a cognition in general with the universal and formal laws of understanding (A 60/B 84). Like Aristotle, therefore, Kant distinguishes the synthesis of imagination, which does not regard the truth, properly speaking, from the pure logical combination of the understanding, which generates assertion and denial.

Without any relation to the content, that is to the object, the formal conditions of truth rely on the universal laws of general logic; in fact, "general logic analyzes the entire formal business of the understanding and reason into its elements, and presents these as principles of all logical assessment of our cognition" (A 60/B 84). It is clear, however, that "logical truth," that is, the agreement of the mere form of cognition with the logical laws, is far from sufficient to constitute the "objective truth" of cognition, in fact, "nobody can dare to judge of objects and to assert anything about them merely with logic without having drawn on antecedently well-founded information about them from outside logic" (A 60/B 85). This is the reason why Kant aims to find out and explain how an "objective truth" of cognition is possible by examining the transcendental synthesis of imagination in the "Transcendental Doctrine of the Power of Judgment," in particular, in the chapter "On the Schematism of the Pure concepts of the Understanding." Here categories, like in Aristotle, are conceived of as schemes. What is at stake is how to apply categories to content, that is, how to combine inhomogeneous elements of cognition like concepts and sensations. This is possible for Kant through a special kind of subsumption, which is the work of imagination that produces a transcendental schema. The transcendental schema is the representation that mediates between sensations and concepts, and provides objective validity, that is, "objective truth," to experience. Here I want to suggest that Kant is following the Aristotelian doctrine of categories and schemes of predication, not only terminologically by employing the same words, but also conceptually by attributing to the "schema" the same function. Schemes determine all possible ways of saying, cognizing, and thinking in relation to the categories. The formula for the application of the categories which in Aristotle was "s (subject) pertains to p (predicate/category)," in Kant is "i (intuition) pertains to c (category)," that is, sensible intuitions correspond to categories. Both conceptions are generalizable in the formula "x pertains to y," and the "procedure" for providing this particular relation is called the schema.

As we have already said, the schema is "always only a product of the imagination." But a schema must be distinguished by an image:

> If I place five points in a row, ... , this is an image of the number five. On the contrary, if I only think a number in general, which could be five or a hundred, this thinking is more the representation of a method for representing [. . .] this representation of a general procedure of the imagination [. . .] is what is call the schema [. . .]. (A 140/B 179)

The difference between "image" and "schema" is better explained through the example of a triangle.

> No image of a triangle would ever be adequate to the concept of it. For it would not attain the generality of the concept which makes this valid for all triangles, right or acute, etc., but would always be limited to one part of this sphere. The schema of the triangle can never exist anywhere except in thought, and signifies a rule of the synthesis of imagination. (A 141/B 180)

The schema is, therefore, a product of the imagination only because it is a rule of the synthesis, a procedure, an operation, not properly speaking a mental object, rather, a mental function that concerns the categories. Kant is quite explicit on this point: the schema of the categories "is something that can never be brought to an image at all, but is rather only the pure synthesis, in accord with a rule of unity according to concepts in general, which the category expresses" (A 142/B 181), In other words, schemes represent the various ways through which categories are applied to possible objects in general, like the schemes of predication in Aristotle, as Brandt cogently argues: "when Kant applies the concept of form to his own logic [. . .], he does so in the wake of the Aristotelian doctrines of schemata and figures."[190] The Aristotelian doctrine of the schemes of categories, which traditionally pertains to general logic, is included by Kant in his transcendental logic, where it is no longer conceived as the relation between a subject and a predicate, but between the manifold of sensible intuitions and the pure concepts of the understanding. This shift from general to transcendental logic is the result of the essential role that "time" assumes. In fact, for Kant, the schema concerns primarily the determination of the application of the categories to the manifold of experience in the inner sense, in accordance with the conditions of its form, that is, time, as we know from the "Transcendental Aesthetic" (A 142/B 181). This temporal component is lacking in Aristotle's theory just because he deals with schema within general logic. In this sense, the application of the Aristotelian conception of schema to transcendental and epistemic logic is Kant's innovation.

Also interesting is the fact that at the end of the chapter on schematism, Kant deals with categories in themselves without considering a possible combination with the manifold of intuition through the schema. Kant points out that "the schemata of the concepts of pure understanding are the true and sole conditions for" providing categories "with a relation to objects, thus with **significance**" (A 146/B 184). Kant therefore suggests that categories "have a significance independent of all schemata and extending far beyond them" (A 147/B 186)—but only a logical significance, since they are "only functions of the understanding for concepts," though alone they do not represent any object (A 147/B 187), which is exactly what Aristotle writes in relation to his conception of the categories.

The strong analogies between the Aristotelian and the Kantian conceptions and the fragments of the 1770s suggest that Kant's doctrine of categories was inspired, at least partially, by Aristotle. There are good reasons to believe that Paul Rabe was his most direct source. First, Rabe's *Commentarius in librum categoriarum Aristotelis* is one of the few eighteenth-century commentaries on Aristotle's categories. Tonelli has already reported the existence of this work, arguing for a strong influence of the problem of categories in Königsberg, a problem that was completely neglected elsewhere, though he did not find any available copy of this work.[191] He also mentioned Johann Jakob Quandt's dissertation *De sede categoriarum propria*,[192] which was written by Rabe and included in his commentary.[193] In Rabe, the question of the proper place of the doctrine of the categories was particularly intense and presented two different interpretations. Some philosophers supported the view that the categories were a part of metaphysics, while others maintained that they were part of logic. The former conception, defended by Scholastic philosophers, considers categories *materialiter*, that is, according to the matter of cognition, in other words, the being that they represent (*sub ratione entis*). The latter interpretation, followed by Rabe, considers categories *formaliter*, that is, according to the form of cognition, meaning, as a part of a possible predication (*sub ratione praedicationis*). This interpretation is traceable back to Paduan Aristotelianism, in particular to Zabarella and Pace, who maintained that categories were concepts through which it was possible to express and to know the being. In his *In Aristotelis categorias commentarius analyticus*, Pace established that categories are not *in rerum natura*, they are not real things, but they are only in reference to their logical function in the judgment (*sub ratione attribuendi et subiiciendi*).[194] Rabe, like all the other Königsberg Aristotelians, refers to this conception, according to which categories are "mental constructions, or concepts of a mental order which did not correspond to an order of things,"[195] therefore categories "only belong to logic because they merely represent our way of conceiving things."[196] Kant's conception of categories as forms of cognition and ways of conceiving things is not so different from this Aristotelian tradition, which is, in my opinion, the real source for Kant.

But my argument may be pushed a little further by saying that in Rabe the doctrine of schema plays a pivotal role in the chapter devoted to the definition of "category." After a short list of the various definitions of "category," Rabe states that there are two ways of conceiving it, one totally a priori, the other a posteriori. A posteriori categories, Rabe explains, are conceived within the proposition, and they are schemes or figures or modes of predication, focusing in particular on Aristotle's *Metaphysics* V.7, VI.2 and *Topics* I.9,[197] and examining every schema of each category.

The schema for Rabe is the way through which a universal predicate, that is category, is attributed essentially and *in concreto* to a subject, and this predication is summarizable in the form "*s* pertains to *p*."[198] Rabe states, like Kant in *The False Subtlety* and in *Critique of Pure Reason*, that a category a priori and in abstract has no real significance, which is acquired only in the judgment. Each category derives from the resolution of a judgment and a priori it is a mere *affirmatio alicujus de aliquo*, that is, a general predicate of a possible object in general, with only a logical significance, without any true connection with reality, exactly as Kant argues in the chapter on transcendental schematism.[199]

But if we look at Rabe's list of the various judgments from which we can derive categories, we can recognize a parallelism with Kant's table of judgments, but with slight differences. In Kant, unlike Rabe, there are no exclusive, exceptive, restrictive, and comparative judgments, because they are derivate judgments and do not concern the transcendental investigation. Kant's categorical judgments correspond to Rabe's copulative judgments, while Rabe's indefinite judgments correspond to Kant's infinite judgments and are located among quantitative rather than qualitative judgments. Indefinite judgments for Rabe are not only judgments such as "the soul is not mortal," (A 72/B 97), as they are for Kant, but they are also of the kind of "the man is animal," which do not determine perfectly the nature of the subject.[200] Kant's problematic, assertoric and apodictic judgments are Rabe's possible, contingent, and necessary judgments. Rabe's impossible judgments are included in Kant's apodictic judgments. With Rabe's textbook, Kant had at his disposal all the possible examples for his table, but some scholars have argued that problematic, assertoric, and apodictic judgments are a Kantian integration.[201] Other possible sources are Weise's *Doctrina logica*, Hollmann's *Philosophia rationalis*, and Darjes's *Introductio in artem inveniendi*, in other words, all authors connected with the Eclectic or Aristotelian traditions. Yet, despite these Aristotelians, Rabe mentions all kinds of judgments listed by Kant. Meanwhile, because of their rhapsodic nature, the Wolffian treatises of Meier and Baumgarten may be ruled out.[202]

It is possible to find a reference to Aristotelian logic in one of the first drafts of the table of the categories in *Philosophical Encyclopaedia* (1778–80). Kant classifies judgments in the following ways: (1) quality: affirmative, negative; (2) quantity: universal, particular, singular; (3) relation: categorical, hypothetical, disjunctive; and (4) modality: problematic that expresses a possibility, assertoric that expresses a matter of fact, apodictic that expresses necessity (29: 36–37). Unlike the version of the *Critique of Pure Reason*, the judgments of quality precede those of quantity, as in Rabe, and the infinite judgments are lacking, which is evidence that Kant had not yet conceived their systematic place. As we have already mentioned, scholars agree that the judgments of modality are a Kantian invention,[203] at least for the words that are used to characterize them. No doubt, however, they are deeply rooted in the Aristotelian tradition of necessary, contingent, and possible judgments. Necessary judgments are apodictic judgments, while problematic judgments are possible judgments. One can question the identification of contingent judgments with assertoric judgment; however, a contingent judgment determines something that is in a particular space and time but could be otherwise: it characterizes the actual existence of something, like the assertoric judgment does through the category of existence.

There are good reasons, therefore, to argue that Rabe was one of the most accredited sources to explain the Aristotelian conceptuality of Kant's doctrine of categories and schema. If we examine the terminology of *Critique of Pure Reason*, we evidently see that Kant is making a terminological shift away from the Wolffian language that he employed in previous decades. The use of concepts and argumentative structures characteristic of the Aristotelian tradition marks a break with Wolffian philosophy and a reassessment of Königsberg philosophical tradition.

The use of the terms *category* and *schema* in the context of the discovery of Aristotle's doctrine of the categories that is related, as I have suggested, to the awakening from the dogmatic slumber, follows the appearance of other terms of Aristotelian logic that characterize a real linguistic and terminological turn in the Kantian philosophy,[204] such as "quaestiones," "paralogismos," "petitiones principii," "demonstratio oppositi," and "organon" (17: 557–58). In particular, in the next section, I focus on two key concepts of Kant's transcendental logic, namely, "analytic" and "dialectic."

ANALYTIC AND DIALECTIC

One of the elements considered unanimously to be of Aristotelian origin is the distinction of transcendental logic into analytic and dialectic. Yet, what Kant's source for this conception was is not so clear, especially since this partition of logic became obsolete at the beginning of the eighteenth century. The schools of both Thomasius and Wolff in fact dropped this division of logic, leaving out dialectic, which was considered the favorite topic of the Aristotelians. Giorgio Tonelli suggested as a possible Kantian source Johann

Georg Darjes,[205] who maintained the Aristotelian partition: "logic is divided in two parts, the first is called analytic, the other is dialectic, or logic of probable things. Analytic is the science of the rules of finding truth with certainty. Dialectic is the science of rules in finding truth with probability."[206] This would be corroborated by the "fact that in one of the first places in which transcendental analytic and dialectic are mentioned, Kant characterizes them respectively as the logic of truth and of illusion, with indubitable reference to the *logica veritatis* and *logica probabilium* of the Aristotelians."[207] Kant, however, completely remolded the meaning of these two concepts, and, as we shall see, included the doctrine of probability in the analytic, distinguishing it from the dialectic as logic of illusion: the doctrine of probability (*Lehre der Wahrscheinlichkeit*) differs from the logic of illusion (*Logik des Scheins*), because the former "is truth, but cognized through insufficient grounds, so that the cognition of it is defective, but not therefore deceptive, and so it need not be separated from the analytical part of logic" (A 293/B 350). The doctrine of probability has an epistemic value, whereas the logic of illusion leads to misleading conclusions. Thus, Tonelli's suggestion of Darjes as a possible source cannot be accepted. Norbert Hinske, on the other hand, pointed to Georg Friedrich Meier as a probable source:[208] in the *Auszug aus der Vernunftlehre*, Meier added a number of Latin terms such as *amphibolia, antithesis, dialectica, disciplina, doctrina, paralogismus, dogmaticus*, etc. . . . .[209] and Kant's employment of this Aristotelian terminology would be explainable by the frequent use of this textbook in his lectures on logic.[210] But again, for Meier analytic is "the logic of firm and complete knowledge," while dialectic is "the logic of probable knowledge."[211] Kant seems to follow Meier's textbook, at least up to 1762–63, as *The Herder Logic* testifies, attributing to dialectic the meaning of the logic of probability (*logica probabilium*) (24: 5). However, at the end of the 1760s, Kant began to distinguish dialectic as logic of probability from the dialectic as logic of illusion. Kant's detachment from Meier's position is documented in *The Vienna Logic*, where he writes that Meier "believes that dialectic is the logic of probability [. . .] but probability is a judgment concerning truth according to correct but insufficient grounds. If its grounds are correct, however, then it belongs to analytics [. . .] dialectic is the logic of illusion" (24: 794). Kant's criticism seems to exclude Meier as a possible source of his partition of logic.[212] Instead, Mirella Capozzi has suggested Johann Jakob Brucker,[213] who in his *Historia critica philosophiae* writes:

> the aim of logic is twofold, probable (*verisimile*) and true, that is probable and firm truth. To the former is devoted dialectic, which deals with truth with probable reasons; to the latter is devoted analytic, which deals with firm demonstrations.[214]

Brucker's position, however, does not explain why Kant conceived dialectic as *logica probabilium* within analytic, since in his work he still distinguishes them. Still, none of these suggestions seem to give adequate explanation for Kant's conception. The problems needing to be solved are (1) why there is a dialectic strictly speaking as logic of illusion distinguished from the doctrine of probability; (2) which is the source of this distinction; and (3) why analytics deals with the concepts and the principles of the understanding.

In order to understand Kant's conception of analytic and dialectic we must go back to Aristotle. According to Aristotle, dialectic is a "method whereby we shall be able to reason from probable opinions about any subject presented to us, and also shall ourselves, when putting forward an argument, avoid saying anything contrary to it."[215] Dialectic is therefore a method for arguing on a problem in general following probable and reputable reasons (ἔνδοξα). A reasoning, which in the Aristotelian mind corresponds properly to the syllogism, is an argument in which "certain things being laid down, something other than these necessarily comes about through them."[216] The deduction of the reasoning is correct if and only if the conclusions derive necessarily from the premises, which can be true, probable, or false. The correctness of the reasoning, even if it does not guarantee truth of what we are saying, is nonetheless its necessary condition: an argument can be correct, but false. If the premises are true, the argument is an apodictic, demonstrative, and scientific syllogism, whose study pertains to analytic. If the premises are only probable, the argument is a dialectic syllogism, whose inquiry pertains to dialectic. Probable premises are properly speaking those "which are accepted by everyone or by the majority or by the wise—i.e. by all, or by the majority, or by the most notable and reputable of them."[217] Dialectic arguments are therefore grounded on the shareability and acceptability of the premises and can have a cognitive value. Besides dialectic and scientific arguments, Aristotle adds sophistic syllogism, which is a syllogism that "starts from opinions that seem to be reputable, but are not really such," or a reasoning that "merely seems to reason from opinions that are or seem to be reputable."[218] The first kind of sophistic syllogism infers an illusion as conclusion, while the second kind appears to conclude, but does not.[219] Aristotle thus distinguishes two kinds of illusion, one that derives from the matter and truth of the premises, the other from the formal correctness of the reasoning. This latter kind of deceiving argument is properly speaking called "paralogism," and it concerns the form, rather than the matter.[220] Besides scientific demonstration, dialectic syllogism, paralogism, Aristotle lists rhetorical syllogism or enthymeme, which is based on probable, but not necessarily reputable, opinions whose aim is persuasion rather than demonstration.

For Aristotle, therefore, a part of dialectic has a relevant cognitive function in providing probable knowledge and in finding truth, while there is another part that concerns the abuses of reasoning, which are to contrast and it is a kind of sophistry. This partition of dialectic is based on Aristotle's distinction at the beginning of the *Topics* between authentic and deceiving ἔνδοξα. The ἔνδοξα of dialectic syllogism are authentic and have a cognitive value, and this is possible because "for Aristotle the ἔνδοξα do not coincide with δοκοῦντα, but only with a special class of the them, that is δοκοῦντα accepted by everyone or by the majority or by the wise."[221] The rhetorical δοκοῦντα are indeed for Aristotle of the same kind of dialectic ἔνδοξα, concerning the objective grounds of the reasoning, that is, the premises, but the aim of rhetorical arguments is not finding truth, but rather persuading subjectively. This is the reason why rhetorical arguments do not have a cognitive value. The sophistic δοκοῦντα, on the other hand, do not have a cognitive value, because they are mere illusions, both objectively and subjectively, whose aim is to deceive. Analytic, instead, concerns those arguments, such as induction and syllogism, whose aim is to find truth and scientific knowledge from necessary objective grounds. For this reason, Aristotle's analytic concerns the formal condition of truth (*Prior Analytics*), which can be applied to finding scientific knowledge starting from sensation (*Posterior Analytics*). Aristotelian analytic is, therefore, at once a general logic of reasoning and an epistemic logic, or a methodology for finding scientific knowledge.

Kant's early conception of "dialectic" and "analytic" is datable to the early 1770s, and seems to be directly influenced by the Aristotelian perspective. His use of this obsolete distinction is probably associated with Kant's discovery of the Aristotelian doctrine of the categories. In fact, we can find the very first occurrences of "analytic" and "dialectic" in fragments dated around 1772, and concerning the pure concepts of the understanding. "Analytic" appears in the *Reflection 4446*, and designates "the house of the intellectual concepts" (*domus conceptuum intellectualium*) in reference to the *Loci Metaphysici Aristotelis* (17: 554). This fragment reveals that Kant's conception of the doctrine of categories as part of analytic was at least partially inspired by the Aristotelian tradition. In *Reflection 1579*, Kant writes that the dialectic is "*disciplina apparentiae logicae*" (16: 21), and he adds that it can be either sophistic, that is, logic of illusion (*Logik des Scheins*), that leads us astray, or critical, that is, skeptical (16: 23).

The conception of "analytic" and "dialectic" is further developed in the chapter "On the Division of General Logic into Analytic and Dialectic" of the *Critique of Pure Reason*, where Kant for the first time defines its transcendental logic in relation to general logic. Kant defines analytic as the part of logic that examines the formal business of the understanding and its elements (A 60/B 84). Nevertheless, Kant states,

> there is something so seductive in the possession of an apparent art for giving all of our cognitions the form of understanding, even though with regard to their content one may yet be very empty and poor, that is general logic, which is merely a **canon** for judging, has been used as if it were an **organon** for the actual production of at least the semblance of objective assertions, and thus in fact it has thereby been misused. (A 60–1/B 85)

This abuse of logic as putative organon is properly speaking dialectic and, as different as the significance of the employment of this designation of a science or art among the ancients may have been, it is a logic of illusion (*Logik des Scheins*):

> A sophistical art for giving to its ignorance, indeed even to its intentional tricks, the air of truth, by imitating the

method of thoroughness, which logic prescribes in general, and using its topics for the embellishment of every empty pretension. (A 61/B 86)

Kant clearly conceives here dialectic as an art of deceiving in the same way that Aristotle understood sophistic. This art of logical illusion deceives by its pretension of extending cognition, while logic should teach us "nothing at all about the content of cognition, but only the formal conditions of agreement with the understanding, which are entirely indifferent with regard to objects" (A 61/B 86). General logic, as an organon, is always dialectic, and it is in itself self-contradictory in its claim to transform a mere canon into a tool of logic, from a canon to an organon, that is, a tool for expanding cognition.[222]

This partition of general logic into "analytic" and "dialectic" can be transferred into transcendental logic. Transcendental analytic becomes the part of logic "that expounds the elements of the pure cognition of the understanding and the principles without which object can be thought at all" (A 62/B 87). It is a logic of "formal truth," what we have called "logical truth." As we have seen, logical truth does not provide any material, objective truth, which comes only in occasion of experience. However, it is very "enticing and seductive" to use this logical truth to go beyond all bounds of experience, and by extending knowledge the understanding can fall "into the danger of making a material use of the merely formal principles of pure understanding through empty sophistries" (A 63/B 88). The part of logic that exposes and criticizes this illusion of the understanding is transcendental dialectic. Kant, however, is at pains to distinguish his conception of transcendental dialectic from a mere dialectic, as "an art of dogmatically arousing such illusion," which is prevalent among what he calls "the manifold works of metaphysical jugglery" (A 63/B 88). Rather, his transcendental dialectic is a critique of the understanding and of reason in their "hyperphysical use," "in order to uncover the false illusion of their groundless pretensions and to reduce their claims to invention and amplification" (A 63–64/B 88).

At this stage, we find in Kant at least two conceptions of dialectic, as *Reflection 1579* suggested: (1) dialectic as an art of deceiving, like the Aristotelian sophistic; and (2) dialectic as critique. In the chapter on "Transcendental Illusion" Kant distinguishes dialectic as logic of illusion from what was usually called dialectic as doctrine of probability (*Lehre der Wahrscheinlichkeit*), in other words, the Aristotelian *logica probabilium*. Like Aristotle, the doctrine of probability aims to find truth, "but cognized through insufficient grounds, so that the cognition of it is defective, but not therefore deceptive" (A 293/B 349). Unlike Aristotle, however, the doctrine of probability according to Kant pertains to analytic rather than to dialectic. The difference is very subtle, but important, and rests on the terminological distinction between what produces an illusion (*Schein*) and what is probable (*wahrscheinlich*).

In the eighteenth century, there was an indistinct, or at least confused, use of the Latin terms *probabile* and *verisimile*.[223] The Latin term *probabile* (*wahrscheinlich, probabel*) meant mainly either the lack of necessary conclusions from premises or the absence of a majority. In these two senses, in the Aristotelian tradition, dialectic was understood as a logic of probability.[224] The Latin term *verisimile* (*scheinbar*), on the other hand, denoted primarily the lack of a principle or rule for truth. Up until the 1760s, Kant himself employed illusoriness (*Scheinbarkeit*) to translate into German the Latin term *verisimilitudo*, and not probability (*Wahrscheinlichkeit*) (24: 196). From the 1770s onward, we can see a strong difference between *verisimilitudo* and *probabilitas*, between illusoriness (*Scheinbarkeit*) and probability (*Wahrscheinlichkeit*), as *Reflections 2209, 2595*, and *The Pölitz Logic* testify.[225] But the Latin terms *probabile* and *verisimile* and their German correspondents do not explain why Kant defines dialectic as logic of illusion. In fact, in *Critique of Pure Reason*, when Kant deals with dialectic, "illusion" (*Schein*) is not related to the consent of majority nor to necessary conclusions (*probabile, wahrscheinlich*), nor does it concern the lack of a rule or a principle (*scheinbar*), since dialectic claims to be an organon. Kant's concept of "illusion," employed to designate dialectic, has no correspondent in eighteenth-century logical textbooks.

However, if we look at the Aristotelian tradition, and Rabe's *Dialectica et analytica* in particular, we can find a similar distinction, which is in my opinion the Kantian source. In the prologue of his logical textbook, Rabe conceives of dialectic as a general name to designate logic, as was customary in Renaissance and early-modern philosophy, because both dialectic and logic have their root in the Greek word λογικός.[226] Properly speaking, however, there is a narrow sense of dialectic, whose intrinsic aim (*finis cujus*) is opinion, and ultimate aim (*finis cui*) the firm truth, that is, scientific knowledge.[227] In general, the purpose is to "produce an opinion in the mind of the audience, λόγῳ δεομένῳ, and to prepare to science."[228] The main tools of dialectic are induction and syllogism, while the matter are the ἔνδοξα or *probabilia*, that is, common propositions or shared opinions.[229] Rabe adds that dialectic differs from analytic because it is always a posteriori, while the latter is always a priori. In fact, dialectic is always concerned with particular opinions and with the matter of cognition, while analytic is a mere formal canon and prescribes a priori the *modus operandi* on the matter acquired a posteriori.[230]

In his treatment of dialectical syllogism, Rabe distinguishes (1) a kind of dialectic as *logica ex probabilibus*, whose aim is truth, from (2) a dialectic as *logica ex apparentibus*, whose aim is to deceive.[231] This is quite a striking distinction, because it reflects Kant's definition of dialectic as *disciplina apparentiae logicae* in Reflection 1579, as well as the Kantian juxtaposition of a doctrine of probability (*Lehre der Wahrscheinlichkeit*) and a logic of illusion (*Logik des Scheins*). Rabe then distinguishes two kinds of reasoning in the *logica ex apparentibus*: (1) sophistic argument; and (2) rhetorical syllogism. The "illusion" generated by rhetorical syllogism is called *verisimilitudo*, and it is different from sophistic illusion because its aim is persuasion, not deception.[232] On the other hand, the sophistic argument deceives in three ways: (1) according to matter, that is, it deals with illusions, and not with probable things; (2) according to the form, that is, it does not conclude correctly from the premises; and (3) according to matter and form, that is, it deals with illusions and concludes incorrectly: this is properly speaking a paralogism.[233] Kant's use of "paralogism" can derive from Rabe. In the *Critique of Pure Reason*, he writes that

> a logical paralogism consists in the falsity of a syllogism due to its form, whatever its content may otherwise be. A transcendental paralogism, however, has a transcendental ground for inferring falsely due to its form. Thus a fallacy of this kind will have its ground in the nature of human reason, and will bring with it an unavoidable, although not insoluble, illusion. (A 341/B 399)

Once again, Kant transfers what he finds in Aristotelian general logic to transcendental logic, characterizing paralogism as an unavoidable illusion of human reason in using logical rules not merely as a canon, but as an organon. Tonelli argues that *paralogism* was a common term in the seventeenth century, but it disappeared almost completely in the eighteenth century.[234] Indeed, it was used, albeit very rarely, not only in the Aristotelian, but also in the Wolffian tradition, hence, in this case, we cannot be sure that Rabe is Kant's only immediate source.[235]

In absence of any other plausible sources thematizing the distinction between dialectic as logic *ex probabilibus* and dialectic as logic *ex apparentibus*, and given the Aristotelian nature of the distinction between analytic and dialectic, I think that there are sufficient reasons to consider Rabe as Kant's source.

As we have seen, besides a negative judgment of dialectic as a logic of illusion, we find in Kant the definition of dialectic as a critique of the understanding and of reason in their hyperphysical use (A 63–64/B 88). Kant conceives of dialectic in a skeptical sense as a *cathartic*. Kant employs the term *cathartic* already at the beginning of the 1770s, as *The Blomberg Logic* testifies, where in relation to the skeptical method, he states that it is the reason's best means of purgation and the path to the truth of what is investigated (24: 208). In *The Jäsche Logic*, Kant associates *katharktikon* with dialectic, which would contain

> the marks and rules in accordance with which we could recognize that something does not agree with the formal criteria of truth, although its seems to agree with them. Dialectic in this sense would thus have its good use as *cathartic* of understanding. (9: 17)

This kind of dialectic should distinguish itself from and therefore decontaminate dialectic conceived of as a logic of illusion, that is, an *ars sophistica, disputatoria* (9: 16), through the rules of the zetetic or skeptical method.[236] The zetetic method would coincide, according to *Reflection 3957*, with the critical method (17: 366). Thus, starting from the *Announcement of the Programme of His Lectures for the Winter Semester 1765–1766*, the zetetic method becomes for Kant the philosophical method par excellence. It consists in opposing one proposition to another and in arguing in favor of the contrary, in such a way as to identify the error, when of a proposition are exhibited proofs and counterproofs. This zetetic method, according to Kant, comes from Zeno:

> **Zeno** the **Eleatic**, a subtle dialectician, was already severely censured by Plato as a wanton sophist who, to show his art, would seek to prove some proposition through plausible arguments and then immediately to overthrow the same proposition through other arguments just as strong. He asserted that God (presumably for him this was nothing but the world) is neither finite nor infinite, is neither in motion nor at rest, and is neither like nor unlike any other thing. To those who judged him, it appeared that he wanted entirely to deny two mutually contradictory propositions, which is absurd. But I do not find this charge can be justly lodged against him [. . .] If two mutually opposed judgments presuppose an inadmissible condition, then, despite their conflict (which is, however, not a real contradiction) both of them collapse, because the condition collapses under which alone either of them would be valid. (A 502/B 530)

Kant's attribution to Zeno of zetetic and critical logic is well established at the beginning of the 1770s. In *The Philippi Logic*, Kant states that the zetetic method

> is immensely useful, provided a correct use is made of it, because it allows the opposition of one proposition to another, and the argument of proofs in support of the contrary, and from this alone derives the examination of reason, because, when of a proposition are exhibited proofs and counterproofs that demonstrate the contrary, since a proposition can be only either true or false, the problem cannot be otherwise than in the subject. (24: 438)

This method, according to Kant, in direct opposition to Plato, "must be considered as a very acute and valuable observation, rather than a reproachable doubt" (24: 209). What is really striking is that Zeno never maintained the doctrine that Kant attributes to him.[237]

Giuseppe Micheli correctly argued that Kant's source was Brucker's *Historia critica philosophiae*, which presents Zeno's arguments as they appear in Kant.[238] But Brucker's source is a pseudo-Aristotelian work titled *De Xenophane, Zenone et Gorgia*, whose title was successively corrected in *De Melisso, Xenophane, Gorgia*.[239] Thus, the doctrine that Brucker and Kant attribute to Zeno must in fact be attributed to Xenophanes of Colophon. Moreover, Zeno's alleged dialectical reasoning infers from the contradiction of a hypothesis the truth of the contrary thesis, a process that is quite different from that mentioned by Kant. Zeno's zetetic method according to Kant consists in showing separately the contradiction of two opposed hypotheses, concluding from this fact that the opposition is a mere illusion.[240] The source of this dichotomous process seems to be Pierre Gassendi, who in turn refers to Proclus's commentary to Plato's *Parmenides*, which was mentioned by Darjes in his *Via ad veritatem*.[241] Hence, from Darjes Kant did not take his conception of dialectic as *logica probabilium*, as Tonelli suggested, but the zetetic method of dialectic as cathartic.

As we have already noted, the Kantian idea of analytic as logic of truth was quite common in the Aristotelian textbooks, and does not present significant conceptual variations in Kant's philosophical developments. Kant did not employ the term *analytic* to designate a part of logic in *The Blomberg Logic* (1771), or in *The Philippi Logic* (1771–72).[242] The notion appears only subsequently, around 1772, as *Reflection 4446* testifies, in opposition to "dialectic" and within the context of the elaboration of the doctrine of the categories. In the transferral from general logic to transcendental logic, analytic shifts from the Aristotelian "logic of truth" to the logic of the transcendental condition of truth. For this reason, transcendental analytic resolves the a priori logical structure of the mind into concepts and principles. In particular, concerning concepts, transcendental analytic determines that concepts are (1) pure, (2) fundamental and elementary, (3) systematized, and (4) belonging to thought. From the resolution of concepts derive fundamental propositions, which are the principles of the understanding (A 149/B 188).

Concepts and principles constitute the core of transcendental analytic, and we can find, as I have already emphasized, a parallelism between Kant's conception and the Aristotelian tradition of gnostology, which deals with the first operation of the mind, that is, the apprehension of concepts, and noology, which deals with the second operation of the mind, namely, the formation of principles. We have also noted that the treatment of the doctrine of the categories within logic is typical of the Aristotelian tradition. But there is also a reason why Kant deals with categories in the analytic. It is not only his systematic spirit or the fact that analytic concerns the resolution of the first a priori elements of cognition that led Kant to devote this part of logic to the study of the categories: we can find an antecedent to Kant's conception in Rabe. If in the *Dialectica et analytica* Rabe includes a brief survey of the categories within dialectic understood as logic in general, because they are the building blocks of every reasoning, and therefore must be taught at the beginning of logic, in the *Primitiae professionis logico-metaphysicae*, he assigns their study very specifically to analytic:

> if we want to look at the utility of categories, we will have to refer them to analytic, because the cognition of categories seems more necessary to analytic than dialectic and it is more useful to it [analytic]: analytic concerns definition, division and demonstration, which without the knowledge of categories cannot be correctly made.[243]

Rabe is quite clear on this point. Categories are that without which cognition would be impossible. We cannot find in any other Königsberg Aristotelian such a conception. In fact, Rabe's mentor, Andreas Hedio, still dealt with categories within dialectic, properly speaking.[244] In Rabe, like in Kant, not only the categories and judgments, as we have seen, but also the principles are part of analytic. The reason of this inclusion is easy to understand. Since analytic deals with demonstrations, and demonstrations are grounded in first, immediate and true principles, the study of these principles must be included in analytic. Rabe presents three kinds of principles: (1) definitions; (2) axioms; and (3) hypothesis.[245] According to their subject-matter and the demonstration in which they are used, principles can concern physics or metaphysics.[246] Principles are therefore never conceived a priori without matter, like the categories, but they must be understood in relation to their possible application.

The insertion of categories, judgments, and principles into analytic is followed by the negation of gnostology as an independent science: it belongs to analytic. Rabe is part of a large group of philosophers for whom "the independent status of gnostology as a whole was very controversial," since for the majority of "philosophers at that time, it belonged either to logic, metaphysics or physics."[247] In the proem to metaphysics in the *Cursus philosophicus*, Rabe writes that new theoretical sciences besides metaphysics have recently been founded: (1) ontology; (2) noology; (3) gnostology; and (4) pneumatology. Ontology deals with the *ens qua ens*, that is, being in general;[248] metaphysics deals with the supreme Being, that is, God;[249] pneumatology studies immaterial substances;[250] while noology is concerned with the first principles of being as being, and is a propaedeutic science to metaphysics.[251] Rabe uses three arguments to refute the autonomous status of gnostology as the science of cognizable qua cognizable. If cognizables were an object of cognition of the mind, gnostology would pertain to the physics that studies the operations of the soul,[252] that is, psychology, or what we have called facultative logic. If the cognizables were affections of being, then gnostology would be a part of metaphysics.[253] If cognizables were considered *sub ratione scibiles*, then it would be possible to invent a new science, but still it would pertain to analytic, which deals with scientific and demonstrative knowledge.[254] Rabe thus conceives of analytic as the science that deals with an object of knowledge in general as far as it can be an object of scientific knowledge, and with the conditions through which a cognizable can become a knowable, which is a similar conception as exposed in *Critique of Pure Reason*.

To sum up, our investigation into Kant's distinction of transcendental logic into analytic and dialectic leads to the following conclusions. The distinction comes from general logic and has an Aristotelian origin. At least up to the first half of the 1760s, Kant conceived of dialectic as logic of probability following Meier's conception, while at the end of the 1760s and in the early '70s he distinguished three kinds of dialectic: (1) *logica probabilium*, whose aim is truth, (2) *logica ex apparentibus*, whose aim is deception, and (3) a zetetic method, which is a skeptical and critical process. The source cannot be Meier, because he is criticized. The source cannot be Darjes, since he maintains the identity between dialectic and *logica probabilium*. The Kantian distinction mirrors the Aristotelian distinction between dialectic and sophistic arguments. Dialectic as *logica probabilium* is included in the analytic because of its cognitive value, and because its ultimate aim is truth. Rabe conceives dialectic as a logic that leads to truth starting from probable premises. In Rabe we have the conception of dialectic as *logica ex apparentibus*, which is typical of Kant. In absence of any other possible source, Kant most likely elaborated his conception of the logic of illusion from Rabe's reflections. Instead, Kant's conception of dialectic as a zetetic and skeptical method comes from Brucker and Gassendi, through the mediation of Darjes.

Analytic is conceived in opposition to dialectic as the logic of truth, and it is divided into the analytic of concepts, which contains also the table of judgments, and analytic of principles. Rabe has a similar conception, and deals with categories, judgments, and principles in the analytic. For Rabe, the object of analytic must be "pure" or "general," meaning that they are considered without matter or content, otherwise they would pertain to specific science such as metaphysics and physics. Rabe includes in the analytic the treatment of gnostology as the science of the cognizable, which should become a knowable. Kant's work follows similar lines of development as Rabe's, using the same terminology and making the same conceptual changes—and this cannot be a mere coincidence.

3

METHODOLOGY

METHOD IN THE ARISTOTELIAN TRADITION

In the previous chapters we examined facultative logic as the discipline of the workings of mind, and transcendental logic as a canon considering only the mere form of cognition. In this chapter, we will focus on Kant's logic as a methodology.

The problem of method is in fact one of the most crucial in Kant's precritical thought. The methodological question is a transversal issue in his precritical works, from *Thoughts on the True Estimation of Living Forces* (1747) to *Inquiry Concerning the Distinctness of the Principles of Natural Theology and Morality* (1764). The seventeen years that elapsed between these two works are marked by profound and significant changes in Kant's conception of method: if at the beginning he wished for the application of a geometrical method in all sciences following his youthful interests in mathematics, alongside a burgeoning interest in metaphysics, he became increasingly aware of the irreconcilability of mathematics and metaphysics. Kant's awareness of the impossibility of applying mathematical methods to metaphysical inquiries, and his loss of confidence in mathematics and its capacity to describe reality, led him to seek a new methodology, which he found only in 1781 with the *Critique of Pure Reason*. Before tackling the methodological issues of the *Critique of*

Pure Reason, however, it is necessary to understand Kant's developments within the intellectual framework of Königsberg, and the new emerging philosophical questions and trends.

In general, the "problem of method" in early modern philosophy concerns many different issues, of which three are of particular relevance for the reconstruction of Kant's conception of methodology: the first is the distinction between order and method; the second is the distinction between resolution, or analysis, and composition, or synthesis; and the third deals with the relation between philosophy and mathematics, which is twofold, the geometrical order of exposition and the application of mathematics to other disciplines such as physics and metaphysics.

Aristotle is the first philosopher to develop a consistent theory of method. In Aristotelian philosophy, method is essentially demonstrative and follows syllogistic reasoning. It is therefore mainly a deductive process, but it would be misleading to consider it exclusively so. In fact, as we have already seen, the method is based on demonstration, and demonstration is grounded in premises, which are grasped by means of an inductive method, starting from sensation, as Aristotle explains in *Posterior Analytics* II.19. Thus, we can say that the inductive method is more foundational than the deductive method, even if the latter leads to scientific knowledge. The interaction between inductive and deductive methods generates knowledge, as Aristotle says in the proem of *Physics*. Knowing (γιγνώσκειν)—he states—means to have acquaintance of first causes, principles, and elements. The natural way of knowing "is to start from things which are more knowable and clear to us and proceed towards those which are clearer and more knowable by nature; for the same things are not knowable relatively to us and knowable absolutely."[1] The method to follow is to proceed from what is less clear and knowable by nature, but more clear and knowable to us, with the aim of attaining what is clearer and more knowable by nature. The search for what is clearer and more knowable by nature corresponds in Aristotle to the search for truth. Searching for the truth, Aristotle writes in *Metaphysics* II.1, is no easy task, since what is more knowable by nature is more obscure to us, "for as the eyes of bats are to the blaze of day," so is the mind "to things which are by nature most evident of all."[2] In knowing, therefore, we must advance "from what is more obscure by nature, but clearer to us, towards what is clearer and more knowable by nature," and only then, by means of analysis, do "the elements and principles become known to us."[3] The knowledge of these elements and principles, however, is not really scientific, "coming from about what is more familiar to us, it is not real demonstration."[4] To know scientifically, in fact, requires starting from true, first, immediate, more knowable premises, which are causes of the conclusions, and not the contrary.[5] The knowledge acquired by means of the analysis of sensation is therefore merely provisional, and must be proved in order to find out if the causes and principles that have been discovered by analysis are the real causes and principles of the particular things. Having established that the principles discovered by analysis are the true and universal causes of the effects observed by sensation, we can then apply them to know particular things scientifically. The verification of the principles, however, that is, the passage from a provisional knowledge of the principles to the acknowledgment that they are true and universal causes, is not clear in Aristotle's treatment, and, as we shall see, shall become so only thanks to Renaissance logicians.

What is important now, however, is that there are two ways of knowing a particular thing: (1) a subjective way, in which the premises are presupposed, and which leads to a knowledge in general; and (2) an objective way, where the premises are already demonstrated, and which leads to a scientific knowledge. The object of knowledge is the same, but there are two different methods of investigation. Aristotle is explicitly emphasizing the importance of the subjectivity of knowledge, in fact, that the same object could be known in two different ways concerns not the object itself, but rather the subjective standpoint of the knowing subject. Without this subjective aspect of cognition, it would be impossible to investigate things in different ways; in fact, there would be only a univocal knowledge of the thing, as Plato argues, which would mean to deny the determining role of experience in acquiring knowledge and in constituting the habits of intellect, science, and wisdom, that is, what we have called the second nature of the subject.[6]

In *Prior Analytics* II.23, 68 b 35–37, Aristotle deals with these two means of cognition. The subjective way is general, by induction (or by demonstration on "that is"), while the objective way is always by means of a deduction: "in order of nature, deduction through the middle term is prior and more familiar, but deduction through induction is clearer to us."[7] Yet, in *Topics* I.12, 104 a 16–19, Aristotle had established that induction is the way from particular to universal, and that it is more persuasive, clear, and knowable as far as sensation is concerned. It is the more apt for the majority, while syllogism is more effective and convincing among those who know logic.[8] In *Metaphysics* VII.4, Aristotle states that "it is an advantage to advance to that which is more intelligible [. . .] to start from what is more intelligible to oneself and make what is intelligible by nature intelligible to oneself."[9] Therefore, even if knowledge at the very beginning at the first step of analysis is particular and generic, it is nonetheless necessary "to understand what is intelligible in itself."[10]

In the final passages of the second book of *Metaphysics*, Aristotle introduces another important issue in his methodology. He states that, in general, one should not expect the same accuracy in all disciplines. He states that "some want to have everything done accurately, while others are annoyed by accuracy, either because they cannot follow the connexion of thought or because they regard it as pettifoggery."[11] Accuracy, Aristotle adds, "is a pettifoggery, so that as in trade so in argument some people think it mean."[12] For this reason one must be already trained to know how accurate the method of research has to be, "since it is absurd to seek at the same time knowledge and the way of attaining knowledge."[13] In fact, Aristotle says:

> the minute accuracy of mathematics is not to be demanded in all cases, but only in the case of things which have no matter. Therefore its method is not that of natural science; for presumably all nature has matter.[14]

Aristotle asserts quite forcefully that physics cannot aspire to the same rigor as mathematics, because the former deals with matter, which is particular and contingent, and not universal like form. Strictly speaking, matter cannot be known scientifically. What is known scientifically is the form that pertains to matter. But one question which fomented endless disputes and controversies among its Renaissance and modern commentators is left tantalizingly open by Aristotle: Does the statement that physics cannot achieve the same degree of accuracy of mathematics not entail that mathematics cannot be applied to physics?

During the Renaissance there was a renewed interest in the Aristotelian conception of method with the integration of the methodological issues of authors such as Euclid, Galen, and Pappus.[15] The most debated issues at the time were the distinction between order and method and the utility of analysis and synthesis. In this context, the logical elaboration of Jacopo Zabarella, who definitively systematized Aristotelian methodology, was crucial. Method, according to Zabarella, is a "logical habit, or intellectual instrumental habit which is useful to acquiring knowledge of things."[16] In other places, it is characterized specifically as the "process from known to unknown through syllogistic discourse."[17] For Zabarella, in general, there is a substantial identity between method and syllogism: "the definition of method does not differ from the definition of syllogism."[18] Order, on the other hand, "is not syllogism, nor the inferential process of a thing from another, but only the correct arrangement of all parts of knowledge."[19] True method "does not arrange the parts of knowledge, but it leads to cognition of the unknown from the known, inferring the former from the latter."[20] Given this distinction between order and method, the methodological discussion shifts to scientific method:

> there are two scientific methods, no more, no less [. . .] perfect (*potissima*) demonstration, or demonstration *propter quid* [. . .] the other, which proceeds from the effect to the cause is called resolutive: for this progress is resolution, like the process from the cause to the effect is called composition.[21]

Synthesis proceeds from the first and simplest elements to the complex ones. On the contrary, analysis proceeds from complex elements to the simplest and first ones, and is in general either induction or demonstration of the "that is." Zabarella establishes also a hierarchy between these two methods: "resolutive method serves demonstrative method."[22] The reason is quite evident: analysis provides the first principles for the synthesis. In fact, Zabarella points out that analysis is necessary when the principles are unknown, while it is useless when they are already known,[23] as in the case of mathematical sciences.[24] Mathematics proceeds only by synthesis, and what is called usually "mathematical analysis" is something completely different from what he understands by analysis.

The aim of the demonstrative method is "perfect science, which is the cognition of a thing through its cause."[25] Meanwhile, the aim of analysis is "discovery rather than science; because with resolution we investigate the causes from effects, to know then the effect from the causes, and in this cognition of causes we rest."[26]

Scientific knowledge can be acquired only in the conjunction between analysis and synthesis, and the crucial point is to explain how the principles discovered by analysis can be converted into the causes and principles of the synthesis. Such passage is possible through Zabarella's theory of regress (*regressus*). Regress leads from an initial, confused, and general knowledge to a final, universal, distinct, and perfect knowledge.[27] In order to explain the effectiveness of regress, Zabarella exemplifies with the following syllogism: "(a) where there is generation, there is matter; (b) in a natural body there is generation, (c) therefore in a natural body there is matter."[28] The major premise (a) is discovered by induction and therefore provides only a confused and generic knowledge, while the minor premise (b) comes from observation. Therefore the conclusion (c) can only be confused and generic, not scientific and universal. What the demonstration from effect (i.e., of the "that is") proves is not the cause itself, but simply that there must be a cause of the effects, perhaps the one we have obscurely recognized, and this recognition constitutes the first part of the regressive method.[29] But in order to acquire knowledge of the effect by means of the distinct knowledge of the cause, and to demonstrate that the cause discovered by the analysis is the one correctly pertaining to the effect, Zabarella introduces a process called "mental examination."[30] Mental examination is constituted by two moments that were left inexplicit in the original Aristotelian treatment. The first moment recognizes the existence of the effect's cause and prepares for the discovery of that cause's essence, or nature, while the second compares the cause (known confusedly) with the effect.[31] If the comparison is successful we can say that the causes and principles we have discovered initially in a confused way are the genuine causes and principles of the effects, now known perfectly. This is the last moment of the regress, and it coincides with the perfect demonstration. Regress is the only process—according to Zabarella—capable of providing scientific knowledge. All the other processes connected with the Platonic and Galenian traditions, such as definition and division, are useless in finding new truths.[32]

A central methodological issue in Zabarella's theory of regress is the distinction between what is most knowable by us and what is most knowable by nature. If we do not understand this distinction, according to Zabarella, regress could be reduced to a form of circular argument. Zabarella, like Aristotle, maintains that what is first and most knowable by nature is the last in the order of mind's cognition, and is the true object of scientific knowledge. Indeed, what is first and most knowable by us is not demonstrated and does not lead to scientific knowledge. Thus, according to Zabarella, it is possible to recognize two orders—(1) analytic and (2) synthetic—which do not designate the order of the things in themselves, but, rather ways of arranging the knowledge of things; that is, they characterize a rational order of the subject.

What is first, Zabarella states, can be said in two ways: what is most knowable by human nature (*humana conditio*), which are sensible objects, and what is most knowable by nature, which are universals.[33] There is, however, a particular kind of "universals," not universals properly speaking, which are most knowable by us, but the first principles of cognition generated by induction and grasped by intellection. These principles are merely hypothetical, that is, they are mere presuppositions that must be further demonstrated as true first principles and causes, and in this way they are not only most knowable by us but also by nature.[34] The cognition of these principles, as we have seen in the previous chapters, is not innate, but is acquired.[35] In his commentary to *Posterior Analytics*, Zabarella emphasizes that to the first principles discovered by induction and grasped by intellection (that is, by the Aristotelian analysis) pertains a kind of universality that is closer to human nature; in other words they are κατ'ἄνθρωπον compared to the universality discovered after perfect demonstration. A universal κατ'ἄνθρωπον is—Zabarella points out—what is valid and common for human nature as if it were one, and not something distributed in various ways in individuals.[36] For Zabarella the Greek expression κατ'ἄνθρωπον is the correct translation of "every man," and therefore the universality of what is first for man concerns not all men, but a man in general.[37] In opposition to the universality κατ'ἄνθρωπον, there is the universality of necessary propositions, which are already demonstrated as universal, and are the foundations of every new scientific demonstration. There are three kinds of universality according to Zabarella, following Aristotle: (1) *omni* (κατὰ παντός); (2) *per se* (κατ' αὐτό); and (3) *universale* (καθόλου).[38] Only the last kind of universality is properly speaking first by nature, and it is the end of scientific knowledge. The passage from a universality κατ' ἄνθρωπον to scientific universality is possible through regress.

At the dawn of the sixteenth century Aristotelian methodology was characterized by five main peculiarities: (1) scientific method consists in the cooperation of analysis and synthesis; (2) method provides scientific knowledge through the demonstration alone; (3) scientific knowledge always concerns universals; (4) method is nonetheless a critical examination of experience and particulars; and (5) the outcomes of the scientific method must always be verified by experience.

In the wake of Zabarella's ideas, as we have already seen, many new philosophical trends were born in Germany in the seventeenth century, in particular, in connection with a new systematization of knowledge. Not only gnostology and noology were invented, but also methodology (*methodologia*) established itself as an autonomous discipline. Abraham Calov was the first to conceive of methodology as a freestanding science independent of logic in his *Tractatus Novus de Methodo docendi et disputandi* (1632), successively published with the title *Methodologia nova* (1651). The extraordinary influence enjoyed by this work in the Aristotelian tradition is testified by the large number of subsequent works it inspired, such as Michael Eifler's *Methodologia thematica* (1635), reprinted with the titles *Methodologia particularis, synthesin et analysin thematicam* (1643) and *Methodologia recognita* (1653); Melchior Zeidler's *De gemino veterum docendi modo exoterico et acroamatico, id est dialectico et analytico, tractatus historico-philologico-philosophicus* (1685), and Paul Rabe's *Methodologia nova atque scientifica sive tractatus de ordine genuino* (1708). All these works are evidence not only of Calov's scientific authority and popularity, but also of the continuity of the Aristotelian methodology up to the first decades of the eighteenth century.

Calov opens his work stating that "our understanding abhors all kinds of confusion [. . .] thus in every cognition it aspires to order."[39] Order requires an ordered cognition, thus a "distinct cognition is better than a confused one."⁴⁰ Cognition is always about something, therefore, method always has to do with a content of knowledge to which it is applied; it is never a pure formal logic, or a canon, rather it is always an organon. For this reason, methodology is an instrumental habit for the teaching of precepts of method and their application in cognizing things. In the absence of the content of knowledge, no precept can be applied.⁴¹ Method is therefore a tool (*instrumentarium*) for organizing every cognition according to particular precepts.⁴² In particular, he calls "organic" (*organica*) the part of the method concerning not the general precepts, but the special precepts of each discipline, such as how to order particular cognitions systematically. But Calov makes another important distinction between the discipline of method, that is, methodology, and what he calls architectonic. While the precepts of methodology in general constitute an organon because they show the specific rules to be obeyed for every cognition of every discipline, the precepts of architectonic show how the various cognitions should be systematized according to the principle of the hierarchy of disciplines, that is, the order of dependence of the various disciplines among them.⁴³ Therefore, methodology shows that cognitions must be arranged in general for attaining a distinct knowledge, while architectonic shows how to systematize them according to specific principles, that is, how to transform an aggregate of cognitions into a system.⁴⁴

The aim of the method is twofold, intrinsic and extrinsic. The intrinsic aim can be either general or special. The intrinsic general aim is the "direction of the mind to distinct knowledge of many things."⁴⁵ Method, however, "does not improve mind; but it directs the ordered process of the mind in an instrumental way; in fact his aim is the direction of the understanding rather than the distinct knowledge of things itself."⁴⁶ The intrinsic special aim is "the direction of the διάνοια of the mind, about the arrangement and resolution of precepts."⁴⁷ In every cognition, two elements must be directed: (1) the inference; and (2) the order, which is not always the same for Calov as for Zabarella.⁴⁸ The extrinsic aim is complete (*ultimatus*) or intermediate. The complete aim is "an easier investigation of truth,"⁴⁹ while the intermediate aim is twofold, that is the "easy perception of things and prompt repetition."⁵⁰

Generally speaking, concerning the object of method, it is "all that in which an ordered arrangement can be given."⁵¹ Specifically, it is twofold, *quod* or *circa quod*. *Objectum quod* is "διάνοια of the mind,"[52] while the *objectum circa quod* "is determined in the thesis."[53] Method is, therefore, the systematic process of directing the mind in the cognition of things according to particular precepts that generate an arranged knowledge.[54] Method differs from order, which is an apt collocation of an aggregate of cognitions according to their natural arrangement.[55]

Zabarella's influence on Calov's conception of method is clear and evident. Unlike Zabarella, however, Calov conceives of method and methodology in the broader context of a new elaboration of the system of sciences. There is in Calov an architectonic concern that goes beyond the mere precepts for the direction of the mind in cognizing things and looks directly at the foundation of a system of sciences and of their reciprocal relations. These relations characterize indelibly the method that must be applied to the subject-matter of each discipline. Nonetheless, this is not at the expense of a common method for all disciplines conceived independently from the content of knowledge and based essentially on basic principles, which constitutes a canon or set of rules,[56] but the task of establishing the rules and general principles governing all sciences belongs, as we have seen in the previous chapter, rather to noology than to methodology.[57]

Calov's methodology extended its influence up to Rabe. With Rabe, for the first time in Königsberg, there is a discussion on Cartesian methodology. Rabe's assessment of Descartes's method is very negative, and probably reflects the opinions popular at that time in Königsberg. In general, Rabe in his *Methodologia* follows Zabarella and Calov and does not make explicit reference to Descartes, at least not as much as in his disputation *De novellis philosophis eorumque philosophia* (1678). There are several characteristic elements of modern philosophy, among which Rabe indicates in particular the lack of method and of reasoning:

> the general character of the new philosophy is the teaching without method and syllogism. While Aristotle not only teaches his doctrines with method and order, but he demonstrates them firmly, these new philosophers, on the contrary, prescribe to neglect the precepts of method and to write arbitrarily, the important thing is that the written things are not stupid. They do not support their statements with any

firm reason, [...], they reject categorically the syllogistic criterion as inappropriate.[58]

Not following the Aristotelian method leads to two negative consequences: (1) "very insolent pride of the mind, intolerable arrogance";[59] and (2) "rejection of truly evident principles and the introduction of others absolutely vain."[60] In Rabe's view, modern philosophers opposed Aristotelian principles, according to which "it is necessary to doubt everything and to free the understanding from prejudice."[61] Specifically to the Aristotelian principles, for which "sensation is the first κρῐτήριον and the law of all the other natural things," and "it is impossible to be and not to be at the same time"; modern philosophers do not propose more than the principles "*cogito, ergo sum* [...] which is like if not worse than the principles: *crepitum ventris emitto, ergo sum*."[62]

Rabe's criticism is not only against Cartesian, but also against Eclectic philosophers, who, despite having maintained many Aristotelian doctrines,[63] dealt with method very confusedly.[64] The acrimonious reference is probably to Christian Thomasius, for whom distinguishing the various methods is simply absurd:

> concerning the foolish quibbles on synthetic and analytic method, it is as if two litigants sit down at a table and quarrelling about whether it was better to make the first cut in the wing or in the thigh, from bottom to top or from top to bottom, from right or from left, and the other diners tried all these ways on chickens served on the table and ate them, while the litigants are still quarrelling. There is only one methodological rule: to order a demonstration or a discovery of truth as one wants, just not in a clumsy and ridiculous way.[65]

Rabe's vocal stand against the Eclectic philosophers was probably prompted by their rapid rise at Königsberg with the backing of the Pietists. Rabe's methodological attempt, beyond being only a genuine defense of Aristotelianism, was also a defense of orthodoxy. In the first decades of the eighteenth century, various new methodological conceptions established themselves in Germany, among which probably the most important was the Wolffian.

MODERN CONCEPTIONS OF METHOD

The first modern methodological work expressly devoted to the renewal of the Aristotelian doctrine of method is Francis Bacon's *Novum Organum* (1620). Bacon's method was based on a preliminary criticism of prejudices—an essential methodological concern of the Enlightenment—and on inductive method, which employed a series of tables of absence, presence, and degrees, as well as crucial experiments to corroborate the hypothesis. However, René Descartes was probably the most influential modern philosopher on method with his unfinished *Regulae ad directionem ingenii* (1627-28) and his *Discours de la méthode* (1637). In the *Regulae*, Descartes explicitly supports the view that "every science is evident and firm knowledge," in the Aristotelian sense of ἐπιστήμη, but unlike the Aristotelians he denies any cognitive value of probable arguments,[66] that is, the ἔνδοξα of dialectic. He adds that he "who searches for the correct way of truth must not be concerned with any object, of which they cannot have a certainty equal to arithmetic and geometrical demonstrations."[67] Unlike the Aristotelian conception, he maintains that true method leads by analysis to accurate demonstrations, such as those of mathematics. According to this idea there are only two operations for acquiring scientific knowledge: (1) intuition and (2) deduction. For intuition he understands "undoubting conception of a pure and attentive mind, generated solely by the light of reason,"[68] while deduction occurs when "many things are known firmly although not self-evident, so long as they are deduced from principles known to be true by a continuous and uninterrupted movement of thought, with clear intuition of each point."[69] Deduction is therefore conceived as a series of intuitive operations, because every moment of deduction consisting in grasping with evidence, that is, intuiting, the reciprocal connections among truths.

On deduction, Descartes develops his conception of method in his *Meditationes de prima philosophia*. In the reply to Mersenne's objection, Descartes establishes the distinction between order and method. Order consists "in putting forward as first what ought to be known without any help from what comes afterward and then in arranging all the rest in such a way that they are demonstrated solely by means of what preceded them."[70] Method, on the other hand, is "the order and arrangement of the things to which the mind's eye must turn so that we can discover some truth."[71] Descartes then states that the method is of two kinds:

> one that proceeds by way of analysis, the other by way of synthesis. Analysis shows the true way by which a thing has been discovered methodically and how the effects depend on the causes [. . .] Synthesis, on the other hand, indeed clearly demonstrates its conclusion by an opposite way; where the investigation is conducted from the effects to the causes (although it is often the case here that this proof is more a priori than it is in the analytics method).[72]

Descartes prefers analysis over synthesis, in open opposition to the Aristotelian tradition. Analysis would be more suitable for teaching, while synthesis always comes after it, and is almost useless for metaphysical disciplines. Beyond this shift of interest toward analysis lies Descartes's new definition of the concept of analysis and synthesis, which led him to attribute to resolution the characteristic elements of composition.

In the *Discours*, Descartes aims for a new reform (*nouvelle réformation*) for mind. This reform had to start from Aristotelian logic.[73] Aristotelian logic, with its syllogisms and rules, would have had no other purpose than to explain what is already known.[74] Lullian art, on the other hand, would be helpful to speak without judgment of things about which one is ignorant, rather than to learn what they are.[75] Instead, the analysis of the ancients and the algebra of the moderns would deal only with very abstract and useless matters. The former concerns figures and numbers that cannot exercise the understanding without a great effort of the imagination.[76] Meanwhile, the latter clutters up the mind with obscure and confused rules and symbols.[77] The main aim of Descartes's new method is to include the advantages of the old conceptions of logic without their defects, that is, the universality of logic, the analytic and synthetic method of geometry and the use of the symbols of algebra. The reform was based on the four methodological rules: (1) evidence; (2) analysis; (3) synthesis; and (4) enumeration. They were not, however, the rules of method, which were probably a companion of contemporary methodologies,[78] or the new relation established between analysis and synthesis, that revolutionized the approach of seventeenth-century philosophical disciplines; rather, they were the application of mathematics to the study of physics and the geometrical order of exposition as Descartes suggested at the end of the second part of the *Discours*:

> those long chains of reasoning, simple and easy as they are, of which geometricians make use in order to arrive at the most difficult demonstrations, had caused me to imagine that all those things which fall under the knowledge of man might very likely be mutually related in the same fashion; and that, provided only that we abstain from receiving anything as true which is not so, and always retain the order which is necessary in order to deduce the one conclusion from the other, there can be nothing so remote that we cannot reach to it, nor so recondite that we cannot discover it.[79]

Descartes explicitly argues that the geometrical method is applicable to every science, that there is a necessary order among the things in nature that is mathematical and geometrical and the base of an exhaustive knowledge of reality. Descartes's mathematicism lies at the very foundations of modern methodology up to Leibniz.

Unlike Descartes, Leibniz sees a substantial difference between mathematics and metaphysics, which is grounded in the distinction between truths of reason and truths of fact. The former are based on the laws of identity and contradiction, the latter on the law of sufficient reason. Truths of reason are necessary truths whose opposite is impossible, and which pertain essentially to the subject. Truths of fact, on the other hand, are contingent truths whose opposite is possible. Admitting only truths of reason would entail that the whole of reality would be structured mathematically and geometrically, as in Descartes and Spinoza. But reality consists also of contingent facts, as our experience testifies. There is therefore irreconcilability between mathematics, grounded in truths of reason, and metaphysics, grounded in truths of fact. But this irreconcilability is only apparent, as truths of fact would be identical to those of reason if it were possible to apply an infinite analysis to them. The difference between mathematics and metaphysics, and the certainty of the former in comparison to the latter, concerns only the limits of human understanding,[80] which, if it were as that of God, could reduce intuitively all truths of fact to those of reason, thereby making it possible to build up a combinatorics.

Leibniz's methodological proposal is quite clear in the essay *Über die rechte Methode der Behandlung der Philosophie und der Theologie*. In this work, Leibniz wishes for the application of mathematics to natural theology and ethics in order to establish definitions and to discover clear basic elements that are even more fruitful than those of Euclid.[81] As geometry is applied to physics, so it must be applied also to the sciences that distinguish what is right and wrong, and also indicate how it is possible to reach happiness.[82] Leibniz criticizes Descartes for his unfulfilled promise to deal with these issues with a geometrical method,[83] in so doing attacking also those who did not believe that mathematical accuracy was not possible outside mathematical sciences because they were unaware that writing mathematically and reasoning formally are the same.[84] Leibniz, as we have seen in the previous chapter, establishes the identity between mathematics and logic, but he emphasizes that we must not be too eager to explain everything mathematically, thereby endangering the truth.[85] In particular, we must not reduce all reality to mere extension and quantity, as Descartes did, in order to apply the mathematical method. Rather, a true mathematical description of reality is primarily concerned with qualities. Only in this way would it have been possible to apply the same method to theology and similar sciences, as well as to natural sciences. This operation is possible only through a radical reappraisal of the mathematical method, or analysis, in opposition to the Cartesian tradition.

Leibniz's new conception of analysis is fully developed in his *De synthesi et analysi universali seu arte inveniendi et judicandi*. Leibniz recalls his discovery of combinatorics, which is the "true analysis of human thoughts," because it resolves all thoughts in the simplest and first notions, from the combination of which all the other notions derive.[86] Leibniz defines these processes of combination and resolution in terms of synthesis and analysis:

> Synthesis is achieved when we begin from principles and run through truths in good order, thus discovering certain progressions and setting up tables, or sometimes general formulas, in which the answers to emerging questions can later be discovered. Analysis goes back to the principles in order to solve the given problems only, just as if neither we nor others had discovered anything before. [. . .] It is more important to establish synthesis, because this work is of permanent value,

> while we often do work that has already been done in beginning the analysis of a particular problem. But it is a lesser art to use synthesis already set up by others and theorems already discovered, than to achieve everything through one's own work, by carrying out analysis, especially since we do not always remember or have at hand the truths which we ourselves or others have already discovered.[87]

In opposition to Descartes, Leibniz reassesses the role of synthesis, but not at the expense of analysis, which remains the basic process for finding the first elements of knowledge. In other words, "combination or synthesis is the better means for discovering the *use* or *application* of something [. . .] Analysis, on the contrary, is best suited for discovering the *means* when the thing to be discovered or the proposed end is given."[88] In this work, Leibniz definitely characterizes combinatorics as the correct method of describing reality:

> The art of combinations in particular [. . .] is that science in which are treated the forms or formulas of things in general, that is quality in general or similarity and dissimilarity; in the same way that ever new formulas arise from the elements a, b, c themselves when combined with each other, whether these elements represent quantities or something else. This art is distinct from common algebra, which deals with formulas applied to quantity only or to equality and inequality. This algebra is thus subordinate to the art of combinations and constantly uses its rules. But these rules of combination are far more general and find application not only in algebra but in the art of deciphering, in various games, in geometry itself when it is treated linearly in the manner of the ancients, and finally, in all matters involving relations of similarity.[89]

Combinatorics does not deal with forms or formulas applied to quantity, like Cartesian algebra, and does not reduce reality to a mere extension. On the contrary, by means a particular kind of analysis called "reductive," the first, simplest, and primitive notions are qualities, which can also, but not only, represent quantity. Combinatorics subordinates under itself algebra, geometry, and every other science: it is the real universal science.

Wolffian methodology emerges from the ashes of Leibniz's project.[90] Wolff's first elaboration of mathematical method is particularly influenced by axiomatics. In the *Anffangsgründe aller mathematischen Wissenschaften* (1710), probably the most successful mathematical textbook of the eighteenth century on which Kant himself studied and taught,[91] mathematical method is conceived as a general method applicable to all sciences[92] and grounded in: (1) definitions; (2) principles and axioms; and (3) proofs. This threefold partition of method has a parallelism in the three logical operations of the mind,[93] which is fully developed in the *Vernünftige Gedancken von den Kräften des menschlichen Verstandes* (1712). At that time mathematical method coincides with geometrical order, as also the *Elementa matheseos universae* (1713) testifies: "for mathematical method I understand the order used by mathematicians to teach their doctrines [. . .] mathematical method is, in fact, geometrical method [. . .] without which it is not possible to attain a firm knowledge of things."[94] In the *Mathematisches Lexicon* (1716) Wolff states that mathematical or geometrical method is:

> the way or manner with which mathematicians, most of all geometricians, want to expose their thoughts on things or with which they proceed in the arrangement and connection of things with each other.[95]

We can find the parallelism between mathematical method and geometrical order also in § 596 of the *Philosophia rationalis sive logica* (1728),[96] but in this context he introduces the distinction between analytic and synthetic method. In § 887, Wolff states clearly that the method of philosophy is synthetic.[97] But since philosophical method is mathematical method, mathematical method is synthetic. The reasons for this identification between synthetic and mathematical method are quite controversial,[98] but what we must keep in mind is that mathematical method for Wolff is not mathematics itself, which is an art of discovery (*ars inveniendi*) based on analysis.[99] The distinction rests on the difference between an *ars inveniendi a priori* and an *ars inveniendi a posteriori*.[100] Pure mathematics requires only *ars inveniendi a priori*, because all the elements are already given, while philosophy requires *ars inveniendi a posteriori*, because the elements must be acquired.[101] This explains the reason why mathematics and philosophy, even if they used the same geometrical method in demonstrating, are grounded respectively in analysis and synthesis. Unlike Leibniz, mathematics does not represent for Wolff the inner structure of philosophy, and this mainly because of a progressive detachment of mathematical method from its ontological foundations.[102] In the *Discursus praeliminaris* of his *Philosophia rationalis*, Wolff distinguishes philosophy from mathematics because the latter deals with quantities, the former with being in general. Wolff clearly dismisses Leibniz's teaching according to which combinatorics concerns qualities rather than quantities, and this probably because such an art had yet to be discovered.[103]

The distinction between mathematics and philosophy became fundamental in the essay *De differentia notionum metaphysicarum et mathematicarum* (1741). In this work, Wolff seems to distance himself from the exaltation of the mathematical method of his youthful writings, but also in this detachment we can recognize the constructive character of mathematics that Kant adopts programmatically in his practical works and in the *Critique of Pure Reason*.[104] The main difference between mathematical and metaphysical notions is what Wolff has already suggested in the *Discursus praeliminaris*, that mathematics deals with quantities, while metaphysics with being in general. Mathematics deals with *notiones imaginariae*, which are useless for knowing the qualities of things,[105] while metaphysics deals with *notiones reales*, where for "real" Wolff means everything that is possible and not contradictory. Imaginary notions are usually more distinct than real ones, for instance, the imaginary concept of extension in geometry is more evident than the real concept in physics and metaphysics.[106] In this sense, philosophers such as Descartes, Johann Clauberg, and Joachim Jungius were wrong in applying the mathematical notion of *res extensa* to ontology.[107] The same kind of error would occur when employing unduly concepts such as "body," "space," "place," "time," "motion," "driving force," "gravity," "centripetal force," and "infinite."[108] Ultimately, "metaphysical notions cannot be inferred from mathematical writings."[109] Real notions are sharply distinguished by imaginary concepts: the former are given, the latter are fictional, in other words, arbitrarily constructed.[110]

To conclude, the distinction between mathematical and metaphysical notions undermines the unity of the deductive model of the system of sciences, mainly because Wolff understands that mathematics is powerless to resolve metaphysical questions and to provide valid concepts for philosophy. The complex history of the relationship between mathematical and metaphysical method in Wolff seems to reflect Kant's philosophical development. From an initial attempt to follow the accuracy and rigor of mathematics in metaphysics, Kant became aware of the irresolvable irreconcilability of these two sciences with the deepening of his ontological interests.

KANT'S PRECRITICAL CONCEPTION OF METHOD

Since the *Thoughts on the True Estimation of Living Forces* (1747), Kant was concerned with methodology. In his first work, Kant is involved in the examination of the concept of force in a *natural body*, even if he suddenly changes his investigation to the notion of force in a *substance*,[111] shifting from a physical to a metaphysical level. This shift implies a rethinking of the possibility of applying Cartesian geometrical method to metaphysics. According to Kant, on a merely physical level, the Cartesian geometrical standpoint is correct, but when the analysis concerns substances from a metaphysical perspective, the Leibnizian method takes over, having on its side the countless proofs of experience. Kant redefines, therefore, the relation between metaphysics and mathematics, establishing the primacy of the former over the latter. In particular, Kant's aim is to free metaphysics from mathematics, considering the latter as science that investigates reality only partially: "they [living forces] will be forever hidden from this type of consideration (namely a mathematical one), and that only a metaphysical investigation, or possibly a special sort of experience, will acquaint us with them. Hence, we do not really contest here the matter itself, but only the *modum cognoscendi*" (1: 60). In fact, mathematics does not deal with the way in which the properties of a body emerge in nature, and they remain entirely indeterminate (1: 70). The lack of distinction between metaphysical and mathematical method led to many errors in philosophy, to the tyranny of mistakes over human understanding, which sometimes lasted whole centuries (1: 95). Already in this first writing Kant is asserting the rights of metaphysics over those of mathematics, giving the former the same degree of evidence as the latter.[112]

Kant's *New Elucidation* (1756) can be considered as his first "geometrical work," structured on propositions, demonstrations, problems, applications, and corollaries. In this work, for the first time, Kant reveals his dissatisfaction with mathematics as an heuristic and descriptive tool of reality. In particular, as we saw in the previous chapter, he mounts a sarcastic attack on the vain attempts of combinatorics because for the human mind an absolute analysis for finding first, simplest and primitive concepts, which pertain only to God, is impossible (1: 389–91). Also in the successive work, the *Physical Monadology* (1756), he follows the geometrical method. The complete title, *The Employment in Natural Philosophy of Metaphysics Combined with Geometry*, is particularly useful for understanding Kant's position at that time: he proposes combining metaphysics with geometry for the explanation of natural phenomena. Metaphysics and geometry differ, however, because the former provides a better understanding of the nature of the things and of their first causes and principles, while the latter explains how phenomena occur. Kant's words reveal an admonition for geometricians rather than metaphysicians, as the former are wont to persuade themselves that they can touch the heavens with their hands, climbing up mountains because they are ignorant of the first causes and principles. In the field of the explanation of the cause and principles, only metaphysics, which many scientists would remove from physics, can provide illumination and clear knowledge (1: 475). In Kant, there seems to emerge a genuine metaphysical interest, an interest that leads to a hierarchical priority of metaphysics over geometry. Indeed, Kant's concept of monad employed in this work cannot be other than metaphysical.

Physical Monadology is the first, if not also the last, Kantian attempt to reconcile the concepts of geometry with those of metaphysics. Kant is aware of the difficulty of the enterprise, which is such that it would seem easier to mate griffins with horses (1: 475). There are many reasons for this difficulty:

> For the former [metaphysics] peremptorily denies that space is infinitely divisible, while the latter [geometry], with its usual certainty, asserts that it is infinitely divisible. Geometry contends that empty space is necessary for free motion, while metaphysics hisses the idea off the stage. Geometry holds universal attraction or gravitation to be hardly

explicable by mechanical causes but shows that it derives from the forces which are inherent in bodies at rest and which act at a distance, whereas metaphysics dismisses the notion as an empty delusion of the imagination. (1: 475–76)

It bears noting that the metaphysical standpoint summarizes Leibnizian and Newtonian positions, while the geometrical perspective supports the Cartesian thesis. It is not important that in this context Newton and Leibniz are substantially reconciled, since Kant maintained this position throughout most of his precritical works, rather that Cartesian philosophy represents geometry.[113] In this sense, the primacy of metaphysics over geometry is already explainable from *Thoughts on the True Estimation of Living Forces*, with Leibniz's superiority over Descartes. But it is quite clear that from 1756 onward, metaphysics surpasses geometry and mathematics.

The Only Possible Argument (1762) cannot be considered a treatise on method, but Kant does introduce some interesting methodological issues that mark a significant development in his thought. Kant states that the rule of thoroughness does not always demand that every concept should be fully analyzed and defined, especially if one "is assured that the clear and ordinary concept by itself can occasion no misunderstanding" (2: 70). For instance, Kant explains, comparing once again metaphysics with geometry, a geometrician discovers "the most secret properties and relations of that which is extended," employing only the ordinary concept of space (2: 70). Therefore, metaphysics can use the common notion of "representation" without an analysis of its meaning by means of definition. But this is not true for all concepts, because some of them can be misleading in the context in which they are employed. This is the case of "existence." However, also in this case, metaphysics should not proceed from a formal definition, in fact such a procedure "is always undesirable when the correctness of the suggested definition is so uncertain" (2: 70). Kant seems to follow Johann Nikolaus Tetens's admonishment in the *Gedancken über einige Ursachen, warum in der Metaphysik nur wenige ausgemachte Wahrheiten sind* (1760), where he writes that:

> since mathematical method has become the trend in metaphysics, metaphysicians are particularly concerned to obey

the rule of logic that proscribes the use any word that has not been previously clarified.[114]

Kant's procedure is indeed like that of someone who is searching for a definition and who assures himself "of what can be said with certainty, either affirmatively or negatively, about the object of the definition" (2: 71). In fact, according to Kant, we can know a lot of things about the subject before we reach its definition. For instance, in the case of space, we are certain that where space exists "external relations must also exist or that it cannot have more than three dimensions, and so on" (2: 71). To aspire always to a certain and perfect definition at the very beginning is to venture on often unnecessary difficulties. Kant contrasts what he calls the "mania for method" (*Methodensucht*), which consists in the imitation of the mathematician, since it has occasioned

> a large number of such mishaps on the slippery ground of metaphysics. These mishaps are constantly before one's eyes, but there is little hope that people will be warned by them, or that they will learn to be more circumspect as a result. (2: 71)

Therefore, around 1762–63, we can say that for Kant it is not possible to apply the mathematical method to metaphysics, as he attempted to do in his *Physical Monadology*. Metaphysics, moreover, proceeds analytically, and should not begin with definitions, rather it should clarify the characteristic marks of the object under investigation.

The definitive evolution of Kant's methodological conception is achieved in the *Inquiry Concerning the Distinctness of the Principles of Natural Theology and Morality* (1764). The work was conceived in answer to the question posed by Johann Georg Sulzer at the Berlin Royal Academy of Sciences in the year 1763, which asked if metaphysical truths in general, and more in particular those of natural theology and morality, were suitable for evident and distinct proofs such as those of geometry, and how certain they were.[115] Kant's *Inquiry* is generally inspired by the works of Crusius and Tetens, but the strongest unacknowledged influence comes in my opinion from Wolff's *De differentia notionum metaphysicarum et mathematicarum*, which has, however, been completely neglected by the scholarship.

The urgency of the methodological problem in Kant is clear from the *incipit* of the book, where in fact only by resolving this question is it possible for metaphysics (*höhere Philosophie*) to acquire a determinate form. Kant's aim is to find a universal method in the metaphysical field, which could pacify the "endless instability of opinion and scholarly sects," as Newton's method transformed the anarchy and turmoil of physical hypothesis "into a secure procedure based on experience and geometry" (2: 275). In the "First Reflection," Kant compares in general the mathematical and philosophical methods. The first great difference is that mathematics finds its definitions by synthesis, whereas philosophy does so by analysis (2: 276).[116] In characterizing mathematical method, Kant has in mind the synthetic demonstrations of Euclid's geometry, thus he denies the analytical approach of Cartesian geometry. Kant explains this difference by stating that a concept in general can have a twofold origin: either by arbitrary composition, or by isolating those cognitions that have already been clarified by resolution or analysis (*Zergliederung*). Mathematics finds its definition following the first method, that is, synthesis and composition, for instance a triangle is constructed by the intersections of three straight lines. Philosophical definitions are completely different because the concept of things is already given, even if in a confused and not sufficiently distinct way. In philosophy, it is therefore necessary to resolve the concept, to compare the various characteristic marks that have been separated out with the aim of determining completely and distinctly the representation of a thing (2: 276). Kant criticizes those philosophers who have the pretension to give synthetic explanations while providing only grammatical definitions, and those mathematicians who are used to employing analytic definitions that would generate in mathematics the same wretched discord of philosophy (2: 277). In short:

> It is the business of philosophy to analyse concepts which are given in a confused fashion, and to render them complete and determinate. The business of mathematics, however, is that of combining and comparing given concepts of magnitudes, which are clear and certain, with a view to establishing what can be inferred from them. (2: 278)

In this sense, Kant seems very close to Wolff, who established that metaphysical concepts were given, real but confused, while mathematical concepts were arbitrary, fictional, and constructed but distinct.

Another important difference between the mathematical and philosophical methods is that mathematics considers the universal *in concreto*, while philosophy considers the universal *in abstracto*. The use of signs in mathematical proofs, which are usually drawn and composed in figures, rather than things themselves, makes it possible to work *in concreto* with easy and certain rules (2: 278). Philosophical signs are nothing other than words which are not "capable of indicating in their combinations the relations of the philosophical thoughts to each other" (2: 279). Their employment is merely *in abstracto*. Here, Kant is undermining the very foundations of the Leibnizian project of combinatorics, establishing a sharp distinction between mathematics and philosophy, as I have noted in the previous chapter. In this particular case, the difference lies in the fact that the nature of mathematical concepts is made evident by figures, in the fact that a quadrangle being composed by the intersection of four straight lines is easily explainable by a drawing, and this figure can be considered as a universal *in concreto* simply because it is realized on paper and is valid for every other possible quadrangle. The nature of philosophical concepts, on the other hand, is not visible by means of a drawing, and the concept substitutes the thing, thus, weakening it and becoming a universal, because in this process of universalization to be universal the concept loses some of its characteristic marks that make it conceivable as a common concept of more objects.

A third important difference is that "in mathematics, irresolvable concepts and indemonstrable propositions are few in number, whereas in philosophy they are innumerable" (2: 279).[117] Concepts like space, time, magnitudes, and unity are irresolvable in mathematics, in other words, their definitions do not belong to this science and this is evident because mathematics does not proceed by analysis. Therefore, in mathematics these irresolvable concepts are not only rare, they do not occur at all, for mathematics "never defines a given concept by means of analysis; it rather defines an object by means of arbitrary combination," through which it is possible to think of such a particular concept (2: 280). Some mathematicians seek to solve or analyze mathematical concepts, but this does not provide any further cognition. Concepts like space, time, and unity in mathematics are only wrongly considered as irresolvable. On the contrary, in philosophy every analysis is necessary for the distinctness of knowledge and the possibility of valid reasoning. But it is obvious for Kant that every analysis leads to irresolvable concepts, at least relatively to the limited powers of our minds to determine the characteristic marks, and it is also quite evident that there are a great many of these irresolvable concepts if we look at the vast complexity of reality, which cannot be known only by means of a few fundamental concepts. Also in this case, Kant warns that one must not succumb to the temptation of analyzing everything, as some philosophers do who commit the error of treating all cognitions as if they were completely analyzable into few simple and first concepts. Such were the early physicists who made the mistake of supposing that all matter was composed of only four elements. Now the task of philosophy and particularly of metaphysics is to draw up a table of irresolvable concepts and indemonstrable propositions (2: 281). Kant outlines here with great foresight the ultimate task of his transcendental philosophy, whose aim is first and foremost to find these concepts and propositions, which became in the critical period the categories and the principles of the understanding. It is clear, therefore, that Kant's elaboration of his tables of judgments, categories, and principles emerges, as we have suggested in the previous chapter, from the ashes of the ruinous projects on irresolvable concepts of his contemporaries.

The last difference, which partially derives from the previous three, concerns the object of investigation: "the object of mathematics is easy and simple, whereas that of philosophy is difficult and involved" (2: 282). In mathematics, from few fundamental doctrines it is possible to acquire by synthesis all mathematical knowledge concerning quantities and magnitudes. In philosophy, on the other hand, many qualities constitute its object, the analysis of which is "an extremely strenuous business," in fact, it is more difficult "to disentangle complex and involved cognitions by means of analysis than it is to combine simple given cognitions by means of synthesis" (2: 282).

The "Second Reflection" concerns the method for acquiring the highest possible degree of certainty in metaphysics. Metaphysics is for Kant, like Baumgarten, the philosophy of the first principles of cognition, and nothing has been more damaging to it "than mathematics, and in particular the imitations of its method in contexts where it cannot possibly be employed" (2: 283). Kant denies once again any value for mathematical method as a demonstrative method in philosophy, but he still holds its immeasurable utility in the application of mathematical method in some parts of philosophy involving cognition of magnitudes (2: 283). Kant repeats once again that mathematics begins with the definition of its object, while in metaphysics definition is the result. He adds that in mathematics there is no concept of the object before definition, while in metaphysics the concept is already given, and its task is to make it more clear, determinate, and distinct. Kant resumes the argument outlined in *The Only Possible Proof*, and states that in metaphysics clear and firm knowledge of an object is possible before the cognition of its definition. In fact, if we find what we were looking for only by knowing some immediate characteristic mark of the object, it is a venture to search for the definition (2: 284). From this very key issue Kant establishes the first rule of the metaphysical method, which is never to start with a definition. Kant's break with the mathematical method is total. The second rule is "to distinguish those judgments which have been immediately made about the object and relate to what one initially encountered in that object with certainty" (2: 285). Kant's model of metaphysical method is Newton's method for natural science: by means of experience one has to seek the fundamental laws of natural events, and it is not important to understand their principle or cause, because their validity will nonetheless be certain. In metaphysics, it is possible to do the same seeking out, by means of an immediate and self-evident inner consciousness, of "those characteristic marks which are certainly to be found in the concept of any general property" (2: 286). If we do not know the essence or the cause of an object, it is nonetheless very useful to know its characteristic marks or proximate causes, because from them we can acquire more cognition of it: in metaphysics "there is a great deal which can be said about an object with certainty, before it has been defined" (2: 289).

Kant sees an intrinsic contradiction in the attempt to conceive metaphysics synthetically by means of a mathematical method. "Scholastic philosophers," in their attempt to imitate the method of mathematicians, start from the more abstract concepts, which are knowable for human understanding only at the end of the investigation, but not at the beginning:

> Those who practice philosophy in this vein congratulate each other for having learnt the secret of thorough thought from geometers. What they do not notice at all is the fact

that geometers acquire their concepts by means of composition (*Zusammensetzen*), whereas philosophers can only acquire their concepts by means of resolution (*Auflösen*)—and that completely changes the method of thought. (2: 289)

Kant does not exclude categorically that metaphysics could employ a synthetic method, but it has a long way to go yet before it can proceed synthetically: "it will only be when analysis has helped us towards concepts which are understood distinctly and in detail that it will be possible for synthesis to subsume compound cognitions under the simple cognition, as happens in mathematics," that is only after the discovery of the categories as pure concepts of the understanding (2: 290). Kant's position, from this perspective, does not differ from Leibniz, who wished for a complete analysis of reality before using combinatorics synthetically. This warning seems to be very significant in the light of the *Critique of Pure Reason*, which, as we have seen, proceeds methodically from the analysis of the first, irresolvable, and simplest concepts, that is, categories, to derivate concepts.

The "Third Reflection" deals with the nature of metaphysical certainty. Kant maintains that mathematics, acquiring its concepts by synthesis, can establish with certainty what is contained in the definition of a concept, while philosophy, dealing with what is given, does not know necessarily a priori all the characteristic marks of the definition of the object. In this sense, metaphysical certainty is weaker than mathematical certainty. Furthermore, being *in concreto*, mathematical signs are means to know with the exact certainty with which we see something with our eyes, whether a characteristic mark pertains or not to the object (2: 291). If a characteristic mark is lacking in philosophy, which deals with concepts *in abstracto*, two objects can be indiscernible and knowledge is everything but not certain (2: 292). Ultimately, Kant states that according to the form, "the certainty of the first fundamental truths of metaphysics is not of a kind different from that of any other rational cognition, apart from mathematics" (2: 293). Concerning matter, however, mathematics is still more intuitive and evident for Kant.

To sum up, in the *Inquiry Concerning the Distinctness* Kant establishes that: (1) metaphysics is grounded in analysis, while mathematics is based on synthesis; (2) metaphysical concepts are real and given, while mathematical concepts are constructed and fictional; (3)

only after a complete analysis, which is however unrealizable due to the limits of human understanding, it is possible to apply synthetic method in metaphysics; and (4) metaphysics has the same certainty of mathematics concerning form, but not matter.

In the "Preface" to the *Attempt to Introduce the Concept of Negative Magnitudes into Philosophy* (1763), Kant summarizes the two main approaches to mathematics of early modern philosophy:

> The use to which mathematics can be put in philosophy consists either in the imitation of its method or in the genuine application of its propositions to the objects of philosophy. (2: 167)

According to Kant, imitating the mathematical method in philosophy, for reasons that have already been discussed, is patently futile, despite high expectations of great advantages to begin with. The application of mathematics to philosophy has been beneficial for the improvement of physics and the doctrine of probability, but not for metaphysics, which considers mathematical concepts as subtle fictions (*feine Erdichtungen*) (2: 167). The hiatus between mathematics and metaphysics exposed in the *Inquiry on the Distinctness* is even wider in this work, probably also because the *Attempt* is an academic program destined for students and not to a committee of famous professors. Mathematics would enjoy absolute certainty, clarity, and distinctness, while metaphysics has only just started out on the path toward these objectives, which shall most likely remain unattained (2: 167–68). In comparison to previous writings, Kant is more severe regarding the metaphysical method. Metaphysicians are obdurate in their use of abstract concepts rather than real concepts, and they charge mathematicians with using invented, arbitrary, and valueless concepts that do not agree with their own abstract concepts (2: 168). Kant specifies that this argument is used by false metaphysics, which loves to avoid the task of becoming a rigorous science like mathematics. Kant was probably thinking about the metaphysics of Crusius, who is mentioned critically in this context and who had a number of followers in Königsberg, such as Daniel Weymann, against whom Kant polemicized in his *An Attempt at Some Reflections on Optimism* (1759).[118] Kant's attack on the metaphysical method must be understood within the scope of the work: harsh criticism leveled at conservative metaphysics should seem more interesting and engaging to students than an impartial assessment of the two methods.

In another academic program, the *Announcement of the Programme of His Lectures for the Winter Semester 1765–1766* (1765), we see the full import of this precritical methodological issue. In this work, Kant states that in spite of the great efforts of past philosophers, metaphysics is still an incomplete and uncertain science because of its method. The metaphysical method is not synthetic like the mathematical method, rather it is analytic. Thus, what is simplest and easiest to know for the doctrine of magnitudes, namely mathematics, is harder and more difficult to know for metaphysics. In mathematics, what is simplest and universal comes first according to the nature of things, while in metaphysics it comes at the very end. In mathematics, one begins with the doctrine of definitions, while in metaphysics definition is the result. As we can see, Kant does not outline any new doctrine, rather, what makes this announcement worth noting is the hope he expresses of presenting in a short period of time a complete survey of what is necessary to understanding metaphysics analytically, in such a way as to expose the errors of the past and to discover the criterion of judgment whereby these errors may be avoided in future enterprises (2: 308). This project of emendation of the errors of metaphysics by means of an analytic method found its fullest achievement only in 1781, with the *Critique of Pure Reason*.

THE METHOD OF *CRITIQUE OF PURE REASON*

In the *Announcement*, Kant promised a work on the methodology of metaphysics, and to Lambert on December 31, 1765, he wrote that it was quite ready, even if he was involved in the drafting of two minor writings titled *First Metaphysical Foundations of Natural Philosophy* and *First Metaphysical Foundations of Practical Philosophy*, which however never came to light:

> For a number of years I have carried on my philosophical reflections on every earthly subject, and after many capsizings, on which occasions I always looked for the source of my error or tried to get some insight into the nature of my blunder, I have finally reached the point where I feel secure

about the method that has to be followed if one wants to escape the cognitive fantasy that has us constantly expecting to reach a conclusion, yet just as constantly makes us retrace our steps, a fantasy from which the devastating disunity among supposed philosophers also arises; [. . .] All of my endeavors are directed mainly at the proper method of metaphysics and thereby also the proper method for philosophy as a whole. Apropos, I must tell you, dear sir, that Herr Kanter, in true bookseller's fashion, did not hesitate to announce the title, somewhat distorted, in the Leipzig catalog when he heard from me that I might have a work with that title ready for the next Easter book fair. (10: 55–56)

Kant's work announced in the Leipzig catalog has to be titled *The Only Method of Metaphysics*, as Johann Heinrich Lambert reports in his letter of November 13, 1765. This work was never published, but the title is extremely significant to understand the direction undertaken by Kant's research during those years. In another letter to Moses Mendelssohn of April 8, 1766, Kant emphasizes his progress in the field of methodology of metaphysics:

I am far from regarding metaphysics itself, objectively considered, to be trivial or dispensable; in fact I have been convinced for some time now that I understand its nature and its proper place among the disciplines of human knowledge and that the true and lasting welfare of the human race depends on metaphysics. [. . .] My feeling is not the result of frivolous inconstancy but of an extensive investigation. Admittedly, my suggested treatment will serve a merely negative purpose, the avoidance of stupidity (*stultitia caruisse*), but it will prepare the way for a positive one. Although the innocence (*Einfalt*) of a healthy but uninstructed understanding requires only an *organon* in order to arrive at insight, a *katharcticon* is needed to get rid of the pseudo-insight of a spoiled head. (10: 70–71)

The method of metaphysics outlined here by Kant is without doubt that of the *Critique of Pure Reason*. A criticism of metaphysics and of its dogmatism is needed to provide a useful tool for philosophy. It is worth noting that Kant in this period was determining the place and the role of metaphysics in the system of sciences, a decisive issue, as we shall see, for understanding his critical enterprise.

In this sense we can argue that the *Critique of Pure Reason* is his answer to methodological problems. It is in fact a treatise on the methodology of metaphysics, as Kant's philosophical development and his own statements testify. In the *Critique of Pure Reason*, there are numerous references to a "secure course" (*sicherer Gang*), "secure path" (*sicherer Weg*), "royal path" (*königlicher Weg*), "high road" (*Heeresstrasse*), "high path" (*Heeresweg*), which refer directly to the Greek etymology of the word *method* (μέθοδος).[119] Moreover, within the Kantian *corpus*, but mainly in the first *Critique*, it is possible to find a number of concepts that relate the critique to applied logic understood as a method (A 708/B 736). The importance of method within the critical system is testified by the fact that each of the three *Critiques* ends with a "Doctrine of Method," or methodology, and that its role, far from being extrinsic, is fundamental and decisive in the construction of the edifice of scientific knowledge. It is significant also that the two final paragraphs of the *Critique of Pure Reason* deal with the problem of method and define what it is (A 855/B 883). If this were not proof enough that the *Critique of Pure Reason* is a methodological work, an interpretation opposed by a number of scholars who maintain that it is a metaphysical or epistemological treatise, Kant himself writes in the second "Preface" that the critique of pure speculative reason is "a treatise on the method" (B XXII). *Critique of Pure Reason* is nothing other than a methodology, or at least, as Tonelli has argued, this the aim in Kant's mind of what was at that time intended by methodology. In order to characterize the kind of methodology that Kant applies to metaphysics, it is necessary to determine the fundamental theoretical issues that are developed in the entire work and not only in the "Doctrine of Method," where the references are no doubt more cogent.

In the "Preface" to the second edition of the *Critique of Pure Reason*, Kant focuses on the status of theoretical sciences involved directly in philosophy. Logic, which is not a real science, had made no advances since Aristotle's times: it is quite a consolidated discipline. Mathematics also found a secure path (*sicherer Weg*) with the Greeks, but it would be an error—Kant warns us—to suppose that it was as easy for mathematics as for logic to find this royal path (*königlicher Weg*); in fact, in logic reason has to do only with itself, while mathematics was left for a long time groping in the dark (*Herumtappen*), and its transformation must be attributed to a one-person revolution, which meant that the road to be taken could no longer be missed. The author of this revolution is unknown, according to Kant, but he states that the revolutionary was the one who for the first time discovered the first elements of geometrical demonstration that require no further demonstration (Euclid). In particular, the one who understood that in order to demonstrate the isosceles triangle, "what he had to do was not to trace what he saw in this figure, or even trace its mere concept [. . .], but rather that he had to produce the latter from what he himself thought into the object and presented (through construction) according to a priori concepts" (B X–XII). It is clear for Kant that the revolutionary aspect of mathematics is that of being synthetic, an element that was already present in various ways in the precritical writings, but which dominates the second edition of the *Critique of Pure Reason*. In physics, the highway of science (*Heeresweg der Wissenschaften*) took much longer, following the suggestion of Francis Bacon and empirical scientists, who understood that "reason has insight only into what it itself produces according to its own design; that it must take the lead with principles for its judgments according to constant laws and compel nature to answer its questions" (B XIII). Kant emphasizes that reason in natural investigation must proceed with its principles in one hand and with experiments thought out in agreement with these principles in the other in order to determine whether its a priori design was more or less valid (B XIII). What strikes Kant is the active role of natural investigators in their attempts to impose on nature the laws they previously conceived of as a priori. Thus was physics first brought to the secure path of science (*der sichere Gang*). Unfortunately, metaphysics did not have the fortune of finding this secure course, despite being the oldest science. A secure method in the metaphysical field may be discovered only by thinking in terms of a revolution such as Copernicus's in astronomy, that is, by thinking that the object must conform to the structures of the mind, not vice versa. In this way, Kant combines in his metaphysical method a revolution in both mathematics and physics, in which mathematics has to do with synthetic a priori elements that prescribe laws to nature. The Copernican revolution in metaphysics would not have been achieved before mathematics and physics had found their methods. Kant is quite explicit on this point: the concern of the critique of pure speculative reason consists in

> the attempt to transform the accepted procedure (*Verfahren*) of metaphysics, undertaking an entire revolution according to the example of the geometers and natural scientists. It is a treatise on the method, not a system of the science itself; but it catalogs the entire outline of the science of metaphysics, both in respect of its boundaries and in respect of its entire internal structure. (B XXII–XXIII)

This is the true nature of the *Critique of Pure Reason*, that is, to be a "treatise on the method" which aims to carry out in metaphysics the same revolution that occurred in mathematics and physics. Only the "critique" can bring metaphysics to the secure path of science and lead it out of its blind groping and aimless wandering (B XXX–XXXI). The "critique"—Kant points out—is not opposed to the dogmatic procedure of reason in its pure cognition as a science, because every science must always be in some sense dogmatic, that is, rigorously demonstrative on the basis of strictly secure and a priori principles (B XXXV). The "critique" is against dogmatism, that is, the pretension to advance in metaphysics only by means of a pure cognition based on concepts and principles without any assessment of their legitimacy in their use (B XXXV). The critique is therefore a preliminary and necessary step toward establishing a well-grounded metaphysics as a science (B XXXVI).

The meaning of a Copernican revolution, therefore, is to find a new method for metaphysics. The critique aims to determine the limits and possibility of all possible a priori cognitions before venturing onto the endless battlefield of metaphysics. The final aim is nonetheless, as we have seen, to determine a method for metaphysics, in other words an organon of the pure reason as a set of principles on which it is possible to base all pure a priori cognitions (A 11/B 24–25). The application of this organon would constitute the true system of metaphysics (A 11/B 25). The "critique," within this organon or method, has a particular place: it is merely a propaedeutic of the system of pure reason, and its utility is merely negative, because it does not extend knowledge, and serves only as a cathartic of reason. The critical part of metaphysics, which represents a large part of the *Critique of Pure Reason*, is not a doctrine, because it does not aim at the extension of knowledge, but only its correction. The "critique" is therefore the preparation of an organon, or at least of a canon, by means of which it is possible to expose both analytically and synthetically the complete system of metaphysics (A 12/B 26). The "critique," for Kant, must provide a complete enumeration of all those concepts that constitute a priori cognition, and in so doing it limits the extension of what can be known. "Critique" itself does not deal with the complete analysis of the primitive or derivative concepts:

> This completeness of the analysis as well as the derivation from the a priori concepts which are to be provided in the future will nevertheless be easy to complete as long as they are present as exhaustive principles of synthesis, and if nothing is lacking in them in regard to this essential aim. (A 14/B 29)

The task of analyzing the concepts of reason pertains to analytic properly speaking. The analysis of concepts does not generate new concepts, rather it provides new insights according to the form of cognition, even if according to the matter it is nothing other than illumination and explanation of what was already thought in a confused way in the concepts. This procedure of resolution provides a real a priori cognition, "which makes secure and useful progress," showing its principles and laws and having as reference the yardstick of experience.

The simple resolution of the object does not suffice to extend knowledge. Kant thus introduces what he calls "synthetic a priori judgments," which, even if they are pure, deal with the cognition of an object in general and therefore with those rules that are at the foundation of every possible knowledge. All theoretical sciences, namely, mathematics, physics, and metaphysics, are grounded in synthetic a priori judgments. In particular, in metaphysics:

> **synthetic a priori cognitions** are supposed **to be contained**, and it is not concerned merely with analyzing concepts that we make of things a priori and thereby clarifying them analytically, but we want to amplify our cognition a priori; to this end we must make use of such principles that

add something to the given concepts that was not contained in them [. . .] metaphysics, at least as far as **its end is concerned**, consists of purely synthetic a priori propositions. (B 18)

Since mathematics and physics are already on the secure path of science, Kantian scholars have maintained that Kant had these two sciences as his model of synthetic a priori judgments of metaphysics.[120] Carl Posy and Michael Friedman recently suggested that "mathematics is, in fact, Kant's paradigm of synthetic a priori knowledge,"[121] and that "Kant's explanation of the possibility of objective human experience in general is built on his explanation of the possibility of the mathematical exact sciences, in that pure mathematics and pure natural science are essential to the a priori constitutive grounding for all objectively valid empirical judgments."[122] There are various reasons to support this interpretation, the last of which but by no means the least being the analytical exposition of the *Prolegomena*, which opens with the question "how is pure mathematics possible?" as a science by means of synthetic a priori judgments. On the contrary, I suggest that Kant did not follow mathematics in conceiving his synthetic a priori judgments for metaphysics, but rather the opposite, that once having established synthetic a priori judgments of metaphysics, he found that also mathematics and physics were grounded in the same kind of judgments. Moreover, I suggest that Kant's conception of synthetic a priori judgments of mathematics comes from Segner's mathematical works.[123] Himself an Aristotelian, Segner is the only pure mathematician mentioned in the *Critique of Pure Reason* besides Descartes and Leibniz, but it is noteworthy that he is mentioned only in the second edition in the crucial argument of the demonstration that mathematics is grounded in synthetic a priori judgments rather than analytic judgments (B 15). Kant states that the explanation of $12 = 7 + 5$ is a synthetic a priori judgment, "as in Segner's arithmetic": we can imagine adding five units or points to seven other units, and we will have twelve units or points, that is, the number twelve. Kant wrote originally the very same passage in the *Prolegomena* (4: 268–69), which is the source of the later insertion in the second edition of the *Critique of Pure Reason*. Moreover, it is important to keep in mind that the example "$7 + 5 = 12$" was already present in the chapter on the "Axioms of Intuition" in the first edition of the *Critique of Pure Reason* (A 164–65/B 205–56), where Kant supported the synthetic character of this kind of proposition, but not the a priori synthetic nature of mathematical sciences in general. We must distinguish in this context the a priori synthetic character of mathematics from the constructivist and arbitrary nature of mathematics itself, which was supported also by other philosophers of the time like Christian August Crusius. From the fact that mathematical concepts are arbitrarily constructed by the mind we cannot derive the synthetic a priori nature of mathematics. In fact, we can arbitrarily construct in our mind any concept whatsoever, but this does not mean that it comes from a synthetic a priori judgment.

Kant's example of the "five points," and therefore an implicit reference to Segner, occurs also in the crucial chapter "On the Schematism of Pure Concepts of the Understanding," which are included only in the second edition (B 179). Kant aims to distinguish schema from image as products of two different faculties, sensibility and the understanding. It is clear that the image constituted by the "five points" characterizes an aesthetical exhibition that is at the foundation of mathematics, while the schema is a construction by concepts that concerns logic, and is the basis of the cognition of an object. The image is always a singular intuition, while the schema is a general construct of what is particular in the image and is valid for every intuition.[124] The importance of Segner in conceiving mathematics as a construction by images that connect mathematical objects to space and time is evidenced by a fragment from the 1790s, where Kant states the "concepts of number require pure sensible images, e.g., Segner" (14: 55). This idea of a pure sensible image is the same that Kant distinguishes from the schema in the *Critique of Pure Reason*. Indeed, in Segner's work, and especially in the tables, we can find what Kant took from him, and in fact it is by images that he shows why arithmetic is a synthetic science (see fig. 1). Since all references to Segner and the synthetic a priori nature of mathematics is included only after the *Prolegomena*,[125] we can argue that Kant did not model his method of metaphysics and its synthetic a priori character on mathematics, but rather that only after the discovery of the very nature of the judgments of metaphysics does he also apply his theory to mathematical sciences. If only synthetic a priori judgments can provide an extension of knowledge and bring metaphysics to the secure path of a science, it is only by a preliminary analysis

```
A - - - -              A . .                A . . . . . . . . . .
B . . . .              B . . .              B . . . . .
C ****                 C . . . . .                           C . . . . .

                       D . . . . . . . . . .

Number                 Sum                  Subtraction


            V .                      A . . . . . .
            A . . .                  B . . .
            B . . . .

                                            . . . . . .
            C . . . . . . . . . . .   C . . . . . .
                                            . . . . . .

                     Multiplication
```

FIGURE 1

of the components of these judgments that we can establish a firm and well-grounded cognition. Therefore, with his "analytic" in the *Critique of Pure Reason*, Kant achieved the desired complete analysis of knowledge that he advocated in the *Inquiry on the Distinctness* (2: 290), resolving all first elements of mind, that is, concepts, judgments, and principles understood as forms in the Aristotelian sense, and preparing them for combination with the aim of finding a priori the conditions of possibility of new knowledge. The complete analysis of these elements is the only warranty of the validity of metaphysics as a science.

Kant, therefore, divides his *Critique of Pure Reason* into a "Doctrine of Elements" and a "Doctrine of Method" for establishing at the very beginning the first elements of cognition by analysis, and then for applying them by synthesis. The "Doctrine of Elements" is a canon, while the "Doctrine of Method" is an organon. Proceeding from the analysis of concepts before their application, even if it is harder and less intuitive, is necessary, "for one must already know the objects rather well if one will offer the rules for how a science of them is to be brought about" (A 52/B 77). Kant states explicitly that the "analytic" is the resolution of all a priori cognition into the first pure concepts of the understanding, and he points out

> 1. That the concepts be pure and not empirical concepts. 2. That they belong not to intuition and to sensibility, but rather to thinking and understanding. 3. That they be elementary concepts, and clearly distinguished from those which are derived or composed from them. 4. That the table of them be complete, and that they entirely exhaust the entire field of pure understanding. (A 64/B 89)

These requirements are identical to those of the combinatorial projects, but Kant, as we know from the previous chapter, conceives these concepts as mere forms of cognition or *modi cognoscendi*, not regarding their matter. Nonetheless, a crucial question for Kant is the simplicity, analyzability, and completeness of these elementary concepts of the understanding. Such completeness cannot be achieved by means of a rough calculation of an aggregate put together, but requires the idea of a whole (*Idee des Ganzen*) constituted by the connection in a system (*Zusammenhang in einem System*) of the division of concepts (*Abteilung der Begriffe*). In this context, the emergence in Kant of the architectonical problem of giving reason and foundation of the a priori cognition is clear. This system of the first elements of the understanding is composed by concepts and principles, from which derives the division of the "Doctrine of Elements" into "Analytic of Concepts" and "Analytic of Principles." By analysis of concepts Kant does not mean

> their analysis, or the usual procedure of philosophical investigations, that of analyzing the content of concepts that present themselves and bringing them to distinctness, but rather the much less frequently attempted analysis of the faculty of understanding itself. (A 65/B 90)

Kant's critical allusion in regard to this "less frequently attempted analysis" is probably to Lambert, who, in his *Neues Organon* and in the *Anlage zur Architektonik*, as we have seen, dealt with elementary concepts; but they were considered for their matter, and they were collected together in a very rhapsodic way. The analytic of principles, on the other hand, is a canon for the power of judgment "that teaches it to apply to appearances the concepts of the understanding" (A 132/B 171). Both "Analytic of Concepts" and "Analytic of Principles" are a canon dealing with the formal criterion of truth. But, as Kant frequently asserts, the mere form of cognition does not suffice to constitute the material objective truth of the cognition, therefore, it is necessary to make the transition from the "Doctrine of Elements" to the "Doctrine of Method," which is no longer a mere canon, but an organon that also considers the material aspect of cognition.

The "Doctrine of Elements" is, therefore, in Kant's eyes an estimation of the "building materials" for the construction of the edifice of the system of reason, but it does not provide the plans of the project to build it. The task of the "Doctrine of Method" is to provide the structure and the plan, in other words, the "formal conditions of a complete system of pure reason" (A 708/B 736). Kant compares his methodology to practical or applied logic concerning the use of the understanding in general. This methodology is absolutely necessary for general logic, which is neither limited to any particular kind of cognition of understanding, nor to any certain object, without borrowing knowledge from other sciences, and can only expound "titles for possible method and technical expressions that are used in regard to that which is systematic in all sorts of sciences" (A 708/B 736). This means that logic cannot only be a mere canon but, after the "critique" and the "estimation," it must become an organon, and an organon that is to be used as a tool, not a mere rule or precept, and must be applied to something, which in Kant's case is to the a priori cognition for the construction of the system of science.

In this passage Kant seems to have learned Calov's methodological lesson, which is reproposed almost identically. As we have seen, for Calov the doctrine of method does not deal only with empty rules for the order of cognition, but is a real tool. To be such, method must be applied to an object.[126] If it were not applied to an object, it would be a mere exposition of abstract precepts, that is, a canon.

The first part of the "Doctrine of Method" is the "discipline of pure reason," which is in general "the **compulsion** through which the constant propensity to stray from certain rules is limited and finally eradicated" (A 709/B 738). The chapter on "The Discipline of

Pure Reason in Dogmatic Use" is particularly interesting for its treatment of the problem of the application of mathematical method to philosophy. In this chapter, we have the impression that Kant is still reworking the precritical doctrines exposed in the *Inquiry on the Distinctness*, integrating them into his transcendental philosophy. Kant adopts the definition of philosophy as a rational cognition from concepts, and mathematics as cognition from the construction of concepts. Kant here is not dealing with the synthetic a priori judgments of mathematics, but rather with the faculty of the mind of constructing arbitrarily mathematical objects, as he explored in his precritical writings.[127] In the *Critique of Pure Reason*, however, Kant points out that to construct a concept means "to exhibit a priori the intuition corresponding to it [...] for the construction of a concept, therefore, a **non-empirical intuition** is required" (A 713/B 741).[128] In this way, the universal validity of all possible intuitions that belong under the same concept is possible for Kant. The construction of a triangle, for instance, Kant states, makes it possible for this particular but a priori construction to be valid for all other triangular figures:

> Philosophical cognition thus considers the particular only in the universal, but mathematical cognition considers the universal in the particular, indeed even in the individual, yet nonetheless a priori and by means of reason, so that just as this individual is determined under certain general conditions of construction, the object of the concept, to which this individual corresponds only as its schema, must likewise be thought as universally determined. (A 714/B 742)

The essential difference between philosophy and mathematics rests on their different way of conceiving the relation between the universal and the particular, that is on the form of cognition and not on the matter. It is wrong, according to Kant, to maintain that philosophy deals with quality, while mathematics with magnitudes, for "philosophy, as well as mathematics does deal with magnitudes [...] and mathematics also occupies itself with the difference between lines and planes as space with different quality" (A 715/B 743). From these statements we can see the great difference of Kant's position from his earlier ideas in the *Inquiry on the Distinctness*, in which he establishes that the objects of mathematics were magnitudes and quantities, while those of philosophy were qualities (2: 286). Also radical is his contraposition to contemporaries such as Rüdiger, Hoffmann, and Crusius, who supported the view that mathematics was the science of magnitudes and philosophy the science of qualities. This breach with his precritical ideas follows Kant's determination in the "Transcendental Aesthetic" of a secure and certain foundation of the mathematical construction, which avoids a conventionalist conception of mathematics as it was in the *Inquiry on the Distinctness*.[129] The real difference between the mathematical and philosophical methods follows, therefore, Kant's discovery of the distinction of the forms of cognition (that is space, time, and categories) from the matter of cognition (that is, the content), which is, as we have seen, an Aristotelian legacy. It is not only the distinction between form and matter of cognition that determines the separation of mathematical and philosophical method, but also that of intuitive and discursive cognition (A 719/B 747). From the "Transcendental Aesthetic" we know that all cognition refers to possible intuitions, through which the objects are given. Kant adds nonetheless that an a priori concept already contains either a pure intuition or a synthesis of the possible intuitions. In the former case, the concept can be constructed, while in the latter case one can judge synthetically and a priori by its means, but "only discursively, in accordance with concepts, and never intuitively through the construction of the concept" (A 720/B 748). Both philosophy and mathematics are based on synthetic a priori judgments, but while in philosophy the object is given by an empirical intuition, in mathematics the object is given by a mere formal intuition that is completely a priori. For there is a twofold use of reason:

> There are two components to the appearance through which all objects are given to us: the form of intuition (space and time), which can be cognized and determined completely a priori, and the matter (the physical), or the content, which signifies a something that is encountered in space and time and which thus contains an existence and corresponds to sensation. With regard to the latter [matter] [. . .] we can have nothing a priori except indeterminate concepts of the synthesis of possible sensations [. . .] With regard to the former we can determine our concepts a priori in intuition

[. . .] The former is called the use of reason in accordance with concepts, because we can do nothing further than bring appearances under concepts, according to their real content; which cannot be determined except empirically, i.e., a posteriori [. . .] the latter is the use of reason through construction of concepts, because these concepts, since they already apply to an a priori intuition, for that very reason can be determinately given in pure intuition a priori and without any empirical *data*. (A 723–54/B 751–52)

Kant traces the two uses of reason, intuitive and discursive, back to the Aristotelian distinction between matter and form.

Another key element in understanding the difference between mathematical and philosophical method is that the validity of mathematics rests on definitions, axioms, and demonstration, which is not the same for philosophy, in fact geometrical method is not enough to establish the truth and certainty of a philosophical argument. This is the reason why "by means of his method the mathematician can build nothing in philosophy except houses of cards, while by means of his method the philosopher can produce nothing in mathematics but idle chatter" (B 727/B 755).

According to Kant "to define properly means just to exhibit originally the exhaustive concept of a thing within its boundaries" (B 727/B 755). Given this meaning of "definition," an empirical concept could never be defined according to Kant, because one will know only some of its characteristic marks, whose correspondence to the word that they would designate is never certain. Kant takes this conception from his theory of definition as exposed in the *Inquiry on the Distinctness* (2: 284).[130] The empirical concept could be only explained, but never defined. Neither can a given a priori concept ever be defined: in fact, it is not certain that the clear representation of a given, albeit still confused, concept has been analyzed exhaustively so that that particular representation is adequate to its object. The problem is the impossibility of a complete analysis of the concept without reference to the object. This analysis could lead to a representation that will surely be adequate to the object, but never apodictically (B 729/B 757). Of empirical and given a priori concepts only an exposition is possible, never a definition. On the contrary, a priori arbitrarily thought concepts can always be the subject of definition, since they are provided by neither experience nor the intellect, and it is impossible to say they have thereby defined a true object (B 729/B 757). Definition is possible only for those concepts that are constructed, and there is no correspondent object relative to them. Mathematics is based on these definitions, while philosophy on the exposition and clarification of a given object. Thus, Kant concludes

> That in philosophy one must not imitate mathematics in putting the definitions first, unless perhaps as a mere experiment. For since they are analyses of given concepts, these concepts, though perhaps only still confused, come first, and the incomplete exposition precedes the complete one, so that we can often infer much from some marks that we have drawn from an as yet uncompleted analysis before we have arrived at complete exposition, i.e., at the definition. [. . .] in philosophy the definition, as distinctness made precise, must conclude rather than being the work. On the contrary, in mathematics we do not have any concept at all a priori to the definitions [. . .] [mathematics] therefore must and also always can begin with them. [. . .] Mathematical definitions can never err. (A 730–31/B 759–60)

Clearly, Kant is simply re-elaborating the doctrine of the *Inquiry on the Distinctness*, allowing us to suppose that from the second half of the 1760s onward, the methodology of metaphysics is thought of in contrast to mathematical method and always in precisely the same way.

A further difference between mathematics and philosophy consists in the fact that the former is based on axioms, but not the latter. Philosophy is always a rational cognition with concepts in which one concept cannot immediately be synthetically combined with another, since a third concept is necessary for mediating cognition (A 732/B 760). Mathematics, on the contrary, admits axioms, because it can connect a priori and immediately the predicates of the object by means of the construction of concept in the intuition of the object itself. The synthetic principles of philosophy are discursive and require a deduction, while axioms of mathematics are intuitive and do not require a proof (A 733/B 761).

The final difference between mathematical and philosophical method is that the former uses demonstration, while the latter does not. Demonstration is for Kant in this particular case an intuitive apodictic proof. However, the empirical cognition does not provide any apodictic proof, and for this reason philosophy must content itself with achromatic discursive proofs.

In the "Doctrine of Method," unlike in his precritical works, Kant emphasizes not only the difference of the object of the two disciplines according to the form, but also their different argumentations and expositions. In this way, Kant fulfils the task of detaching philosophy from mathematics begun in his youth, maintaining the scientific nature and accuracy of both sciences.

In the chapter "The Discipline of Pure Reason with the Regard to Its Polemical Use," Kant introduces a pivotal element of his critical methodology, namely the distinction between κατ'ἄνθρωπον and κατ'ἀλήθειαν.[131] This distinction has a twofold meaning in Kant's writings. In one sense, κατ'ἄνθρωπον coincides with the *argumentum ad hominem*, and is opposed to the argument κατ'ἀλήθειαν, that is, an argument in which premises are considered to be true. In this case, the two expressions occur separately (12: 40; 16: 850). In a second sense, Kant employs the distinction κατ'ἄνθρωπον-κατ'ἀλήθειαν, following the Aristotelian tradition. Kant began to use it around 1776 and 1779, when he was particularly involved in the study of Aristotelian logic. In *Reflection 5103* (1776–1778), Kant mentions the demonstration κατ'ἄνθρωπον in the same sense as used in the *Critique of the Power of Judgment*, employing the very same words and explaining the same argument. Kant writes that the laws of the intelligible world are not the object of intuition, therefore every physico-teleology, that is, the proof of God from the teleologism of nature, is impossible. They are in fact a matter of faith, and concern the reflecting use of the understanding. The connection between the sensible and the intelligible world is possible only by means of logical inference such as analogy. Analogous inferences and *argumenta practica* κατ'ἄνθρωπον allow for the conception of the *transitum* from one world to the other. According to Kant, the proof of God's existence and of the intelligible world is possible only by an argument κατ'ἄνθρωπον, that is, "*argumentum ad modulum humanitatis*" (18: 88). This *Reflection* has a striking similarity to Zabarella's conception of the argument κατ'ἄνθρωπον, which is "*secundum assumpta humanae naturae*" and "*non hominis singularis.*"¹³² This argument is valid subjectively for every human being, not as an individual, but as a kind, that is, for his nature. In *Reflection 5508*, Kant states, again in reference to God's proof that it can be only κατ'ἄνθρωπον and never apodictic, that it is grounded only in the subjective condition of thought (18: 203). Like the Aristotelians, Kant juxtaposes an apodictic demonstration to the argument κατ'ἄνθρωπον. In *Reflection 6428*, Kant writes that not only is God demonstrable κατ'ἄνθρωπον, but also freedom and the immortality of the soul. These three ideas are not cognizable from a theoretical standpoint, but they are necessary from the practical standpoint for the realization of the morality of the subject (18: 713).

In the *Critique of Pure Reason*, Kant states that an argument κατ'ἄνθρωπον is a valid justification for every human being, but is not necessarily valid κατ'ἀλήθειαν, being rather only a subjective proof (A 739/B 767). The kind of proof of the argument κατ'ἄνθρωπον is that which is investigated also in § 90 of the *Critique of the Power of Judgment* concerning the subjective ethical-teleological proof of God's existence. In order to explain the legitimacy of this proof, Kant introduces the κατ'ἄνθρωπον-κατ'ἀλήθειαν, as he did in *Reflection 5103*. Kant states that a proof whose aim is conviction is of two kinds: the first kind is the argument κατ'ἀλήθειαν, which provides universal and objective validity and theoretical conviction (5: 462). But such a kind of proof concerning God is impossible for speculative reason. The second kind of proof is the argument κατ'ἄνθρωπον, which establishes "what it is for us (the human being in general) according to the necessary rational principles for our judging" (5: 463). It produces a moral conviction. Kant emphasizes that κατ'ἄνθρωπον refers to the human being in general, that is, how something can be the object of cognition according to the subjective constitution of its cognitive faculties. The concepts of reason are not, therefore, in relation to the object coming from experience, but only to the cognitive faculties and their use. The argument κατ'ἄνθρωπον is the only possible argument for transcendental philosophy, if we look only at how something can be an object of cognition for us. It aims to know whether something is cognizable or not, not compared to itself, but merely with the cognitive faculties (5: 467). In the *What Real Progress Has Metaphysics Made in Germany?* Kant writes that the moral argument can be called *argumentum* κατ' ἄνθρωπον valid for men as rational creatures generally, and not merely for the contingently adopted thought-habit of this man or that; and would have to be distinguished from the theoretico-dogmatic κατ' ἀλήθειαν which claims more to be certain than man can possibly know. (10: 306)

In *Religion within the Boundaries of Mere Reason*, Kant states that we cannot know the morality of an action κατ' ἀλήθειαν, because its moral character pertains to the intelligible world. In order to understand the moral character, a kind of analogy is required starting from an argument κατ' ἄνθρωπον (6: 64). An argument κατ' ἄνθρωπον is universally valid, even if it is subjective concerning the form. This kind of argument κατ' ἄνθρωπον, even if it seems marginal, is indeed essential for Kant in establishing the universal validity of moral, aesthetic, and teleological judgments, in other words to assure the passage from physics to metaphysics.

The most original part of the "Doctrine of Method" is the "Architectonic of Pure Reason," which has received scant attention from scholars who view it as an unessential and clumsy part of Kant's philosophical system.[133] On the contrary, I maintain that the "Architectonic" is essential for understanding Kant's transcendental philosophy and its sources.

Architectonic is the art of the system. In particular, the systematic unity is what turns ordinary cognition into science, in other words transforms a mere aggregate of cognitions into a system. Architectonic is therefore the doctrine of what is properly speaking "scientific" in cognition, and for this reason it pertains to methodology (A 823/B 860). The systematic unity guarantees that all possible cognitions are not a mere rhapsody, an idea that comes from Kant's concern with the a priori completeness of every possible cognition. The system is defined by Kant as "the unity of the manifold cognitions under one idea" (A 823/B 860). The notion of "idea," not in the sense of "transcendental idea," plays a crucial role for Kant in the architectonic since it is the end, that is, "the rational concept of the form of a whole, insofar as through this the domain of the manifold as well as the position of the parts with respect to each other is determined a priori" (A 823/B 860). The idea is therefore fundamental to determine the end and the form of the whole. The form of the whole is articulated (*articulatio*) according to the idea, not heaped together (*coacervatio*) (A 833/B 861). The whole can grow up only internally according to the end that determines the form, but cannot grow up externally by means of contingent additions.

With these architectonical considerations, Kant summarizes more than a decade of reflections on the problem of the system of knowledge. The concept of system in opposition to the aggregate is datable back to the early 1770s, and has its origin in the logic lectures from Meier's textbook, which is probably the primary source for his ideas.[134] In § 104 of his *Auszug aus der Vernunftlehre*, Meier writes that "a doctrinal edifice (*Lehrgebäude*) (*systema*) is a set of dogmatic truths which are related to one another, and that combined together constitute a knowledge which can be considered as a whole."[135] Meier's definition is based on § 889 of Wolff's *Philosophia Rationalis*, where the system is "a set of truths related one to each other and to their principles."[136] In a remark on Meier's § 104 in *The Blomberg Logic*, Kant writes that "a system is a multitude or manifold of many simple cognitions and truth combined together, such that taken together these constitute a whole [. . .] a *systema* is, however, A. historical B. rational" (24: 100). In *The Philippi Logic* Kant comments:

> The author [Meier] calls doctrinal edifice [*Lehrgebäude*], system, a set of dogmatic principles combined together [. . .] All systems of knowledge are either rational or historical [. . .] A dogmatic system is therefore a relation of various rational truths, which are taken together by a principle. There is therefore a system of philosophy, of ethics, of the influences of the soul on the body [. . .] Only a system, at the expense of technique, can serve for an evident correct cognition of truth. He who believes that truth can be known individually [that is concerning only one case and not the manifold taken together] deceives himself. In a system one must start from the whole, from the fundamental concept (*Hauptbegriff*), [. . .] and not from the parts. The schema for the whole must be designed in advance, only after it the parts have sense. The ideal (*Ideal*) or whole comes first, and only in the whole the parts are thinkable. The encyclopedias are such a system or companion, by means of which we learn, as the cognitions are combined and how they are held together to form

a whole [. . .] Not every mosaic is a system. This is not the way to the ideas. The schema must come from a main separate idea, and not from the parts. [. . .] Now it seems that the systems of almost all sciences were given, however it is still lacking a system that is limited only to the method of finding and examining truth, and this would be really necessary. (24: 399–400)

Unlike *The Blomberg Logic*, in *The Philippi Logic* the problem of an a priori ordering idea and the necessity of a plan to constitute the system appear prominently.[137] It is also interesting that Kant focuses on the theoretical enterprise of the encyclopedias as a system of sciences, because it will influence his way of conceiving the architectonic.

From *Reflection 4643*, which is datable back to the early 1770s, we know that Kant's interest in the theory of system is born with the architectonical problem. In this fragment, after the definition of "transcendental" as what concerns every pure a priori cognition in which no sensation is given, philosophy is divided into aesthetics, logic, critique, and architectonic (17: 623). In *Reflection 4858*, Kant states that transcendental philosophy requires a critique, a discipline, a canon and an architectonic (18: 11), which means that already in the 1770s he had in mind his "Doctrine of Method," as the letter to Herz of November 24, 1776, testifies (10: 199). In this period, Kant definitively elaborated his idea of architectonic in the lectures on the philosophical encyclopedia, where he states that there is a system when the idea of the whole precedes the parts, while when the parts precede the whole there is an aggregate (29: 5). A system of cognitions constitutes a science in which the idea of the whole is original, and from the division of the whole the parts are determined.

In the "Architectonic," Kant states that for its execution the idea requires a schema, that is, "an essential manifoldness and order of the parts determined a priori from the principle of the end" (A 833/B 861), which he conceived in *The Philippi Logic* (24: 400). If the schema is outlined empirically, the unity is called technical, while if it is designed according to the idea, the unity is architectonic. A science cannot arise technically if it aims to highest certainty and completeness. It must be grounded only architectonically (A 833/B 861).

The contraposition between a "technique" and an "architectonic" is strongly rooted in Kant's philosophy, and, as we will see, it comes from the seventeenth-century Aristotelian tradition. In *Reflection 2702*, Kant writes that the totality or the sum (*Inbegriff*) of knowledge as an aggregate characterizes an ordinary knowledge, while as a system it characterizes a science. The former kind of knowledge is contingent, while the latter represents a necessary unity (16: 476). In *Reflection 2703*, on the other hand, Kant states that the manifold of knowledge constitutes either an aggregate or a science. In the former case, the manifold is combined in a fragmentary and rhapsodic way, or properly speaking technically by means of successive additions. In the latter case, the manifold is combined systematically according to a hierarchy (16: 477). In *Reflection 1837*, Kant states that a cognition based on an idea is architectonic, while based on an aggregate it is merely technical (16: 133). The problem of establishing a science on a schema is that only after a long, technical, and rhapsodic collection of the material of the edifice of science is it possible to design architectonically according to the end of reason. Architectonic thus becomes an essential part of Kant's philosophical system, because it is properly speaking what makes of various cognitions a science.

The importance that Kant attributes to architectonic as part of methodology is an apax in the eighteenth century. Contrary to Tonelli and Manchester, I do not think that Kant's most immediate architectonical antecedent, Lambert's *Anlage zur Architectonic*, is sufficient to explain the central role architectonic plays in his philosophical system.[138] First of all, because in Lambert architectonic is not a part of a methodology, but of ontology. Second, for Lambert, as the subtitle of the work reveals, architectonic is "a theory of what is simple and primitive in philosophical and mathematical cognition,"[139] that is, a system of the first, simplest concepts of every cognition, not only concerning form but also the matter of knowledge. In a letter dated November 13, 1765, Lambert wrote to Kant that

> I take architectonic to include all that is *simple* and *primary* in every part of human cognition, not only the *principia* which are grounds derived from the form, also the *axiomata* which must be derived from the matter of knowledge and actually only appear in simple concepts, thinkable in

themselves and without self-contradiction, also the *postulata* which state the universal and necessary possibilities of composition and connection of simple concepts. (10: 52)

Therefore, Lambert conceived architectonic differently from Kant, and the original intention seems closer to the Kantian "transcendental analytic" in finding concepts and principles. Indeed, Lambert himself reveals that the title of his work itself, "Architectonic," derives from Baumgarten's *Metaphysica*:

On the title of this work I have only to note that the word "Architectonic" comes from Baumgarten's *Metaphysica*. The term is derived from architecture, and it has a similar meaning in connection with the edifice of human cognition, in particular as it refers to the first foundations, to the first disposition, to the materials, to their preparation and order in general, and with the intention of producing a purposeful whole.[140]

But despite Baumgarten, Lambert believes that architectonic is a special kind of ontological lexicon of all primitive concepts of which reality is constituted.[141] In particular, it has the task of establishing the origin of concepts through different methods and their immediate use. The reference to a purposeful whole, which seems to have a parallel in Kant's conception, means for Lambert that by listing all these concepts one can find more easily and exactly the clue, which one has to follow in order to establish a real science. Such a clue, according to Lambert, is completely different from the common topics, that is, from a generic and rhapsodic disposition of commonplaces usually employed by logicians. In fact, "the subject-matter and the order of the exposition in each particular science must be determined by the ends it has to serve," and these ends are peculiar to each science, so that, if each science is to take its genuine shape, no general mold is admissible in which all of them can be cast.[142] In this case, Lambert shares with Kant the point that architectonic has to establish a classification of the sciences according to their own ends. In the *Logische und philosophische Abhandlungen*, Lambert outlines a "theory of system" in which he aims to define "the set of ideas and propositions that considered together can constitute a whole."[143] The main characteristics of a system are subordination and the connection of things among them in such a way that what proceeds can explain what follows. Lambert adds that Wolff completely neglected this theory of system (*Eintheilungen*), while Meier was more concerned with a logical topic.[144] Lambert's suggestion of looking at Baumgarten is not very helpful in explaining Kant's position. In Baumgarten, architectonic is nothing other than one of the many names of ontology as the "science of the general predicate of the being."[145] Neither is the characterization of the architectonic attributed to the *facultas fingendi*, quite common in the Wolffian school, significant in understanding Kant.[146] It is probable, however, that Kant conceived his architectonic during his lectures on Baumgarten's metaphysics, and in fact, in *Reflection 5039* (1776–78), Kant outlines the structure of his methodology: the nomothetic of pure reason has a negative part, which is the discipline, and a positive part, which is a canon, and at the very end an architectonic (18: 70). Going back in Wolff's *De notionibus directricibus et genuino usu philosophiae primae* we find that the architectonical science is ontology, or first philosophy, which is the sense of "architectonic" employed by Baumgarten and Lambert.[147]

We can find a striking parallelism to Kant's doctrine in the Aristotelian Calov. It is so suggestive, in fact, that Tonelli himself was prompted to boldly state that the only clear precedent to Kant's use of "architectonic" is "in Calov, and possibly other Aristotelians sharing his views [. . .] Kant had probably been informed of this by his Aristotelian teachers at Königsberg University."[148] There are at least two elements pointing to Calov's influence. The first element is that in Calov, like in Kant, architectonic was a part of methodology, which organized philosophical cognitions hierarchically according to principles.[149] A second element is the constant tension between "system" and "aggregate" in Calov's work, which is absent in other eighteenth-century philosophers:

> I call aggregate that which considers various objects combined together by some bond. It is necessary that they are combined together, regardless the kind of union. [. . .] it is not sufficient to share the mere name without the criterion of the essence, as happens to equivocal names that cannot generate a common concept beyond our mind, from which

derive distractions: and thus they cannot found the unity of the unity of the aggregate system.[150]

It is quite clear for Calov that a system is not possible by means of a merely casual and rhapsodic addition of cognitions, without considering the relations between them. Only by establishing the principles and the precepts according to which cognitions are combined together is it possible to make a system from a mere aggregate.[151] Given such a marked and unusual analogy between Calov and Kant, Tonelli correctly states that "Kant may have had Calov in mind when he set system in opposition to aggregate."[152]

In conclusion, we have sufficient reason to say that the *Critique of Pure Reason* is a treatise on the method of metaphysics: this was Kant's intention, as the text explicitly reveals. In the light of Kant's project, his "Doctrine of Method" assumes a pivotal role in the critical system. Indeed, the "Analytic" and the "Dialectic" merely have the negative role of limiting the boundaries of cognitions or to list the first elements of knowledge, that is, to determine the material and the confines of the metaphysical system; the "Doctrine of Method," on the other hand, has the task of building the edifice of metaphysics. Kant's methodological doctrines have their origin in his early interests in mathematics and Newtonian physics. However, with his progressive study of metaphysics he became aware of the distinction between the metaphysical and mathematical method, and of the limits of the latter. In the *Inquiry on the Distinctness*, in parallel with his break with the tradition of combinatorics, Kant abandons the possibility of applying mathematics to metaphysics, and developed a new doctrine of method that recalls the Aristotelian and Eclectic methodologies. Kant's use of concepts such as "organon," "canon," "architectonic," and κατ'ἄνθρωπον-κατ'ἀλήθειαν shows unequivocally that its reference is the Aristotelian tradition.

CONCLUSION

ARISTOTLE IN KANT

With the research carried out in this volume, I have attempted to highlight a neglected aspect of Kant's philosophy: namely, the marked influence of the Aristotelian tradition on the genesis and development of his thought. If we consider the most important reconstructions of Kantian philosophy, we find no reference to Aristotle and modern Aristotelianism; rather, Kant is often pictured as an anti-Aristotelian philosopher. Only occasionally are a few Aristotelian authors mentioned as a reminder that their textbooks were widespread in Königsberg and read by Kant, but they are considered first as textbook writers without philosophical standing. This book grew out of my dissatisfaction with the traditional scholarship, which consistently denies Aristotelianism and scholastic or academic philosophy any share in the rise of Kant's transcendental philosophy. My investigation, by contrast, has tried to show the historical and philosophical importance of Aristotle and Aristotelianism from the late sixteenth century to the first half of the eighteenth century.

My investigation of Königsberg's intellectual context shows that it was a melting pot for various philosophical traditions, and that, at least up until the first three decades of the eighteenth century, the dominant philosophy was Aristotelianism. Aristotle's supremacy had its root in the foundation of the university and the strict relationship with Melanchthon's teaching. In the seventeenth century, Königsberg Aristotelianism was characterized by its original interpretation and by the new philosophical perspective in the logical field with figures such as Abraham Calov and Melchior Zeidler. Other philosophers such as Michael Eifler, Andreas Hedio, and Paul Rabe pursued their respective lines of inquiry in the wake of these two authors. Rabe in particular, the last important Königsberg Aristotelian, was particularly influential on the educational system in Königsberg for at least forty years, both in the *Collegium Fridericianum* and in the university. His *Dialectica et analytica* was the regular textbook for knowledge of the rudiments of logic at the collegium and the university, while his *Cursus philosophorum* was one of the most important university manuals for accessing the higher faculties of medicine, law, and theology. His works were so successful that Hieronymus Georgi summarized the *Cursus* in his *Philosophia propaedeutica*, while Johann David Kypke summarized the *Dialectica et analytica* in the *Brevissima delineatio scientiarum dialecticae et analyticae ad mentem philosophi*. At the beginning of the eighteenth century, with the rise of Pietism, the dissemination of Eclectic and Wolffian philosophy, and also the import of British philosophy, the hegemony of Aristotelian philosophy began to wane. This does not mean, as we have shown, that Aristotle was no longer taught, or that he was not the cornerstone for every philosophical doctrine: his philosophy was taught for a large part of the first half of the eighteenth century.

My claim is that this Aristotelianism had a decisive impact on Kant's philosophy. One of the fields in which Aristotelianism was more influential is facultative logic, which concerns the study of the origins and the structure of cognitive faculties. The rise of facultative logic was possible thanks to a rethinking of the problem of habit within the Renaissance and early-modern Aristotelian tradition. Melanchthon was still anchored to the examination of the three operations of the mind, that is, simple apprehension, judgment, and reasoning, modeled on the three logical inferences, that is, concept, proposition, and syllogism, rather than a true analysis of the faculties of the mind. It was with Jacopo Zabarella that the topic of facultative logic took a central role in the doctrine of the habit. The dissemination of Zabarella's work in Germany generated a new field of research among the Calvinists with the birth of the *hexiologia*, while in the Lutheran area, and especially in Königsberg, it led to the rise of gnostology and noology. In particular, it was Abraham Calov who was the true maker of the systematization of these two disciplines in Königsberg, which enjoyed great success up to the beginning of the eighteenth century. Gnostology emphasizes the problem of the different kinds of objects of cognition, that is, the cognizable and the knowable. Instead, noology concerns the study of the first principles of knowledge. Besides Aristotelian facultative logic, Lockean philosophy had a wide dissemination from the fourth decade of the eighteenth century onward, getting into its stride in 1770.

Aristotle and Locke are Kant's two main points of reference in facultative logic, and his early works on the topic show the strict conceptual relationship between these two philosophers. From his reflections on the Aristotelian facultative logic Kant supported: (1) the three operations of the mind; (2) the idea that there are special sciences concerning the study of the cognizable qua cognizable and the first principles of cognition, that is, gnostology and noology; (3) the conception of a science that deals with the origin of cognition distinguished by logic; and (4) space, time, and categories are originarily acquired like a mental habit.

One of the most important contributions of Aristotelianism in this sense is the distinction between the matter and form of knowledge. The distinction concerns the various ways in which the object of knowledge is considered and investigated. This doctrine was particularly elaborated by Zabarella's works, in which matter is the *res considerata*, while form is the *modus considerandi*. The *modus considerandi* characterizes the perspective of the subject, in other words, the subjective standpoint on the object, which is properly speaking the *res considerata*. Zabarella's doctrine became extremely popular in Germany, and Calov employed it in the broader field of epistemology. Leibniz himself uses this distinction and states well before Kant that space and time are *modi considerandi*, which had a foundation in reality. It is in the wake of this tradition that Kant in the *Inaugural Dissertation* employs the distinction between the form and matter of knowledge. The distinction became fundamental in the "Transcendental Aesthetic" and in the "Transcendental Logic," in which space, time, and categories are the forms of knowledge by means of which the subject can know.

Having established the Aristotelian matrix of Kant's conception of the origin of the faculties of the mind and the forms of cognitions, we went on to examine their functions. Kant's doctrine of categories arises from the failure of the precritical attempts at finding first, simplest, and primitive concepts that, once combined, can explain reality in its complexity: it is the failure of the syllogistic and combinatoric project. Leibniz represents a turning point for a mathematical conception of Aristotelian syllogistic with his idea to find a universal science, an *ars characteristica combinatoria*, through which reality can be described by means of the combination of few mathematical signs. The Leibnizian project was carried out by the Bernoullis and by eclectic philosophers such as Johann Andreas Segner, Gottfried Ploucquet, Johann Heinrich Lambert, and Joachim Georg Darjes, who were Kant's primary references during his precritical period. Kant's interest in these authors is clear, not only in *The False Subtlety*, which is expressly devoted to syllogistic, but also in many other places of the Kantian *corpus*. The result of Kant's investigation is essentially threefold: (1) the impossibility of finding first, simplest, and primitive concepts that, once recombined, can describe the whole of reality; (2) concepts are merely heuristic devices to explain reality, but they are in no way constituent building blocks of it; and (3) logical investigation cannot start from concepts, but from judgments from which the concepts are determined. Starting from these results, at the beginning of the 1770s, Kant adopts the Aristotelian doctrine of categories, understood not as the highest kinds or first concepts, but as *modi considerandi* and *cognoscendi*. Categories as *modi considerandi* are what gives determinate significance to the object of knowledge. This notion of "category" is traceable back to early-modern Aristotelianism in authors such as Zabarella and Pace, but was followed in particular by Rabe in his commentary to Aristotle's categories. Also the idea of schema, the figure of the process of the attribution and arrangement of categories for describing reality, has an Aristotelian origin, and has in Rabe Kant's most immediate precursor.

Kant's most Aristotelian element is probably the distinction of logic into analytic and dialectic. In Kant, dialectic has three major meanings. The first meaning is dialectic as doctrine of probability, that is the logic that starting from premises that are not necessarily true, but which have a cognitive value, draws probable conclusions.

CONCLUSION

The second meaning conceives dialectic as a logic of illusion, that is the art of deceiving and of showing false cognitions as true. In the third meaning, dialectic is understood as the zetetic method and probably comes from Darjes's reading. In the first two cases, Kant's conception of dialectic comes from Rabe's distinction of a *logica ex probabilibus* and a *logica ex apparentibus*. Concerning analytic as the logic of truth, it was quite a common conception within the Aristotelian tradition, but the idea of an analytic as a part of logic that deals with the first elements of knowledge, that is, concepts and principles, occurs in Rabe, who conceives analytic as an a priori logic containing gnostology and noology which dealt with concepts and principles.

Aristotelianism exerted its influence also on Kant's methodology. Unlike the new methodology of Descartes, Spinoza, and Leibniz, which relied on the new mathematical method and geometrical order, in Königsberg the Renaissance Aristotelian conception of method survived, in particular in relation to Zabarella. In Königsberg, Calov established a new discipline called "methodology" with his *Methodologia nova*, which aimed to reassess Aristotelian primacy for its conceptions of method. Calov's work was the beginning of a new interest in Aristotelian methodology, which lasted up to the eighteenth century with Eifler's *Methodologia thematica* and Rabe's *Methodologia nova*. Of particular importance in this context was Christian Wolff's position, which was a synthesis between the Scholastic tradition and modern mathematism. From an initial panmathematism, Wolff's work progressively distinguished mathematical from metaphysical methods, establishing the impossibility of using mathematical concepts in philosophy. Kant followed Wolff's suggestion from his early writings, and in particular in the *Inquiry on the Distinctness*, in which he shows the failure of the application of mathematics to philosophy and the necessity of establishing a new methodology, which is the real aim of the *Critique of Pure Reason*. In this context, Kant revived some seminal methodological issues of Königsberg Aristotelianism.

The impact of the Aristotelian methodology is recognizable in the *Critique of Pure Reason*. In the second "Preface," Kant explicitly characterizes the *Critique of Pure Reason* as a treatise of method, no more no less. The search for a new methodology for metaphysics among the ashes of the failure of precritical projects led Kant to new solutions for assessing the relation between mathematics and metaphysics, and in general the system of science. Several methodological issues follow the Aristotelian model, not only Kant's conception of "architectonic," which most likely comes from Calov, but also the distinction κατ' ἄνθρωπον-κατ' ἀλήθειαν, which has its origin in the Aristotelian tradition.

THE ARISTOTELIAN KANT

At the end of this book, one might wonder why it was only between the late 1760s and the beginning of the '70s that Kant found in the Aristotelian tradition possible solutions to his problem. At the end of the 1760s, Kant was facing two important issues: (1) the search for a new methodology of metaphysics, sharply distinguished from that of mathematics; and (2) ensuring the possibility of a universal and objective knowledge starting from experience—namely, its Copernican revolution.

The *Critique of Pure Reason* in Kant's eyes should respond exactly to these demands, in other words, it must provide a methodology for metaphysics and for determining a new transcendental theory of knowledge. In so doing, Kant broke radically with contemporary philosophical projects he had explored in the precritical period, and he began to focus on the Aristotelian tradition. I believe that Kant was aided in the reappropriation of the Aristotelian tradition by his job as librarian at the *Schlossbibliothek* during 1766 and 1772, which is exactly the period of his terminological shift toward an Aristotelian conceptuality. Since its foundation in 1529, the *Schlossbibliothek* was one of the richest libraries in Protestant Germany, counting by the mid-sixteenth century around two thousand volumes.[1] According to the catalog inventoried in 1758, the library had 966 volumes on philosophy.[2] The auction catalog of private libraries acquired by the *Schlossbibliothek* includes the collections of the Aristotelians Hedio and Rabe, their publisher Heinrich Boye, and Kant's mentor Knutzen.[3] Unfortunately, only Hedio's catalog is available and can provide a reliable inventory of the books, listing 174 on Plato and Aristotle and another 103 on various philosophical topics.[4] From the auction catalog it is possible to evince that between 1759 and 1773, a period that includes Kant's employment as a librarian, there were no new acquisitions, but there was a general overhaul of the library in which

Kant must have participated.[5] Moreover, the first important acquisition after 1759 was that of the library of the Aristotelian Quandt in 1773,[6] a sign that the Aristotelians and their libraries still aroused some interest. Kant thus had available to him a large collection of books, as well as the opportunity to read Aristotelian doctrines at a crucial time in the genesis of critical philosophy.

To conclude, we can say for certain that Kant finds in Aristotelian philosophy clues to solving important puzzling questions in his own philosophy, and that probably the very first years of the 1770s were crucial to his understanding of the Aristotelian tradition. The influence is testified by his drastic and radical conceptual and doctrinal changes. Some reading this book may find the evidence presented here inconclusive, or the sources unconvincing, but the right to rebuttal is entirely the reader's. In absence of other sources, I think it is extremely difficult, if not impossible, to explain Kant's Aristotelianism and his Aristotelian terminology in any other way.

It remains to be asked whether Kant was or was not an Aristotelian. Kant certainly never professed to be one, but as we have seen, over the years he used Aristotelian doctrines and strategies to solve problems that contemporary philosophy was unable to handle. This does not mark a complete revival of Aristotle, but only the adoption and updating of certain elements that were decisive in the formation of his thought and in the genesis of the *Critique of Pure Reason*, and without which it is not possible to fully appreciate Kant's thought.

NOTES

INTRODUCTION

1. See McDowell 1994; Van Cleve 1999; McDowell 2009a; McDowell 2009b.
2. See Ameriks 1982; Allison 1983; Guyer 1987; Allison 1990; Kitcher 1990; Makkreel 1990; Allison 2001; Ameriks 2003; Ameriks 2006; Kitcher 2011.
3. See Ameriks 2000; Rockmore 2006; Rockmore 2007; Rockmore 2011.
4. See Beck 1969; Brandt 1991; Laywine 1994; Schönfeld 2000; Watkins 2004.
5. See Hinske 2006.
6. See Bird 2006.
7. See Görland 1909; Campo 1939; Campo 1953; Tonelli 1956a; Tonelli 1956b; Tonelli 1958; Tonelli 1959a; Tonelli 1962; Tonelli 1964; Tonelli 1966; Tonelli 1971; Tonelli 1974a; Fries 1975; Tonelli 1975; Tonelli 1976a; Tonelli 1976b; Pozzo 1989; Brandt 1991; Tonelli 1994; Pozzo 1995; Pozzo 1998a; Micheli 2002; Tommasi 2003a; Tommasi 2003b; Pozzo 2004a; Pozzo 2004b; Tommasi 2005; Santozki 2006; Pozzo 2008; Mosser 2008; Walter 2013.

8. Tonelli 1974a, 189.
9. Brucker 1742–44, 4: 333.
10. See Petersen 1921; Wundt 1939; Wundt, 1945: Beck 1969; Tonelli 1975; Sparn 2001; Pozzo 2008; Rohls 2012/2013.
11. See Freedman 1985a; Freedman 1993.
12. See Freedman 1985b.
13. See Dieter 2001.
14. Brucker 1742–44, 4: 333.
15. Rabe 1704: 212.
16. Professors of dialectics in the sixteenth century were Nikolaus Jagenteufel (1552–67), Martin Lauben (1569–78), Michael Scrinius (1579–85), Lorenz Pantän (1585–89), Martin Winter (1589–95), and Johann von Geldern (1595–1620). Cf. Arnoldt 1746, 2: 381.
17. Dreier 1644: 7.
18. For example, Melchior Zeidler published two different Aristotelian handbooks for the theological faculty, the *Prodromus introductioni in lectionem Aristotelis praemissus* (1680) and the *Introductio in lectionem Aristotelis* (1681), each of them of more than one-thousand pages. The use of Aristotelian handbooks also in the faculty of theology illustrates the degree to which Aristotelianism had taken root in Königsberg.
19. See Pozzo 2002: 53–65. In the seventeenth century, professors of logic were Georg Crusius (1621–25), Levin Pouchen in 1626, Lorenz Weger (1626–29), Michael Eifler (1630–57), Melchior Zeidler (1658–63), Lambert Steger (1663–67), and Andreas Hedio (1667–1703). Influenced by Zabarella were both Crusius's *Collegium logicum* (1618), a collection of dissertations on the nature of logic, and Weger's *Quaestiones in omnes Organi Aristotelici libros* (1628). Weger's *Quaestiones* considered the nature of logic as *habitus instrumentalis speculativus* and its subject as "second notions" or *ens rationis* in a very Zabarellean way. It is possible to find Zabarellean traces also in Eifler's works such as the *Methodologia particularis, synthesin et analysin thematicam* (1643), the *Frontispicium logicum* (1644), the *Lineamenta logicae* (1645), the *Primordia pansophiae* (1645), and the *Methodologia recognita* (1653). The last important Aristotelian logical work of the seventeenth century in the wake of Zabarella was Andreas

Hedio's commentary to Aristotle's *Organon* (1686), which unfortunately remained incomplete and thus dealt only with dialectics.
20. See Brucker 1742–44, 4: 334–35.
21. On the synthetic and analytic method, Zeidler also devoted a short treatise titled *De gemino veterum docendi modo exoterico et acroamatico, id est dialectico et analytico, tractatus historico-philologico-philosophicus* (1685). Also, Francis Bacon's *Novum Organum* was read and interpreted from an Aristotelian perspective as a book of methodology whose aim was not to substitute Aristotelianism but to integrate and improve it.
22. Christian Dreier was very interested in dialectics, more than in the methodology of science. His writings were collected by Bussmann in the *Dialectica Regiomontana sive compendium Topicorum Aristotelis* (1690). In Dreier's wake, Steger published a collection of ten dissertations about Aristotle's *Topica* and *Elenchi sophistici* (1665). Against Descartes's principle, Steger wrote also the dissertation *De primo cognoscendi principio* (1656). See Morhof 1688–92: 477; Brucker 1742–44, 4: 334.
23. See Wundt 1939: 242–57.
24. After Weger's death in 1630, his writing and lectures were collected and published in the *Prima mentis operatio*, which analyzed the activities of the mind in the act of apprehension.
25. In 1651 in the *Scripta philosophica* Calov collected his two main treatises on facultative logic: the *Gnostologia* and the *Noologia*. Followers of Calov were Georg Meier, who published in 1662 a *Gnostologia*, and Georg Wagner, who published in 1670 a *Synopsis noologica* and a *Synopsis gnostologica*. In Königsberg, Eifler continued the tradition of *noologia* and *gnostologia*, publishing in 1639 the *Collegii philosophici*, in which noological topics played a central role. In 1651, Eifler published a collection of dissertations on the topic of noology titled *Habitus intelligentiae disputatio*. The interest in gnostology and noology was widespread also in the theological field, as the appearance of Kaspar Witzel's dissertation *De noologia, an peculiaris aliqua et distincta sit scientia* (1662) directed by Zeidler testifies. See Leinsle 1998.
26. See Rohde 1722: 1, now in Sgarbi 2013.
27. In the preface to the *Philosophia propaedeutica*, Georgi defines Rabe not simply as an Aristotelian commentator, but as an

autonomous Aristotelian thinker, capable of new and original philosophical ideas (Georgi 1716).

28. There is little information about Rabe's life. He was born on April 11, 1656, in Königsberg, where, on September 22, 1678, he became *magister legens* of philosophy. In 1682, he became inspector of the *Collegium Fridericianum*, on which he exerted a strong and long lasting influence due to his "scientific authority"; see Horkel 1855: 29. From 1685 to 1703, Rabe was professor of Greek at Königsberg University, which allowed him to teach classes of rudimentary logic. From 1703 to 1713, as Andreas Hedio's successor, Rabe became full professor of logic and metaphysics. For a general introduction to Rabe, see Sgarbi 2009.

29. See Pisanski 1886: 530. Most likely, Rabe's textbook was conceived only after 1686, when Andreas Hedio's edition of Aristotle's *Organon* came out, because the Aristotelian text seems to be based on this version.

30. On the adoption of Rabe's textbook at the *Collegium* at Kant's time, see Arnoldt 1746, 3: 314–93, in particular 319, Gotthold 1853; Arnoldt 1881: 614; Zippel 1898: 70; Schumacher 1913; Sommerfeldt 1918: 451, 458, 460; Vorländer 1924: 22; von Selle 1956: 139–40; Vorländer 1986: 15, Pozzo 1991: 176; Klemme 1994; Sgarbi 2009. Rabe's *Dialectica et Analytica* was taught also at the Albertina by Johann David Kypke. Even Kypke's *Brevissima delineatio scientiarum dialecticae et analyticae ad mentem philosophi* (1729) was nothing more than a companion to Rabe's work. In his logic, Kypke used tables very similar to those used by Kant in his "Transcendental logic" (Pisanski 1886: 531–32). It is nonetheless the case that Kant lived in Kypkes's house for a while during his first years of university teaching, and that he might have become acquainted with Aristotelian doctrines in such a context. It is impossible to establish for sure whether Kant lived in the house of Johann David Kypke, or in that of Georg David Kypke. However, what is important is Kant's familiarity with environment. See Stark 1994: 88.

31. The *Cursus* was recommended for its completeness to university students of the higher faculties, such as theology, law, and medicine, as the subtitle of the work suggests (Erdmann 1876: 21; Pozzo 1989: 4–5; Kühn 2001: 74–75). The success of this work

is also shown by the wide dissemination of the *Philosophia propaedeutica sive Philosophiae Fundamenta praerequisita, ad ductum et methodum Cursus Philosophici b. Professoris Raben in tres tomos iuxta triplicem Philosophiam breviter et perspicue distributa*, a companion of the *Cursus* published for his lectures in 1716 in Königsberg by Hieronymus Georgi (see Pisanski 1886: 529). Furthermore, Rabe's *Cursus* was the only textbook able to cover all six disciplines required by Rogall's decree to gain access to theological studies (Pozzo 1991: 175). On the use of Rabe's *Cursus* at the Albertina, see Sgarbi 2009. Rabe's *Cursus philosophicus* was probably the manual used by Thomas Burckhard, professor of rhetoric, poetics and ancient languages, for his lectures (see Oberhausen-Pozzo 1999: 98, 104, 107, 110, 119, 122, 137, 140, 143, 146). Kant undoubtedly followed Burckhard's lectures: (1) philosophy students were required to know Latin, rhetoric and classical poetics; and (2) Kant's well-known juvenile interests in philology would have led him to attend Burckhard's classes. Moreover, Burckhard was known to use the *Dialectica et analytica*, and the announcements of his lectures frequently specified the Aristotelian nature of his teaching, thus there is no reason to rule out the possibility that he taught Rabe's *Cursus*.

32. Von Selle 1956: 104.
33. See Tonelli 1975: 129–30.
34. See Rohde 1722, now in Sgarbi 2013.
35. See Pisanski 1886: 532.
36. This work, more than any other, provides some evidence of what Kant could have known about logic in his youth. First of all, Knutzen's logic deals with facultative logic, epistemic logic, logical prejudices and errors, and methodology. Knutzen's treatment of logic is particularly indebted to Cartesian logic, Wolffian logic, Port-Royal logic, as well as authors such as Nicolas Malebranche, Jean-Pierre de La Crousaz, Francis Bacon, Isaac Watts, John Locke, Philipp Melanchthon, Melchior Zeidler, Johann Franz Budde, Christian Thomasius, Andreas Rüdiger, and Ehrenfried Walther von Tschirnhaus. These were probably the works and ideas that Kant was exposed to during his youth. A particularly relevant influence would seem to be John Locke, whom, as we will see in the chapter 1, Knutzen was one of the

first in Germany to appreciate, and the translation of whose *Of the Conduct of the Understanding* Knutzen undertook but failed to complete by the time of his death (see Locke 1996: 11).
37. See Tonelli 1975: 126–27.
38. For Eclecticism and Eclectic school with the capital *E*, I characterize that particular philosophical movement which arose between the end of seventeenth and the beginning of the eighteenth century, led by Christian Thomasius and Johann Franz Budde, whose aim was to select the best opinions from ancient and modern philosophers, thus reflecting a new independent thought. The adjective *eclectic*, with the lowercase *e*, indicates a general attitude toward employing material, doctrines, and ideas from various traditions without being attached to one particular school.
39. See Pozzo 2008.
40. Lecture catalogs give us a very clear picture of the teaching of logic in Königsberg. Beginning in WS 1703/1704, when he first became professor, Rabe taught a course on Aristotle's *Categories* and *On Interpretation*, the result of which was the *Primitiae professionis logico-metaphysicae, sive Commentarius in librum categoriarum Aristotelis*. In parallel, he lectured privately on methodology, probably on Calov's *Tractatus novus de methodo docendi et disputandi*. The entire *cursus* was taught using his own textbook. From SS 1704, he also began to use *Dialectica et analytica*. The teaching of metaphysics concerned the agreement and disagreement of Scholastic philosophers with Aristotle. In 1706, Rabe was nominated vice rector, but he continued to teach his *Dialectica*. From SS 1707 to SS 1713, he taught on his *Dialectica* and on his *Cursus*. Also Johann Böse, from WS 1713/1714 to SS 1714/1715, taught on Rabe's textbooks. Between SS 1715 and WS 1719/1720, Hieronymous Georgi, Heinrich Oelmann, Micheal Gehrke, and Christian Gabriel Fischer taught on Aristotelian manuals such those of Calov, Zeidler, and Rabe.
41. See Wundt 1945: 37–60.
42. For instance Christian Friedrich Baumgarten, Theodor Reinhard That, and Johann Heinrich Kreuschner.
43. This reconstruction is very much indebted to Tonelli 1975, even if his research was not substantiated by the examination of the *Vorlesungsverzeichnisse*. Whereas the lectures catalog for the

years between 1720 and 1804 was published by Riccardo Pozzo and Michael Oberhausen in 1999, no one to my knowledge has ever considered the documents that are available from the period between 1703 and 1720.

44. In WS 1719/1720, there was the first Wolffian teaching of logic on the *Vernünfftige Gedanken von den Kräften des menschlichen Verstandes* (1712) by Oelmann in conjunction with Budde's *Elementa philosophiae instrumentalis* (1703). However, Gehrke and Burckhard continued their lectures on Aristotelian manuals. In SS 1720, Rohde taught logic and metaphysics on Budde's *Elementa philosophiae instrumentalis* and *Elementa philosophiae theoreticae*, as well as on Christian Weise's *Doctrina logica* (1681). Oelmann taught Wolffian logic and Rabe's *Cursus*. Georg Henrich Rast had private lectures on *cursus philosophicus* and a class of logic following Wolffian manuals. Gehrke, on the other hand, lectured privately on Rabe's *Cursus*. In SS 1720/1721, Rohde lectured publicly on Aristotelian logic using Weise's textbook, and privately using Budde's manual. Oelmann taught publicly on logic using Budde's works and Thomasius's *Einleitung zu der Vernunfft-Lehre* (1699). Privately, he taught Rabe's *Cursus philosophicus*. Fischer taught Budde's *Elementa philosophiae theoreticae* (1703). Gehrke continued his private lectures on Rabe's *Cursus*. Abraham Wolf had private classes on Budde's *Elementa philosophiae instrumentalis*, while Rast taught logic on Wolffian manuals. In SS 1721, Rohde taught logic privately using Thomasius's *Introductio in philosophiam aulicam* (1688), and mentions Budde's works as an alternative. Oelmann taught Budde's *Philosophia instrumentalis* and Thomasius's *Einleitung zu der Vernunfft-Lehre* publicly, and Wolff's German metaphysics and Zeidler's *De gemino veterum docendi modo exoterico et acroamatico* privately. In the same semester, Thomas Burckhard taught logic on Rabe's *Dialectica et analytica*. Gehrke taught Rabe's *Cursus* privately. Rast, on the other hand, continued his private teaching of logic. Johann Arnd taught a course of logic and rhetoric using Jean Le Clerc's works. In SS 1721/1722, Rohde publicly taught logic on Joachim Lange's *Genuina methodus disputandi* (1719). Oelmann in his public lecture on logic used Thomasius *Einleitung zu der Vernunfft-Lehre* and the fourth part of Budde's *Philosophia instrumentalis*. Burckhard preferred to adopt Rabe's *Dialectica et*

analytica. In SS 1722, Oelmann used Wolff's textbook for logic in public, while privately he taught the *cursus philosophicus*, probably with Rabe's work. Burckhard continued his teaching on Rabe's *Dialectica et analytica*. Rast taught logic privately, while Arnd had a course on Le Clerc's logic. In WS 1722/1723, Rohde publicly taught logic using Budde's manual. Oelmann held public lectures on logic using Wolffian works, and Burckhard adopted Rabe's textbook for the exercises on dialectic and analytic. In SS 1723, Rohde publicly taught Aristotelian logic, probably with Rabe's textbooks, as propaedeutic to Cartesian and Eclectic logic, while Oelmann used Wolffian manuals for his teachings. In WS 1723/1724, Oelmann publicly taught Wolffian philosophy, but most continued to use Rabe's *Cursus* privately. Burckhard remained loyal to Rabe's *Dialectica et analytica*. Also in SS 1724, Olemann still continued to use Wolffian manuals publicly and Aristotelian textbooks in private. In the same semester, Burckhard chose not to follow Rabe, preferring rather to adopt Samuel Grosser's *Pharus intellectus sive logica electiva* (1697).
45. See Ritschl 1844, 2: 290.
46. See Wotschke 1928; Riedesel 1937: 30.
47. See Von Selle 1956: 139–40.
48. The lectures clearly show the Eclectic tendency. In WS 1724/1725, Rohde publicly taught Le Clerc's *Ars critica* (1697–1700), while both Oelmann and Burckhard continued to use the textbooks of the previous semester. In SS 1725, Rohde publicly taught logic in Latin using Rabe's works, as did Burckhard. In WS 1725/1726, Rohde publicly taught logic with Rabe's *Methodologia* and Johann Friedemann Schneider's *Tractatus logicus in singularis quo processus disputandi seu officia aeque ac vitia [. . .] exhibentur* (1718). Gregorovious used Andreas Hedio's *Prolegomena de philosophia*, which I did not find listed in any library catalog. In SS 1726, Rohde taught Rabe's *Methodologia*, and Budde's work against atheism and Port-Royal logic. Burckhard taught from Rabe's textbooks; Georg Friedrich Rogall, on the other hand, taught Wolffian logic, with a polemical intent. Kypke probably taught from Rabe's *Dialectica et analytica*, and Hebrew and Greek metaphysics from an unknown manual. In WS 1726/1727, Rohde publicly taught Port-Royal logic and Le Clerc's *Ars critica*. Privately, he taught Jean-Pierre de la Crousaz's *Logicae systema* (1724), Le

Clerc's logic, Johann Jakob Syrbius's *Institutiones philosophiae rationalis eclecticae* (1719), and Schneider's *Fundamenta philosophiae rationalis* (1703). In SS 1727, there was no specific course for logic. In WS 1727/1728, after Rohde's death, Kypke began to lecture on natural theology and logic. In SS 1728, Teske began to teach logic as well. Kypke taught logic in WS 1728/1729, and from his lessons he derived his *Brevissima delineatio scientiarum dialecticae et analyticae ad mentem philosophi* (1729); meanwhile, Teske taught syllogistic, probably using Rabe, and Wolff's *Philosophia rationalis* for the other parts of logic. Kypke publicly taught hermeneutics in SS 1729, and logic privately, probably from his own manuals, while Burckhard taught logic from Rabe. In WS 1729/1730, Kypke taught natural theology publicly, and privately logic from his own manual. Burckhard taught logic from Rabe. Alongside the course on logic, Salthenius added courses on criticism, hermeneutics, didactics and *ars disputandi*, probably from Aristotelian or Eclectic textbooks. In SS 1730, Kypke and Burckhard taught Aristotelian logic, while Salthenius taught from Eclectic textbooks. In WS 1730/1731, Kypke taught logic and metaphysics from the manuals used in the previous years. Salthenius taught "special logic" again, in particular criticism, hermeneutics, didactics and *ars disputandi*. Privately, however, he taught Rabe's *Cursus philosophicus*, which was also the base of Marquardt's lectures. In SS 1731, Kypke privately taught Rabe's *Cursus*, in conjunction with Eclectic authors such as Budde and Johann Georg Walch (1730), whose manuals were adopted also by Marquardt. In WS 1731/1732, Kypke taught natural theology, while Salthenius continued to teach disputatory exercises. Daniel Heinrich Arnoldt taught the *cursus philosophicus* privately for the three following semesters. In SS 1732, Kypke taught logic from his own manual, while Burckhard and Marquardt taught the *cursus*, probably from Rabe's textbook. Karl Heinrich Rappolt held lectures on logic and metaphysics, probably from Eclectic textbooks. In WS 1732/1733, Kypke continued his public lectures on logic, and Burckhard his lectures on Rabe's *Cursus*, while Marquardt privately taught Budde's *Elementa philosophiae rationalis*. Marquardt's teaching on this textbook continued also in SS 1733. In WS 1733/1734, Kypke lectured publicly on logic, while Marquardt privately taught metaphysics. Bock, on the other hand, who had been extraordinary professor of logic and metaphysics for two semesters, taught his *De pulchritudine carminum*. In SS 1734, Kypke publicly taught logic and metaphysics, while Marquardt and Knutzen privately taught Rabe's *Cursus*, but Knutzen also held public lectures on logic. In WS 1734/1735, Kypke taught natural theology and Marquardt taught the *cursus* privately, but it is not possible to ascertain which manual he used.

49. See Fehr 2005.
50. See Pozzo 2008: 182.
51. See Kühn 2001: 50; Stark 1994: 88.
52. See Rohde 1722.
53. Starting from the SS 1734, there are some faint traces of Wolffian teachings. Knutzen publicly taught "practical rational philosophy," while lecturing privately on metaphysics. In WS 1735, Kypke taught logic, while Marquardt continued his private lectures on the *cursus*. Knutzen taught Wolff's *Philosophia rationalis* publicly, and privately the *Cursus philosophicus*. In WS 1735/1736, Burckhard taught logic and metaphysics on Samuel Christian Hollmann's *In universam philosophiam introductio* (1734). Knutzen taught Rabe's *Cursus* and Wolff's *Philosophia rationalis*. Things did not change in the following two semesters. In SS 1736 and in WS 1736/1737, Karl Andreas Christiani taught *cursus philosophicus* using Ludwig Thümmig's *Institutiones philosophiae wolffianae* (1725–26). In SS 1737, Kypke probably taught Aristotelian logic, while Burckhard and Marquardt used Rabe's *Cursus philosophicus*. Christiani taught the *cursus* on Thümming's works, and Knuzten lectured logic on Wolff's *Philosophia rationalis* (1728). In WS 1737/1738, Burckhard taught the *cursus*, probably on Budde's textbooks, Marquardt held private lectures, most likely on Rabe's *Cursus*, while Knutzen publicly taught Wolff's Latin logic. Rappolt, on the other hand, taught logic probably from Eclectic manuals. Christiani continued his private lectures using Thümmig's *Institutiones*. In SS 1738, Burckhard, Marquardt, Knutzen, and Christiani used the same manuals as the previous semester. In WS 1738/1739 Kypke, Marquardt, Knutzen, Burckhard, and Christiani continued their teachings of logic and metaphysics. It is worth noting that Gregorovious taught *philosophia contemplativa, practica et effectiva* from

Hedio's *Prolegomena*, which is not listed in any library catalog and is now probably lost. In SS 1739, Marquardt, Knutzen, and Christiani taught the *cursus*. Knutzen used Wolff's *Philosophia rationalis* for his teaching of logic. Between WS 1739/1740 and WS 1742/1743, there were no significant changes in the teaching. In SS 1743, besides the usual teaching of the *cursus*, Knutzen taught Wolff's *Philosophia rationalis*, Rappolt taught Thümmig's *Institutiones philosophiae wolffianae*, while Christiani and Kypke lectured on metaphysics from Baumeister's textbooks. From WS 1743/1744 to WS 1746/1747, Knutzen and Kypke continued his teaching of the *cursus*. In this last semester, Knutzen taught logic on his *Elementa philosophiae rationalis*, which had just been published. Throughout this period, Kypke alternated between logic and metaphysics, while Knutzen taught both contemporaneously. In SS 1747, Coelestin Christian Flottwell, professor of eloquence, gave private lessons on the *cursus*, which he repeated in WS 1750–51. Up to WS 1750/1751, Kypke and Knutzen taught logic and metaphysics with the assistance of Christian for the teaching of the *cursus*. From this semester onward, Johann Bernhard Hahn, professor of eloquence, taught logic and *ars disputatoria*. In SS 1751, Flottwell taught logic and metaphysics from Gottsched's *Erste Gründe der gesamten Weltweisheit* (1733–734), standing in for Knutzen's premature death. In SS 1752, Henrich Wilhelm Johanssen had a private teaching of logic. The situation did not change until SS 1753, when Buck held private lectures of metaphysics based on Wolffian textbooks. Also based on Wolffian manuals was Rappolt's private teaching of the *cursus*. In SS 1755, Georg David Kypke held private lectures on logic and metaphysics based on Baumeister's textbooks. In SS 1756, Jakob Friedrich Werner taught logic from Crousaz and metaphysics from Baumeister. In the same semester, Michael Friedrich Watson taught logic from Knutzen's *Elementa philosophiae rationalis*, Johann Gottlieb Heineccius's *Elementa philosophiae rationalis* (1738) and Johann Gotthelf Linder's *Anweisung zur guten Schreibart überhaupt und zur Beredsamkeit* (1755). In WS 1758/1759, Watson used Baumeister's logic.

54. From WS 1760/1761 to WS 1765/1766, for the first time in Königsberg University, Buck used Christian August Crusius' *Weg zur Gewißheit und Zuverläßigkeit der menschlichen*

Erkenntniß (1747) for the teaching of logic. From SS 1766 to the WS 1769/1770, Buck adopted Knutzen's *Elementa philosophiae rationalis* in conjunction with Crusius's logic as his manual of logic. Between WS 1766/1767 and WS 1768/1769, Christiani taught logic and metaphysics from Baumeister's textbooks.

55. Pozzo 2008: 181–83.
56. See Locke 1996: 11.
57. See Wundt 1945: 254–64.
58. See Harnack 1900: 317–53.
59. See Sgarbi 2010e.
60. See Tonelli 1959a: XIX.
61. See Tonelli 1959c.

CHAPTER 1. FACULTATIVE LOGIC

1. Buickerood 1985: 163.
2. See ibid.: 164.
3. See Schuurman 2004: 44–50.
4. See Nuchelmans 1998: 105
5. See Auroux 1993; Michael 1997: 1–20.
6. Arnauld-Nicole 1878: 27.
7. Keckermann 1601: 8.
8. See Falkenstein-Easton 1997: I.
9. See Pozzo 2003; Pozzo 2007a.
10. Boh 1993: XI.
11. See Yolton 1955; McRae 1965; Yolton 1975.
12. See Pozzo 2007c.
13. See Plato, *Republic*, 477 D7–E3.
14. Plato, *Republic*, 477 C1.
15. See Smith 2000.
16. Aristotle, *On the Soul*, II.5, 417 b 242–45.
17. Aristotle, *On the Soul*, II.3, 427 b 16–17.
18. See Aristotle, *On the Soul*, II.3, 427 b 28–29.
19. See Aristotle, *On the Soul*, III.3, 428 a 3–5.
20. Aristotle, *On the Soul*, III.3, 429 a 1–2.
21. See Kahn 1981.
22. Aristotle, *Posterior Analytics*, II.19, 99 b 35.

23. See Bazan 1981.
24. See Melanchthon 1846: 142. Melanchthon traces this division of the three operations of the mind back to Simplicius.
25. See ibid.: 142–43. Melanchthon focuses in particular on the operation of the enumeration that according to him is the expression of the maximum power of the human mind. In this context, we cannot exclude Melanchthon's influence on René Descartes' *Discours de la méthode*.
26. Brandt 1991: 99.
27. Ibid. See A 130–31/B 169.
28. Kant's reading of Wolff is not correct. We can find this partition in his *Philosophia rationalis*.
29. Knutzen 1747: 60. See Capozzi 2002: 299.
30. Barone 1957: 222.
31. Ibid.: 225.
32. See Conrad 1994: 77.
33. Brandt 1991: 46.
34. Adickes 1889: XIX.
35. See Capozzi 2001: 303.
36. See Zabarella 1597: 502e. See Pozzo 1998b: 157–58.
37. See ibid.: 504f.
38. See ibid.: 505b.
39. See ibid.
40. See ibid.: 506b.
41. See Alsted 1612.
42. Ibid.: 260. According to Alsted, principles are intelligible, but not cognizable; they are necessary for demonstration, but are in themselves indemonstrable.
43. See Gutke 1625.
44. See Fromme 1631.
45. See Wundt 1945: 242–57.
46. See Weger 1630.
47. The science of *habitus primorum principiorum* as a discipline was probably founded by Georg Gutke in the wake of Zabarella's work, as we shall see in the following pages. On Gutke, see Wundt 1939: 242–54; Sparn 2001: 582–85.
48. Calov 1640: 1.
49. Ibid.

50. See Timpler 1607: 38.
51. Calov 1640: 10.
52. Calov 1640: 25.
53. See Tonelli 1964: 183.
54. Calov 1640: 26.
55. See Ibid.: 183.
56. See Sgarbi 2011.
57. See Ibid.: 198.
58. Ibid.: 206.
59. See Timpler 1607: 38.
60. See École 2001. It is well known that Wolff refers to Timpler's position in his *Ontologia*.
61. See Wolff 1736: 62; Baumgarten 1779: 3.
62. Calov 1651: 10.
63. Ibid.: 38.
64. Ibid.
65. See Ibid.
66. Ibid.: 49.
67. See ibid.: 50.
68. See ibid.: 40.
69. See Nöbe 1636.
70. See Zeidler 1662.
71. See Calov 1651: 40. In Kant, this distinction will lead to the *Metaphysical Foundations of Natural Science* and to *The Metaphysics of Morals*.
72. See Calov 1640: 2–17.
73. See Vollrath 1962; Rompe 1968; Sparn 1976.
74. See Duchesneau 1974.
75. See Oberhausen 1997. In the *Critique of Pure Reason*, as we shall see below, Kant calls this process "reflection" (A 261/B 317).
76. See Aristotle, *Categories*, I.8, 8 b 26–27.
77. See Aristotle, *Categories*, I.8, 8 b 27–29.
78. See Aristotle, *Categories*, I.8, 9 a 1–4.
79. See Aristotle, *Categories*, I.8, 9 a 10–11.
80. See Aristotle, *Rhetoric*, I.10, 1369 b 6.
81. Aristotle, *Rhetoric*, I.11, 1370 a 4–7.
82. See Aristotle, *Nicomachean Ethics*, VI.3, 1139 b 16–17.
83. See Aristotle, *Nicomachean Ethics*, VI.3, 1139 b 20–21.
84. See Aristotle, *Nicomachean Ethics*, VI.3, 1139 b 33–34.

85. See Aristotle, *Nicomachean Ethics*, VI.6, 1141 a 6–8.
86. See Aristotle, *Nicomachean Ethics*, VI.7, 1141 b 1–2. See Aristotle, *Nicomachean Ethics*, VI.7, 1141 a 18–20.
87. See Lohr 1999: 281.
88. See ibid.: 288.
89. See Zabarella 1597: 6a–7b.
90. See ibid.: 16a–c.
91. See ibid.: 16e–18b.
92. See ibid.: 16c–d.
93. Ibid.: 21b.
94. See ibid.: 1262 f.
95. See ibid.: 1263d.
96. Ibid.: 1265f.
97. Ibid.: 1266c.
98. Ibid.: 1282f–1283a.
99. See Keckermann 1606; Timpler 1607; Timpler 1618; Nolle 1617; Gutke 1625; Fromme 1631; Eifler 1651; Meier 1662; Geilfus 1662; Wagner 1670.
100. See Alsted 1612: 254.
101. Ibid.: 260.
102. Ibid.
103. Ibid.: 261.
104. Ibid.
105. See Ibid.: 264.
106. See Ibid.
107. Ibid.: 268.
108. Ibid.: 270.
109. Ibid.: 271.
110. Ibid.: 274.
111. See Lohr 1999: 292.
112. Alsted 1612: 274.
113. Ibid.: 277.
114. See ibid.
115. Ibid.: 278.
116. Calov 1640: 27.
117. Ibid.
118. See ibid.: 1.
119. See ibid.
120. See ibid.: 1–2.

121. Ibid.: 29.
122. Ibid.: 47–8.
123. See ibid.: 48.
124. Wolff 1738: 339.
125. See ibid.: 342.
126. See ibid.
127. See ibid.: 347.
128. Ibid.
129. Ibid.: 353.
130. Ibid.: 354.
131. See ibid.: 354–355.
132. Ibid.: 356.
133. See ibid.
134. See ibid.: 357.
135. See ibid.: 358.
136. See Pozzo 2007a, 45–52.
137. Wolff 1740: 107.
138. Ibid.
139. Ibid.: 108.
140. Ibid.: 109.
141. See ibid.
142. See ibid.: 114.
143. Baumeister 1774: 8.
144. See ibid.
145. See ibid.
146. See ibid.: 10.
147. Ibid.
148. Ibid.: 24. In this context "subjective" does not mean "arbitrary," rather what pertains to the subject.
149. Ibid.: 25.
150. Baumgarten 1779: 206.
151. See ibid.
152. Ibid.: 222.
153. Ibid.: 219–20.
154. Ibid.: 220.
155. Ibid.: 220–221.
156. See Meier 1752a: 771.
157. See ibid.: 772–73; Lu-Adler 2016b.

158. Meier 1752b: 148.
159. See Oberhausen 1997; Rumore 2007.
160. See De Pierris, 1987; Zöller 1989; Falkenstein 1990.
161. See Malebranche 1688, 340–56.
162. Kant here uses the word *categories* for the first time. Before this letter Kant never used it, even if the search for the pure concepts of the understanding started vigorously from the *Dreams of a Spirit-Seer*.
163. "Locke has to do with the physiology of reason, with the origin of concepts" (18: 14), "Locke examines and search for the genesis and the origin of our ideas" (28: 176), "Locke: origin of concepts" (16: 48), "Locke: origin of human concepts" (16: 62), "Locke and Leibniz worked in the previous century at the physiology of reason" (28: 377).
164. As we shall see, habits are also related to the origin of concepts in other passages (see 28: 333–34).
165. See Tonelli 1994, 226; Nuzzo 2008, 264. From the late 1760s, Kant employs the expression "transcendental physiology" to characterize either the science in which "the data from experience in accordance with the relations of space and time are given in such a way that the most universal concept of the object of all outer and inner sensations can be taken and the ground thereof can be sought" (17: 362), or the transcendental knowledge of the world and of God (A 846/B 874).
166. See Kant 1998, 28.
167. Paton 1936: 78.
168. See Tonelli 1994: 285.
169. Capozzi 2002: 303. 1770 was a crucial year for Locke in Prussia. Frederick II established that his *Essay* had to be the reference for the teaching of logic and metaphysics in all the universities of the realm (see Brandt 1981: 45). The impact of facultative logic in Königsberg, mediated on the one hand by Eclectic textbooks such as Budde's *Elementa philosophiae instrumentalis* (1703) and Syrbius's *Institutiones philosophiae primae novae et eclecticae* (1719), and, on the other hand, by Wolffian manuals such as Meier's *Vernunftlehre*, is well known. Knutzen's *Elementa philosophiae rationalis seu logica* was even an attempt to meld the Lockean perspective with Wolffian philosophy. In

addition, as we have seen, Georg David Kypke was the author in 1755 of a successful translation of Locke's *Of the Conduct of the Understanding*. We know that Kant had read Locke's *Essay* in a Latin edition, probably from Gottfried Heinrich Thiele's Latin edition (see Locke 1741; Pollock 2004).

170. On the relation between Locke and Kant, see the papers in Thompson 1991.
171. See Capozzi 2002: 257. I agree with Hanna's position; see Hanna 2001: 16–44; Hanna 2006: 77–115.
172. See Oberhausen 1997: 151–53, 165–76; Longuenesse 1998: 251–53; Rumore 2007: 217.
173. Tonelli 1974b: 437. On the impact of the *Nouveaux Essais*, see Böhm 1906; Merten 1908; Vaihinger 1922, 1: 49; De Vleeschauwer 1934: 147.
174. Tonelli 1974b: 453.
175. See Tonelli 1974b: 438.
176. See *GP* 5: 67.
177. See *GP* 5: 74.
178. See *GP* 5: 83.
179. See *GP* 5: 97.
180. See *GP* 5: 75.
181. See Eberhard 1789a; Eberhard 1789b.
182. See Eberhard 1789b: 388. Rumore 2007 has particularly insisted on this point.
183. Schmid 1788: 9–10.
184. Eberhard 1789b: 388.
185. See Rosales 2000: 87; Longuenesse 1998: 221–25, 251–53. Kant summarizes this conception in *The Dohna Metaphysics* (1792/93) (28: 619).
186. For minor differences in the theory of original acquisition between the *Inaugural Dissertation* and *On a Discovery*, see Quarfoord 2004, 86–87.
187. There is a little agreement about what epigenesis really was for Kant and many scholars have emphasized his ambivalent attitude toward this theory, see Wubnig 1969; Genova 1974; Zöller 1988; Ingesiep 1994; Piché 2001; Sloan 2002; Zammito 2003; Mensch 2013.
188. See Zammito 2003, 85; Zöller 1988, 80–84.

189. Piché 2001, 187–91.
190. Piché 2001, 189.
191. For Kant, as we shall see, dispositions are not unfolded or expanded, but progressively developed in the course of experience.
192. Sloan 2002: 230–41.
193. In B 168 Kant is quite explicit on this point stating that the categories of cause, "which asserts the necessity of a consequent under a presupposed condition, would be false if it rested only on a subjective necessity, arbitrarily implanted in us, of combining certain empirical representations according to such a rule of relation."
194. Zammito 2002: 1–14.
195. Of this opinion are Quarfoord 2004: 109; Mensch 2013: 204.
196. Leibniz 1778: 165–66, 204.
197. Tetens 1777, 2: 434.
198. Ibid.: 429.
199. Ibid.: 440.
200. Ibid.: 447.
201. Ibid.: 434.
202. Ibid.: 428.
203. Ibid.: 445.
204. Ibid.: 446
205. Tetens 1777, 1: 732.
206. Ibid.
207. Ibid.
208. Ibid.: 733.
209. Ibid.
210. Ibid.: 734.
211. Ibid.
212. Ibid.: 730.
213. Zammito 2003: 93, 96.
214. See Mensch 2013: 110–24.
215. Ingesiep 1994: 385.
216. Quarfoord 2004: 102–3.
217. See Wubnig 1969: 151.
218. Genova 1974: 270.
219. Zöller 1988: 88.

220. See De Vleschauwer 1934: 270.
221. Zöller 1988: 86.
222. Zöller 1988: 87.
223. Kant in this *Reflection*, however, crosses out "transcendental."
224. Van Cleve 1999: 105.
225. Keeping in mind that in Aristotle's logic the temporal dimension is lacking in the characterization of the categories.

CHAPTER 2. TRANSCENDENTAL LOGIC

1. For instance in a judgment, the subject and the predicate are the matter, while the copula is what gives the form. In a syllogism, the matter is the content of the premises, while the consequence, as containing premises, is the form (9: 91, 101, 105).
2. Wolff 1740: 155.
3. For a detailed reconstruction of the topic see Rumore 2007: 195–96.
4. See Aristotle, *Metaphysics*, I.1, 981 a 15–16.
5. See Aristotle, *Metaphysics*, I.1, 981 b 10–11.
6. See Aristotle, *Metaphysics*, I.1, 981 b 21–28.
7. Aristotle, *Nicomachean Ethics*, I.7, 1098 a 25–35. See Pozzo 1998b.
8. See Pozzo 1998b: 153.
9. See Alsted 1621: 11; Calov 1640: 26.
10. Zabarella 1597: 502e. On this shift, see Pozzo 2012.
11. Calov 1640: 28.
12. Ibid.: 28–29.
13. See Nuchelmans 1983: 223–24.
14. *CL*, 432–34.
15. *CL*, 520.
16. Ibid.
17. See Crusius 1766: 48.
18. Knutzen 1747: 5.
19. Ibid.: 6.
20. See Pollok 2001: 267–73; Friedman 2013: 164.
21. See Euler 1750: 328.
22. Ibid.: 324.
23. Ibid.: 331.
24. See Falkenstein 1995: 48.

25. See Falkenstein 1995: 338–39.
26. See Euler 1960: 325.
27. See Menne 1974; Wilson 1975; Fries 1975; Capozzi 1980; Capozzi 1981; Capozzi 1982; Capozzi 1983; Martin 1985; Capozzi 1989; Capozzi 1994; Malzkorn 1995; Barone 1999; Capozzi 2002: 211–20.
28. Aristotle, *Topics*, I.1, 100 a 25–27.
29. Aristotle, *Prior Analytics*, I.4, 25 b 37–39.
30. See Bochenski 1951: 44.
31. Aristotle, *Prior Analytics*, I.4, 25 b 37–26 a 1.
32. Llull 1984: 174.
33. Ibid.
34. See Rossi 1960.
35. Goclenius 1613: 13–14.
36. See Welch 1990.
37. *OP* 1: 419.
38. *OP* 1: 162.
39. See ibid.
40. See *GP* 4: 30; *OP*, 1: 162.
41. See *OP* 1: 163.
42. See *OP* 1: 164.
43. *CL*: 430.
44. See *CL*: 431.
45. *OP* 1: 82.
46. *GP* 7: 204–5.
47. *GP* 7: 198–99.
48. See *GP* 7: 199.
49. *GP* 7: 200.
50. *GP* 7: 20, see GP 7: 297–98.
51. For a detailed examination of these three aspects, see Mori 1996: 482–83.
52. Barone 1999: 71.
53. Hobbes 1839: II.9.
54. Ibid.: III.3.
55. Locke 1975: III.3.3.
56. Ibid.: III.8.1.
57. Ibid.: III.8.2.
58. Brucker 1723: 238–39.
59. Baumgarten 1779: 43.
60. Baumgarten 1773: 17.

61. Ibid.: 17–18.
62. Ibid.: 21.
63. Ibid.
64. Ibid.
65. Ibid.: 22.
66. Hollmann 1767: 136.
67. Ibid.: 131–32.
68. Crusius 1747, 169.
69. Ibid.: 170.
70. Ibid.: 171.
71. Ibid.: 216–17.
72. Ibid.: 217.
73. *CL*: 511.
74. Wolff 1718: 121.
75. Gerhardt 1860: 18. See Corr 1975.
76. See Campo 1939: 43.
77. See Arndt 1965; Corr 1972.
78. Wolff 1738: 210.
79. Ibid.: 216.
80. See Campo 1939: 90–96.
81. See Wolff 1740: 377. Kant shares with Wolff many other views on logic, but they were quite common in eighteenth-century textbooks on logic, while the doctrine of prosyllogism and episyllogism was particularly stressed by the Wolffian position.
82. See Meier 1752b: 112. See Pozzo 2000.
83. Wolff 1740: 377.
84. See Warda 1922: 38.
85. See Bernoulli 1744: 220.
86. See Capozzi 1994: 57.
87. Bernoulli 1744: 217.
88. Ibid.: 218.
89. See Sgarbi 2010e.
90. See Warda 1922: 35.
91. See ibid.: 32.
92. Segner 1732; Segner 1734. For an exhaustive and extremely rich analysis of Segner see Capozzi 1988, to which I am very indebted.
93. Segner 1740: 9.
94. See Segner 1740: *Dedication*.
95. See Capozzi 1988: CLIV.
96. Segner 1740: *Dedication*.

97. See Capozzi 1989: 307.
98. Segner 1740: 105.
99. Ibid.: 3.
100. See Capozzi 1989: 307–8.
101. Segner 1740: 65.
102. Ibid.
103. Ibid.: 66.
104. Ibid.: 67.
105. See Capozzi 1988: CLXV–CLXVI.
106. See Bök 1766.
107. Ibid.: 31.
108. Ibid.
109. Ibid.
110. Ibid.: 36.
111. Bök 1766: 257–59.
112. Barone 1999: 90.
113. Bök 1766: 46–47.
114. Ibid.: 50.
115. Ibid.: 51.
116. Bernoulli 1781, 1: 96.
117. Lambert 1765: 442.
118. See ibid.: 444, 446.
119. See Lambert 1782: 15.
120. See ibid.: 16.
121. See ibid.: 17.
122. See ibid.: 55.
123. See ibid.: 56.
124. For an insightful analysis of Leibniz's standpoint, see Barone 1999: 117.
125. Lambert 1764: 5–6.
126. Ibid., 418.
127. Barone 1999: 115
128. See Darjes 1738.
129. Darjes 1742: *Preface*.
130. Ibid.
131. Ibid.: 101.
132. Ibid.: 104.
133. See Warda 1922: 55.
134. Sulzer 1755: 34.
135. See ibid.: 9.

136. See ibid.
137. See ibid.: 10.
138. See ibid.: 11.
139. See ibid.
140. See ibid.: 15.
141. See ibid.: 16.
142. See ibid.: 17–18.
143. See ibid.: 32.
144. See ibid.: 7–8.
145. Bernoulli 1782: 412.
146. Tonelli 1959a: 204.
147. Sulzer 1758, 437–38.
148. Segner 1742: 18.
149. Thomasius 1688: 166.
150. Ibid.: 167.
151. Ibid.: 167–68.
152. See ibid.: 168. See Thomasius 1710: 185.
153. Kant 1998: 279.
154. Schultz replies to Kant: "The ingenious idea of using the table of categories to invent an *ars characteristica combinatoria*, which you were kind enough to suggest to me, is most excellent and I agree completely that if such an invention were possible at all it would have to be done in this way" (10: 354).
155. See Capozzi 2001: 217–19.
156. Riehl 1908, 310.
157. For a complete overview on the debate, see Ertl 2002.
158. We must be wary of taking too seriously Kant's statements on his own life, because his frequent mistakes or inaccuracies are well known.
159. See Crusius 1747: 243–45; Lambert 1764: 472–77; Lambert 1771, 1: 1; Lambert 1782, 15–56. In Crusius, the doctrine of the irresolvable concepts is compared with the doctrine of the Aristotelian categories, but the latter is criticized because categories are primarily conceived as the highest kinds of being.
160. Beck 1969: 464.
161. See Lee 2004.
162. Lambert 1782: 518.
163. Ibid.: 517.
164. Ibid.
165. We cannot establish with certainty that Kant knew Lambert's

thought. In the correspondence there is no evidence to support this hypothesis.
166. See Seung 1969: 55; Tonelli 1976b.
167. Thomasius 1688: 140; Hollmann 1767: 127.
168. See Görland 1909.
169. See Huhn 1926; Paton 1931; Lugarini 1956.
170. See Seung 1989.
171. See Tonelli 1958; Tonelli 1964; Tonelli 1976.
172. Owens 1960–1961: 73–90.
173. See Aristotle, *Categories*, 2, 1 a 16–17.
174. See Aristotle, *Categories*, 2, 2 a 5–10.
175. See Engmann 1976, 259–65.
176. See Aristotle, *Metaphysics*, V.7, 1017 a 22–23.
177. See Aristotle, *Metaphysics*, VI.2, 1027 a 13–15.
178. See Longuenesse 2005: 97–8. See Martin 2006: 42–73.
179. On the completeness claim see Lu-Adler 2016a.
180. See Tolley 2012: 426–28.
181. See Seung 1969: 5.
182. See Aristotle, *On Interpretation*, I.5, 17 a 8–9.
183. See Aristotle, *On Interpretation*, I.5, 17 a 21–22.
184. See Aristotle, *On Interpretation*, I.7, 17 a 38–40.
185. See Aristotle, *On Interpretation*, I.12, 21 a 34–36.
186. See Brandt 1991: 87.
187. See ibid.: 65.
188. See Pozzo 2007b.
189. This examination of Aristotelian categories probably comes from Johann Jakob Brucker, who not only shares with Kant some depreciative opinions but also employs a similar terminology. See Brucker 1742–44, 1: 806–7.
190. Brandt 1991: 70–71.
191. See Tonelli 1958: 132.
192. See Gilde 1933: 162.
193. See Rabe 1703c.
194. See Pace 1597: 26.
195. Tonelli 1994: 165.
196. Ibid.: 166. See Risse 1964: 280, 348; Risse 1970: 315.
197. See Rabe 1704a, 66. Rabe quotes from the *Aristotelis opera omnia quae extant graece et latine, veterum ac recentiorum interpretum ut Adriani Turnebi, Isaaci Casauboni, Julii Pacii studio emendatissima*, which is likely the same edition listed in

Kant's library with the signature "Aristotelis opera gr. et lat. in 8°," see Warda 1922, 45. See Walter 2013.
198. See ibid.: 67.
199. See ibid.: 65.
200. See Rabe 1703b, 327.
201. See Tonelli 1956a, 120–39.
202. See Tonelli 1966, 135–42.
203. See Tonelli 1964: 240; Seung 1969: 16; Brandt 1991: 65.
204. See Conrad 1994: 75–118; Hinske 1995; Pozzo 2001.
205. See Tonelli 1964: 239.
206. Darjes 1742: 206.
207. Tonelli 1964, 239–40.
208. See Hinske 1983: X; Hinske 1998: 28; Hinske 1999: 27–31.
209. See Hinske 1999: 28.
210. Ibid. Elfriede Conrad substantially agrees with Hinske; see Conrad 1994: 75–118.
211. Meier 1752a: 2.
212. I share Capozzi's view; see Capozzi 2001: 31–44.
213. See Capozzi 2001: 32–33.
214. Brucker 1742–44, 1: 805.
215. Aristotle, *Topics*, I.1, 100 a 18–21. Translation mine.
216. Aristotle, *Topics*, I.1, 100 a 25–27.
217. Aristotle, *Topics*, I.1, 100 b 21–23.
218. Aristotle, *Topics*, I.1, 100 b 24–26. Emphasis mine.
219. See Aristotle, *Topics*, I.1, 101 a 4.
220. See Aristotle, *Topics*, I.1, 101 a 5.
221. Berti 2004: 326. On the cognitive value of Aristotle's dialectic, see Bolton 1990.
222. On "canon" and "organon," see Carboncini–Finster 1982; Tonelli 1994, 37–134.
223. See Funaki 2002: 63–77.
224. See Berti 1987: 149.
225. See Funaki 2002: 222–30.
226. See Rabe 1703a: 1.
227. See ibid.: 2–3.
228. Ibid.: 3.
229. Ibid.
230. See Rabe 1703b: 302. Rabe does not state explicitly that analytic is a science a priori like Kant, however he distinguishes the two uses of this science. Analytic is a priori if the analysis of the

logical structure is aimed at finding the formal conditions and rules of reasoning in themselves (*in se*), while it is a posteriori if these rules and conditions are applied to something else (*per alium*). See Rabe 1703b, 306.
231. See Rabe 1703a: 11.
232. See ibid.: 12.
233. See ibid. 10–11.
234. See Tonelli 1964: 240.
235. See Wolff 1740: 463.
236. See Micheli 1980: 90–97.
237. See Micheli 1980: 132.
238. Brucker 1742–44, 1: 1169–70.
239. See Micheli 1980: 132–33.
240. See ibid.: 134–35.
241. See ibid.: 136–39.
242. See Hinske 1991: L–LII.
243. Rabe 1704: 43.
244. See Hedio 1686: 80–86.
245. See Rabe 1703a: 59–60.
246. See Rabe 1703b: 1222–23.
247. Tonelli 1994: 168. Despites Tonelli's assertion, in my research I have never found a philosopher supporting gnostology as a part of physics.
248. See Rabe 1703b: 1205.
249. See ibid.
250. See ibid.: 1206.
251. See ibid.
252. See ibid.: 1207.
253. See ibid.
254. See ibid.

CHAPTER 3. METHODOLOGY

1. Aristotle, *Physics*, I.1, 184 a 16–18. Translation mine.
2. Cf. Aristotle, *Metaphysics*, II.1, 993 b 7–11.
3. Aristotle, *Physics*, I.1, 184 a 21–b 1.
4. Aristotle, *Posterior Analytics*, I.3, 72 b 32–35.
5. See Aristotle, *Posterior Analytics*, I.2, 71 b 21–22.
6. Aristotle, *Nicomachean Ethics*, I.2, 1095 b 6–7.

7. Aristotle, *Prior Analytics*, II.23, 68 b 35–37.
8. See Aristotle, *Topics*, VIII.1, 156 a 4–7.
9. Aristotle, *Metaphysics*, VII.4, 1029 b 3.
10. Aristotle, *Metaphysics*, VII.4, 1029 b 10–12.
11. Aristotle, *Metaphysics*, II.3, 995 a 8–10.
12. Aristotle, *Metaphysics*, II.3, 995 a 10–11.
13. Aristotle, *Metaphysics*, II.3, 995 a 11–14.
14. Aristotle, *Metaphysics*, II.3, 995 a 14–16.
15. For a general discussion on the argument, Gilbert 1960; Risse 1963; Vasoli 1968.
16. Zabarella 1602: 135 A.
17. Zabarella 2009: 7.
18. Zabarella 1602: 226 C.
19. Zabarella 2009: 7.
20. Zabarella 1602: 139 B.
21. Ibid.: 230 E–F.
22. Ibid.: 266 E.
23. Ibid.: 266 F.
24. Ibid.: 267 A–B.
25. Ibid.: 267 D.
26. Ibid.: 267 D–E.
27. Ibid.: 481 A–B.
28. Ibid.: 485 B.
29. Ibid.: 486 C–D.
30. Ibid.: 486 F.
31. Ibid.: 487 A–B.
32. Ibid.: 235 A, 247 A–B.
33. See Zabarella 1597: 663 F.
34. See ibid.: 667 A–670 F.
35. See ibid.: 672 B.
36. See ibid.: 1271 E.
37. See ibid.: 1271 F.
38. See ibid.: 345 C.
39. Calov 1651: 1039.
40. Ibid.
41. See ibid.
42. See ibid.: 1040.
43. Ibid.
44. See ibid.: 1040–41.

45. Ibid.: 1048.
46. Ibid.
47. Ibid.: 1049.
48. Ibid.
49. Ibid.: 1050.
50. Ibid.: 1051.
51. Ibid.
52. Ibid.
53. Ibid.: 1052.
54. See ibid.: 1058.
55. See ibid.: 1059.
56. See ibid.: 1148.
57. Ibid.: 584.
58. Rabe 1704: 187.
59. Ibid.: 188.
60. Ibid.: 190.
61. Ibid.: 190.
62. Ibid.: 191. For a similar defense of Aristotelianism and attack to modern philosophy, see also the *Dissertatio prima de orthodoxia Aristotelis philosophica a recentioribus temere impugnata*, published by Martin Coelestin Kowalewski in 1729 in Königsberg.
63. See ibid.: 184.
64. See ibid.: 190–93.
65. Thomasius 1699: 170.
66. See *AT* 10: 362.
67. *AT* 10: 366.
68. *AT* 10: 368.
69. *AT* 10: 369.
70. *AT* 7: 155.
71. *AT* 10: 379.
72. *AT* 7: 155–57.
73. See *AT* 6: 17.
74. See ibid.
75. See ibid.
76. See *AT* 6: 17–18.
77. See *AT* 6: 18.
78. See Risse 1963: 281.
79. *AT* 6: 19.
80. See Tonelli 1959d.

81. See *GP* 7: 323
82. See ibid.
83. See *GP* 7: 324.
84. See ibid.
85. See *GP* 7: 325.
86. See ibid.
87. *GP* 7: 296–27.
88. *GP* 7: 297. Italics is mine.
89. *GP* 7: 297–28.
90. On Wolff's methodological conceptions, see Campo 1939: 39–123; Wagner 1939; Paolinelli 1974; Frängsmyr 1975; Engfer 1986; Marcolungo 1989; Marcolungo 2004; Gómez Tutor 2004; Gómez Tutor 2007; Goubet 2007.
91. See Martin 1967.
92. See Wolff 1710: 5.
93. Ibid.: 31.
94. Wolff 1713: 5, 16.
95. Wolff 1716: 889–90.
96. See Wolff 1740: 445.
97. See ibid.: 634.
98. See Tonelli 1976a: 199; Gómez Tutor 2004: 100–101.
99. See Wolff 1740: 635.
100. See Wolff 1738: 356.
101. See Wolff 1740: 444.
102. See Paolinelli 1974: 37.
103. Wolff 1938: 215–16.
104. Ibid.
105. See Wolff 1741: 386, 391.
106. See Wolff 1736: 91.
107. See Wolff 1741: 394.
108. See ibid.: 392–449.
109. Ibid.: 449.
110. Wolff shares this view with some of his opponents such as Andreas Rüdiger and Christian August Crusius, who maintained that mathematical notions were imaginary and arbitrarily constructed. See Tonelli 1959b: 56.
111. See Tonelli 1959a: 1.
112. See Tonelli 1959a: 24.
113. See Tonelli 1959a: 18–21.
114. See Tetens 1760: 16.

115. See Harnack 1900: 306–7.
116. Kant has a different opinion from Moses Mendelssohn, the winner of the Academy prize, who maintains that mathematics was a completely analytical science. See Mendelssohn 1985, 2: 273–79.
117. I translate *unauflöslich* with *irresolvable* rather than *unanalyzable*.
118. See Stark 1999; Sgarbi 2010e.
119. Tonelli emphasizes particularly this aspect in Tonelli, 1994: 4.
120. Cohen 1871: 11–12.
121. Posy 1992: 3.
122. Friedman 2005: 263.
123. See Sgarbi 2010d.
124. See Ferrarin 1995: 149–51, 160, 163, 174; Ferrarin 2006.
125. There is no systematic theory of the synthetic a priori nature of mathematics in Kant's reflections before 1783, or in the lecture notes such as the *Wiener Logic*, *Hechsel Logic*, *Pölitz Logic*, or in the *Philosophical Encyclopedia*. See Sgarbi 2010d.
126. See Calov 1651: 1039.
127. See Peters 1962–66; Peters 1966; Ferrarin 1995; Micheli 1998: 29–47.
128. Kant is referring here to the formal intuition (B 160).
129. See Micheli 1998: 32.
130. Beck 1969.
131. The Aristotelian distinction of κατ'ἄνθρωπον-κατ'ἀλήθειαν has huge repercussions among the Eclectic philosophers. Christian Thomasius expresses the distinction in terms of *notiora natura* and *notiora nobis*, and it almost completely exhausts his doctrine of method (Thomasius 1688: 177–80). In Adolf Friedrich Hoffmann the distinction κατ'ἄνθρωπον-κατ'ἀλήθειαν occurs to characterize the difference of the postulates within a demonstration, to determine the kind of truth and demonstration (Hoffmann 1737: 5–6, 573, 992–93). Christian August Crusius follows his mentor Hoffmann and employs the distinction to define the kinds of postulates and demonstration (Crusius 1747: 64–6, 939–40). Also in Samuel Christian Hollmann, κατ'ἄνθρωπον-κατ'ἀλήθειαν characterizes different kinds of demonstration grounded in alleged various true principles (Hollmann 1767: 650).

132. See Zabarella 1597, 1271e.
133. Kemp Smith 1923: 579: "the section is of slight scientific importance, and is chiefly of interest for the light which it casts upon Kant's personality. Moreover the distinctions which Kant here draws are for the most part not his own philosophical property, but are taken over from the Wolffian system." For a partial re-evaluation of Kant's architectonic, see Manchester 2003.
134. See Hinske 1999: 133–55.
135. Meier 1752b: 26. On Meier's concept of "system," see Schwarz 2001, 85–93.
136. Wolff 1740: 635.
137. Also in the lectures on logic of the 1780s and in the fragment of the same period, Meier's passage is commented on in the same way (24: 530–1; 16: 476; 9: 72, 139).
138. See Tonelli 1994: 254; Manchester 2003: 288.
139. Lambert 1771, 1: front matter.
140. Lambert 1771: XVIII–XXIX.
141. See ibid.: VIII.
142. See ibid.: 35–36.
143. Lambert 1782: 510.
144. See ibid.: 514.
145. Baumgarten 1779: 2.
146. See ibid.: 213.
147. See Wolff 1729: 314.
148. Tonelli 1994: 255.
149. Calov 1651: 1040.
150. Ibid.: 1074.
151. See ibid.: 1076.
152. Tonelli 1994: 251.

CONCLUSION

1. See Kuhnert 1926; Krollmann 1927.
2. See Lavrinovic 2004: 350.
3. See Tondel 2004: 400, 402, 404, 413.
4. See Stich 2004: 428.
5. See Tondel 2004: 413.
6. See ibid.

BIBLIOGRAPHY

PRIMARY SOURCES

Alsted, J. H. 1612. *Philosophia digne restituta. Libros quatuor praecognitorum philosophicorum complectens.* Herborn.

———. 1621. *Metaphysicae brevissima delineatio.* Herborn.

Arnauld, A., and Nicole, P. 1878. *La logique de Port-Royal.* Paris.

Arnoldt, D. H. 1746. *Ausführliche und mit Urkunden versehene Historie der Königsbergischen Universität.* Königsberg.

Baumeister F. C. 1774. *Institutiones philosophiae rationalis methodo Wolfii conscriptae.* Wittenberg.

Baumgarten, A. G. 1753. *Acroasis logica.* Halle.

———. 1779. *Metaphysica.* Halle.

Bernoulli, J. 1744. *Opera omnia.* Geneve.

———. 1781. *Heinrich Lamberts deutscher gelehrter Briefwechsel.* Berlin.

Bök, A. F. 1766. *Sammlung der Schriften, welche den logichen Calcul Herrn Prof. Ploucquets betreffen mit neuen Zusätzen.* Frankfurt-Jena.

Brucker, J. J. 1723. *Historia philosophica doctrinae de ideis.* Augsburg.

———. 1742–44. *Historia critica philosophiae.* Leipzig.

Calov, A. 1640. *Metaphysica divina.* Rostock.

———. 1651. *Scripta philosophica.* Lübeck.

Crusius, C. A. 1747. *Weg zur Gewissheit*. Leipzig.
———. 1766. *Entwurf der nothwendigen Vernunft-Wahrheiten*. Leipzig.
Darjes, J. G. 1738. *De arithmetica quod sit summae scientiae species*. Jena.
———. 1742. *Introductio in artem inveniendi, seu Logicam theoretico-practicam, qua Analytica atque Dialectica usum et jussu auditorum suorum methodo iis commoda proponuntur*. Jena.
Dreier, C. 1644. *Sapientia sive philosophia prima*. Königsberg.
Eberhard, J. A. 1789a. "Ueber den Ursprung der menschlichen Erkenntniß." *Philosophisches Magazin* 1: 290–306.
———. 1789b. "Ueber den wesentlichen Unterschied der Erkenntniß durch die Sinne und durch den Verstand." *Philosophisches Magazin* 1: 369–405.
Eifler, M. 1651. *Habitus intelligentiae disputatio*. Königsberg.
Euler, L. 1750. "Réflexions sur l'espace et le tems." *Memoires de l'Académie des Sciences de Berlin* 4: 324–33.
Fromme, V. 1631. *Gnostologia*. Wittenberg.
Geilfus, J. G. 1662. *Intelligentia seu primorum principiorum habitus*. Tübingen.
Georgi, H. 1716. *Philosophia propaedeutica*. Königsberg.
Gerhardt, C. 1860. *Briefwechsel zwischen Leibniz und Christian Wolff aus den Handschriften der Königlichen Bibliothek zu Hannover*. Halle.
Goclenius, R. 1613. *Lexicon philosophicum*. Frankfurt.
Gutke, G. 1625. *Habitus primorum principiorum seu intelligentiae*. Berlin.
Hedio, A. 1686. *Organum Aristoteleum ad vera Aristotelis et ad Graecorum mentem ac methodum ex optimis interpretibus vetustioribus ac recentioribus concinnatum*. Königsberg.
Hobbes, T. 1839. *Opera philosophica quae latine scripsit*. London.
Hoffmann, A. F. 1737. *Vernunft-Lehre*. Leipzig.
Hollmann, S. C. 1767. *Philosophia rationalis quae logica vulgo dicitur*. Göttingen.
Kant, I. 1998. *Logik-Vorlesungen. Unveröffentlichte Nachschriften I–II*. Hamburg.
Keckermann, B. 1601. *Systema logicae*. Hanau.
Knutzen, M. 1747. *Elementa philosophiae rationalis seu Logicae cum generalis tum specialioris mathematica methodo in usum auditorum suorum demonstrata*. Königsberg-Leipzig.

Lambert, J. H. 1765. "De universaliori calculi idea, disquisitio, una cum adnexo specimine." *Nova acta eruditorum* 6: 441–73.

———. 1768. *Neues Organon*. Leipzig.

———. 1771. *Anlage zur Architectonic, oder Theorie des Einfachen und des Ersten der philosophischen und mathematischen Erkenntnis*. Riga.

———. 1782. *Logische und philosophische Abhandlungen*. Berlin.

Llull, R. 1984. *Ars Brevis*. Turnhout.

Leibniz, G. W. *Philosophische Werke*. Halle.

Locke, J. 1741. *Libri IV. de intellectv hvmano: denvo ex novissima editione idiomatis anglicani, longe accvratiori in pvriorem stylvm latinvm translati*. Leipzig.

———. 1975. *An Essay Concerning Human Understanding*. Oxford.

———. 1996. *Of the Conduct of the Understanding: Anleitung des menschlichen Verstandes. Eine Abhandlung von den Wunderwerken in der Übersetzung Königsberg 1755 von Georg David Kypke*. Stuttgart-Bad Cannstatt.

Malebranche, N. 1688. *De la récherche de la vérité*. Amsterdam.

Meier, G. 1662. *Gnostologia*. Wittenberg.

Meier G. F. 1752a. *Vernunftlehre*. Halle.

———. 1752b. *Auszug aus der Vernunftlehre*. Halle.

Melanchthon, P. 1846. *Erotemata dialectices*, in *Corpus Reformatorum*. Halle.

Mendelssohn, M. 1985. *Gesammelte Schriften*. Vol. 10. Stuttgart-Bad Cannstatt.

Morhof, D. G. 1688–1692. *Polyhistor sive de notitia auctorum et rerum commentari*. Lübeck.

Nöbe, G. 1636. *De functionibus intellectus humani rectificandis ac dirigendis a logica*. Königsberg.

Nolle, H. 1617. *Gnostica*. Steinfurt.

Pace, G. 1597. *In Porphyrii Isagogen, et Aristotelis Organum Commentarius Analyticus*. Frankfurt am Main.

Rabe, P. 1703a. *Dialectica et Analytica scientiarum biga utilissima, omnibusque ad solidam eruditionem contendentibus maxime necessaria*. Berlin.

———. 1703b. *Cursus philosophicus, seu Compendium praecipuarum scientiarum philosophicarum, Dialecticae nempe, Analyticae, Politicae, sub qua comprehenditur Ethicae, Physicae atque Metaphysicae, ex evidentioribus rectae rationis principiis deductum, methodo scientifica adornatum, et brevi atque perspicuo stylo concinnatum, gratiam non solum Philosophiae cultorum ex professo, sed et imprimis eorum, qui tantum ex ea modo haurire desiderant, quantum sibi superioribus Facultatibus usui esse potest Theologia nempe, Jurisprudentia et Medicina.* Königsberg.

———. 1703c. *Disputatio philosophica, de sede categoriarum propria, quam rectore magnificentissimo, serenissimo atque excelsissimo principe ac domino, domino Friderico Wilhelmo, regni Prussiae, et electoratus Brandenburgici haerede, &c. jussu magnifici domini pro-rectoris et amplissimi senatus, regia ad pregelam academia, pro loco ordinario, logicae et metaphysicae professionis obtinendo solenni ventilationi submittit M. Paulus Rabe, ord. respondente Johanne Jacobo Qvandt, reg. pruss. auditorio majori horis ante & pomeridianis d. 18. octobris anno MDCCIII.* Königsberg.

———. 1704. *Primitiae professionis logico-metaphysicae, sive Commentarius librum categoriarum Aristotelis.* Königsberg.

———. 1706. *Methodologia nova atque scientifica.* Berlin.

Rohde, J. J. 1722. *Meditatione philosophica qua Aristotelica sapientissimus de veritate judice.* Königsberg.

Schmid, C. C. E. 1788. *Wörterbuch zum leichtern Gebrauch der Kantischen Schriften.* Jena.

Segner, J. A. 1732. *De syllogismo.* Jena.

———. 1734. *De syllogismo dissertationem alteram.* Jena.

———. 1740. *Specimen logicae universaliter demonstratae.* Jena.

Sulzer, J. C. 1755. *Facies nova doctrinae syllogisticae qua multo plures modi figurarum syllogisticarum facillimis et certissimis reguilis proponuntur quam hactenus exhibiti sunt.* Zürich.

Sulzer, J. G. 1758. "Analyse de la raison." *Histoire de l'Académie Royale des Sciences et Belles Lettres* 1: 414–42.

Tetens, J. N. 1760. *Gedancken über einige Ursachen, warum der Metaphysik nur wenige ausgemachte Wahrheiten sind, als eine Einladungs-Schrift zu seinen den 13ten October auf der neuen Bützowschen Academie anzufangenden Vorlesungen.* Bützow-Wismar.

———. 1777. *Philosophische Versuche über die menschliche Natur und ihre Entwicklung.* Leipzig.

Thomasius, C. 1688. *Introductio ad philosophiam aulicam.* Leipzig.

———. 1699. *Einleitung zu der Vernunfftlehre.* Halle.

———. 1710. *Einleitung zur Hof-Philosophie.* Frankfurt-Leipzig.

Thümmig, L. 1725–1726. *Institutiones philosophiae wolfianae.* Frankfurt.

Timpler, C. 1607. *Metaphysicae systema methodicum*. Marburg.
———. 1618. *Exercitationum philosophicarum sectiones X*. Hannover.
Wagner, G. 1670. *Disputatio gnostologica tradens affectiones gnostologicas partim genere*. Wittenberg.
Weger, L. 1630. *Prima mentis operatio logica*. Königsberg.
Wolff, C. 1710. *Der Anfangs-Gründe Aller Mathematischen Wissenschafften*. Halle.
———. 1713. *Elementa Matheseos Universae*. Halle.
———. 1716. *Mathematisches Lexicon*. Leipzig.
———. 1718. *Ratio praelectionum*. Halle.
———. 1729. *Horae subsecivae marburgenses*. Frankfurt-Halle.
———. 1736. *Philosophia prima sive Ontologia*. Frankfurt-Leipzig.
———. 1737. *De differentia nexus rerum sapientis et fatalis necessitatis nec non systematis harmoniae praestabilitae et hypothesium Spinosae luculenta commentatio*. Halle.
———. 1738. *Psychologia empirica methodo scientifica pertractata*. Frankfurt-Leipzig.
———. 1740. *Philosophia rationalis sive Logica*. Frankfurt-Leipzig.
———. 1741. *De differentia notionum metaphysicarum et mathematicarum*. Frankfurt-Leipzig.
Zabarella, J. 1597. *Opera logica*. Köln.
Zabarella, J. 1607. *De rebus naturalibus libri triginta*. Frankfurt.
Zeidler, M. 1662. *Discursus philosophicus de noologia, an peculiaris aliqua et distincta sit scientia*. Königsberg.

OTHER WORKS CITED

Adickes, E. 1889. *Immanuel Kants* Kritik der reinen Vernunft *mit einer Einleitung und Anmerkungen*. Berlin.
Allison, H. E. 1983. *Kant's Transcendental Idealism*. New Haven-London.
———. 1990. *Idealism and Freedom*. Cambridge.
———. 2001. *Kant's Theory of Taste*. Cambridge.
Ameriks, K. 1982. *Kant's Theory of Mind*. Oxford.
———. 2000. *Kant and the Fate of Autonomy*. Cambridge.
———. 2003. *Interpreting Kant's Critiques*. Oxford.
———. 2006. *Kant and the Historical Turn*. Oxford.

Arndt, H. W. 1965. "Christian Wolffs Stellung zur *ars characteristica combinatoria*." *Filosofia* 16: 743–53.

Arnoldt, E. 1881. "Kants Jugend und die fünf ersten Jahre seiner Privatdozentur im Umriss dargestellt." *Altpreußische Monatsschrift* 18: 606–86.

Auroux, S. 1993. *La logique des idées*. Montréal: Bellarmin.

Barone, F. 1999. *Logica formale e logica trascendentale. Da Leibniz a Kant*. Turin.

Bazan, B. C. 1981. "*Intellectum speculativum*: Averroes, Thomas of Aquinas, and Siger of Brabant on the Intelligibile Object." *Journal of the History of Philosophy* 19: 425–46.

Beck, L. W. 1962. "Kant's Theory of Definition." *Philosophical Review* 65: 179–91.

———. 1969. *Early German Philosophy*. Cambridge.

Berti, E. 1987. *Contraddizione e dialettica negli antichi e nei moderni*. Palermo.

———. 2004. *Nuovi studi aristotelici: I–Epistemologia, logica e dialettica*. Brescia.

Bird, G. 2006. *The Revolutionary Kant*. Chicago–La Salle.

Bochenski, I. M. 1951. *Ancient Formal Logic*. Amsterdam.

Boh, I. 1993. *Epistemic Logic in the Later Middle Ages*. London.

Böhm, P. 1906. *Die vorkritischen Schriften Kants: Ein Beitrag zur Entwicklungsgeschichte der kantischen Philosophie*. Strassburg.

Bolton, R. 1990. "The Epistemological Basis of Aristotelian Dialectic." In *Biologie, logique, et métaphysique chez Aristote*, 185–236. Edited by D. Devereux and P. Pellegrin, Paris.

Brandt, R. 1981. "Materialien zur Entstehung der *Kritik der reinen Vernunft* (John Locke und Johann Schultz)." In *Beiträge zur Kritik der reinen Vernunft*, 37–68. Edited by I. Heidemann. Berlin–Zürich–New York.

———. 1991. *Die Urteilstafel*. Kritik der reinen Vernunft *A 67–76/B 92–101*. Hamburg.

Buickerood, J. 1985. "The Natural History of the Understanding: Locke and the Rise of Facultative Logic in the Eighteenth Century." *History and Philosophy of Logic* 6: 157–90.

Campo, M. 1939. *Cristiano Wolff e il razionalismo precritico*. Milan.

———. 1953. *La genesi del criticismo kantiano*. Varese.

Carboncini, S. and Finster, R. 1982. "Das Begriffspaar Kanon-Organon." *Archiv für Begriffsgeschichte* 26: 25–59.

Capozzi M. 1980. "Osservazioni sulla riduzione delle figure sillogistiche in Kant." *Annali della Facoltà di Lettere e Filosofia dell'Università di Siena* 1: 79-98.

———. 1981. "Legge di specificazione e teoria dei concetti in Kant." In *Atti del Convegno Nazionale di Logica*, 655-84. Edited by S. Bernini. Naples.

———. 1982. "Sillogismi e proposizioni singolari: Due aspetti della critica di Wolff a Leibniz." In *La grammatica del pensiero. Logica, linguaggio e conoscenza nell'età dell'Illuminismo*, 103-50. Edited by D. Buzzetti and M. Ferriani. Bologna.

———. 1983. "Sillogismi e *ars inveniendi* in J. H. Lambert." In *Atti del Convegno Internazionale di Storia della Logica*, 271-76. Edited by V. M. Abrusci, E. Casari, and M. Mugnai, Bologna.

———. 1988. "Introduzione." In *Specimen logicae universaliter demonstratae*, XI-CLXXII. Edited by J. A. Segner. Bologna.

———. 1989. "La sillogistica di Segner." In *Atti del Convegno Internazionale di Storia della Logica: Le Teorie della Modalità*, 307-12. Edited by G. Corsi, C. Mangione, and M. Mugnai. Bologna.

———. 1994. "Il *Parallelismus* di Jakob Bernoulli." In *Atti del Congresso Internazionale Logica e filosofia della scienza: Problemi e prospettive*, 54-74. Edited by C. Cellucci, M. C. Di Maio, and G. Roncaglia. Pisa.

———. 2001. "Dialectic, Probability and Verisimilitude in Kant's Logic." In *Prospettive della logica e della filosofia della scienza*, 31-44. Edited by V. Fano, G. Tarozzi, and M. Stanzione. Soveria Mannelli.

———. 2002. *Kant e la logica I*. Naples.

Cohen, H. 1871. *Kants Theorie der Erfahrung*. Berlin.

Conrad, E. 1994. *Kants Logikvorlesungen als neuer Schlüssel zur Architektonik der* Kritik der reinen Vernunft: *Die Ausarbeitung der Gliederungsentwürfe den Logikvorlesungen als Auseinandersetzung mit der Tradition*. Stuttgart-Bad Cannstatt.

Corr, C. A. 1975. "Christian Wolff and Leibniz." *Journal of the History of Ideas* 36: 241-62.

De Pierris, G. 1987. "Kant and Innatism." *Pacific Philosophical Quarterly* 68: 285-305.

De Vleeschauwer, H. J. 1934. *La déduction transcendentale dans l'oeuvre de Kant*. Antwerpen.

Dieter, T. 2001. *Der junge Luther und Aristoteles: Eine historisch-*

systematische Untersuchung zum Verhältnis von Theologie und Philosophie. Berlin–New York.

Duchesneau, F. 1974. "Kant et la physiologie de l'entendement humain." In *Akten des 4. Internationalen Kant-Kongresses*, vol. 2: 270–6. Edited by G. Funke. Berlin–New York.

École, J. 2001. "Christian Wolffs Metaphysik und die Scholastik." In *Vernunftkritik und Aufklärung: Studien zur Philosophie Kants und seines Jahrhunderts: Norbert Hinske zum siebzigsten Geburtstag*, 115–28. Edited by H. Delfosse, M. Oberhausen, and R. Pozzo. Stuttgart–Bad Cannstatt.

Engfer, H.-J. 1986. "Zur Bedeutung Wolffs für die Methodendiskussion der deutschen Aufklärungsphilosophie: Analytische und synthetische Methode bei Wolff und beim vorkritischen Kant." In *Christian Wolff 1679–1754. Interpretationen zu seiner Philosophie und deren Wirkung*, 48–65. Edited by W. Schneiders. Hamburg.

Engmann, J. 1976. "Imagination and Truth in Aristotle." *Journal of the History of Philosophy* 14: 259–65.

Erdmann, B. 1876. *Martin Knutzen und seine Zeit: Ein Beitrag zur Geschichte der wolfischen Schule und insbesondere zur Entwicklungsgeschichte Kants*. Leipzig.

Ertl, W. 2002. "Hume's Antinomy and Kant's Critical Turn." *British Journal for the History of Philosophy* 4: 617–40.

Erler, G. 1911–12. *Die Matrikel und die Promotionsverzeichnisse der Albertus-Universität zu Königsberg*. Leipzig-Berlin.

Falkenstein, L. 1990. "Was Kant a Nativist?" *Journal of the History of Ideas* 51: 573–90.

———. 1995. *Kant's Intuitionism: A Commentary on the Transcendental Aesthetic*. Toronto.

Fehr, J. J. 2005. *"Ein wunderlicher nexus rerum": Aufklärung und Pietismus in Königsberg unter Franz Albert Schultz*. Hildesheim–Zürich–New York.

Ferrarin, A. 1995. "Construction and Mathematical Schematism: Kant on the Exhibition of a Concept in Intuition." *Kant-Studien* 86: 131–74.

———. 2006. "Lived Space, Geometric Space in Kant." *Studi Kantiani* 19: 11–30.

Frängsmyr, T. 1975. "Christian Wolff's Mathematical Method and Its Impact on the Eighteenth Century." *Journal of the History of Ideas* 36: 653–68.

Freedman, J. 1985a. "Philosophy Instruction within the Institutional Framework of Central European Schools and Universities during the Reformation Era." *History of Universities* 5: 117–66.

———. 1985b. *Deutsche Schulphilosophie im Reformationszeitalter (1500–1650). Ein Handbuch für den Hochschulunterricht.* Münster.

———. 1993. "Aristotle and the Content of Philosophy Instruction at Central European Schools and Universities during the Reformation Era (1500–1650)." *Proceedings of the American Philosophical Society* 137: 213–53.

Friedman, M. 2005. "Kant on Science and Experience." In *Early Modern Philosophy: Mind, Matter, and Metaphysics*, 262–75. Edited by C. Mercer and E. O'Neill. Oxford.

———. 2013. *Kant's Construction of Nature: A Reading of the* Metaphysical Foundations of Natural Science. Cambridge.

Fries, E. 1975. *Aristotelische Logik bei Kant.* Göttingen.

Funaki, S. 2002. *Kants Unterscheidung zwischen Scheinbarkeit und Wahrscheinlichkeit.* Frankfurt am Main.

Genova, A. C. 1974. "Kant's Epigenesis of Pure Reason." *Kant-Studien* 65: 259–73.

Gilbert, N. W. 1960. *Renaissance Concept of Method.* New York.

Gilde, L. 1933. *Beiträge zur Lebensgeschichte des Königsberger Oberhofpredigers Johann Jacob Quandt.* Stallupönen.

Görland, A. 1909. *Aristoteles und Kant.* Gießen.

Gómez Tutor, J. I. 2004. *Die wissenschaftliche Methode bei Christian Wolff.* Hildesheim–Zürich–New York.

———. 2007. *Die wissenschaftliche Methode bei Christian Wolff.* In *Christian Wolff und die europäische Aufklärung*, vol. 2: 113–23. Edited by J. Stolzenberg and O.-P. Rudolph. Hildesheim–Zürich–New York.

Gotthold, F. G. 1853. "Andenken an Johann Cunde, einen Freund Kant's und Ruhnken's." *Neue Preußische Provincial-Blätter* 3: 241–58.

Goubet, J.-F. 2007. "Das Verhältnis zwischen mathematischer Methode und Logik." In *Christian Wolff und die europäische Aufklärung*, vol. 2: 141–52. Edited by J. Stolzenberg and O.-P. Rudolph. Hildesheim–Zürich–New York.

Guyer, P. 1987. *Kant and the Claims of Knowledge.* Cambridge.

Hanna, R. 2001. *Kant and the Foundation of Analytic Philosophy.* Oxford.

———. 2006. *Kant, Science, and Human Nature*. Oxford.
Harnack, A. 1900. *Geschichte der königlich-preussischen Akademie der Wissenschaften zu Berlin*. Berlin.
Hinske, N. 1974. "Kants neue Terminologie und ihre alten Quellen. Möglichkeiten und Grenzen der elektronischen Datenverarbeitung im Felde der Begriffsgeschichte." In *Akten des 4. Internationalen Kant-Kongresses Mainz April 6–10, 1974*, vol. 1: 68–85. Berlin–New York.
———. 1983. *Lambert-Index: Stellenindex zu Johann Heinrich Lamberts* Neues Organon I. Stuttgart–Bad Cannstatt.
———. 1991. *Kant-Index Bd. 14: Personenindex zum Logikcorpus*. Stuttgart-Bad Cannstatt.
———. 1995. "Kants neue Theorie der Sinnlichkeit und ihre Sprachregelungen." In *Sensus: Sensatio*, 527–40. Edited by M. Bianchi. Florence.
———. 1998. *Zwischen Aufklärung und Vernunftkritik: Studien zum Kantschen Logikcorpus*. Stuttgart-Bad Cannstatt.
———. 1999. *Tra illuminismo e critica della ragione: Studi sul corpus logico kantiano*. Pisa.
———. 2006. "Che cosa significa e a qual fine si pratica la storia delle fonti? Alcune osservazioni di storia delle fonti sulla antinomia kantiana della libertà." *Studi Kantiani* 19: 113–20.
Horkel, J. 1855. *Der Holzkämmerer Theodor Gehr und die Anfänge des Königl: Friedrichs-Collegiums zu Königsberg nach handschriftlichen Quellen dargestellt*. Königsberg.
Ingesiep, H. W. 1994. "Die biologischen Analogien und die erkenntnistheoretischen Alternativen in Kants Kritik der reinen Vernunft B § 27." *Kant-Studien* 85: 381–93.
Kahn, C. 1981. "The Role of *Nous* in the Cognition of First Principles in Posterior Analytics II 19." In *Aristotle on Science: The Posterior Analytics*, 385–416. Edited by E. Berti. Padua.
Kemp Smith, N. 1923. *A Commentary to Kant's* Critique of Pure Reason. London.
Kitcher, P. 1990. *Kant's Transcendental Psychology*. Oxford.
———. 2011. *Kant's Thinker*. Oxford.
Klemme, H. 1994. *Die Schule Immanuel Kants*. Hamburg.
Kohnen, J. 1994. *Königsberg: Beiträge zu einem besonderen Kapitel der deutschen Geistesgeschichte des 18. Jahrhunderts*. Frankfurt am Main.

Krollmann, C. 1927. "Die Schloßbibliothek in Königsberg": *Altpreußische Forschungen* 4: 128–49.

Kühn, M. 2001. *Kant. A Biography*. Cambridge.

Kuhnert, E. 1926. *Geschichte der Staats- und Universitäts-Bibliothek zu Königsberg: Von ihrer Begründung bis zum Jahre 1810*. Leipzig.

Langel, H. 1909. *Die Entwicklung des Schulwesens in Preussen unter Franz Albrecht Schultz (1733–1763)*. Halle.

Lavrinovic, K. 2004. *Kataloge der Königsberger Bibliotheken aus der Zeit des Siebenjährigen Krieges*. In *Königsberger Buch- und Bibliotheksgeschichte*, 425–52. Edited by A. Walter. Köln-Weimar-Wien.

Laywine, A. 1993. *Kant's Early Metaphysics and the Origins of the Critical Philosophy*. Atascadero, CA.

Lee, S.-K. 2004. "The Determinate-Indeterminate Distinction and Kant's Theory of Judgment." *Kant-Studien* 95: 204–25.

Leinsle, U. G. 1988. *Reformversuche protestantischer Metaphysik im Zeitalter des Rationalismus*. Augsburg.

Lohr, C. 1999. "Metaphysics and Natural Philosophy as Sciences: The Catholic and the Protestant Views in the Sixteenth and Seventeenth Century." In *Philosophy the Sixteenth and Seventeenth Centuries: Conversations with Aristotle*, 280–95. Edited by C. Blackwell and S. Kusukawa. Aldershot.

Longuenesse, B. 1998. *Kant and the Capacity to Judge: Sensibility and Discursivity in the Transcendental Analytic of the* Critique of Pure Reason. Princeton.

———. 2005. *Kant on the Human Standpoint*. Cambridge.

Lu-Adler H. 2016a. "Kant on Proving Aristotle's Logic as Complete." *Kantian Review* 1: forthcoming.

———. 2016b. "Epigenesis of Pure Reason and the Source of Pure Cognitions: How Kant is No Nativist about Logical Cognition." In *Rethinking Kant 5*. Edited by P. Muchnik, forthcoming. Newcastle upon Tyne.

Lugarini, L. 1956. "Il principio categoriale in Aristotele e Kant." *Giornale critico della filosofia italiana* 2: 160–90.

Makkreel, R. 1990. *Imagination and Interpretation in Kant: The Hermeneutical Import of the* Critique of Judgment. Chicago.

Malzkorn, W. 1995. "Kants Kritik an der traditionellen Syllogistik." *History and Philosophy of Logic* 16: 75–88.

Manchester, P. 2003. "Kant's Conception of Architectonic in Its Historical Context." *Journal of the History of Philosophy* 41: 187–207.

Marcolungo, F. L. 1989. "Wolff e il problema del metodo." *Il cannocchiale* 2–3: 11–38.

———. 2004. "Matematica e metafisica in Christian Wolff." In *Scienza e conoscenza secondo Kant*, 333–48. Edited by A. Moretto. Padua.

Martin, G. 1985. *Arithmetic and Combinatorics: Kant and His Contemporaries*. Carbondale.

Martin, W. 2006. *Theories of Judgment*. Cambridge.

McDowell, J. H. 1994. *Mind and World*. Cambridge, MA.

———. 2009a. *Having the World in View: Essays on Kant, Hegel, and Sellars*. Cambridge, MA.

———. 2009b. *The Engaged Intellect: Philosophical Essays*. Cambridge, MA.

McRae, R. 1965. "Idea as a Philosophical Term in the Seventeenth Century." *Journal of the History of Ideas* 26: 175–90.

Menne, A. 1974. "Kants Kritik der Syllogistik." In *Akten des 4. Internationalen Kant-Kongresses*, 2: 130–4. Edited by G. Funke. Berlin–New York.

Mensch, J. 2013. *Kant's Organicism: Epigenesis and the Development of Critical Philosophy*. Chicago.

Merleker, C. F. 1847. *Annalen des Königlichen Friedrichs-Collegiums*. Königsberg.

Merten, R. 1908. *Über die Bedeutung von Leibniz Nouveaux essais sur l'entendement humain für den Standpunkt Kants der Dissertation De mundi sensibilis atque intelligibilis forma et principiis von 1770*. Erlangen.

Michael, F. S. 1997. "Why Logic Became Epistemology: Gassendi, Port Royal and the Reformation in Logic." In *Logic and the Workings of the Mind*, 1–20. Edited by P. Easton. Atascadero, CA.

Micheli, G. 1980. *Kant storico della filosofia*. Padua.

———. 1998. *Matematica e metafisica in Kant*. Padua.

———. 2002. "La terminologia aristotelico-scolastica e il lessico kantiano." In *La presenza dell'aristotelismo padovano nella filosofia della prima modernità*, 445–70. Edited by G. Piaia. Rome-Padua.

Mosser, K. 2008. "Kant's General Logic and Aristotle." *Proceedings of the XXII World Congress of Philosophy* 16: 181–89.

Mori, M. 1996. "Calcolo combinatorio e ricerca dei principi." In *Storia della filosofia IV*, 482–96. Edited by P. Rossi and C. A. Viano. Rome-Bari.

Nuchelmans, G. 1983. *Judgment and Proposition*. Amsterdam.
———. 1998. "Logic in the Seventeenth Century: Preliminary Remarks and the Constituents of the Proposition." In *The Cambridge History of Seventeenth-Century Philosophy*, 103–17. Edited by D. Garber and M. Ayers. Cambridge.
Nuzzo, A. 2008. *Ideal Embodiment: Kant's Theory of Sensibility*. Bloomington.
Oberhausen, M. 1997. *Das neue Apriori: Kants Lehre von einer "ursprünglichen Erwerbung" apriorischer Vorstellungen*. Stuttgart–Bad Cannstatt.
Oberhausen, M. and Pozzo, R. 1999. *Vorlesungsverzeichnisse der Universität Königsberg (1720–1804)*. Stuttgart–Bad Cannstatt.
Owens, J. 1960–1961. "Aristotle on Categories." *Review of Metaphysics* 14: 73–90.
Paolinelli, M. 1974. "Metodo matematico e ontologia in Christian Wolff." *Rivista di Filosofia Neo-Scolastica* 66: 3–39.
Paton, H. J. 1931. "The Key to Kant's Deduction of the Categories." *Mind* 159: 310–29.
———. 1936. *Kant's Metaphysic of Experience: A Commentary on the First Half of the* Kritik der reinen Vernunft. London.
Peters, W. S. 1962–1966. "Zum Begriff der Konstruierbarkeit bei I. Kant." *Archive for History of Exact Science* 2: 153–67.
———. 1966. "Widerspruchfreiheit und Konstruierbarkeit als Kriterien für die mathematische Existenz in Kants Wissenschaftstheorie." *Kant Studien* 57: 178–85.
Petersen, P. 1921. *Geschichte der aristotelischen Philosophie im protestantischen Deutschland*. Leipzig.
Piché, C. 2001. "The Precritical Use of the Metaphor of Epigenesis." In *New Essays on the Precritical Kant*, 182–200. Edited by T. Rockmore. New York.
Pisanski G. C. 1886. *Entwurf einer preußischen Literärgeschichte*. Königsberg.
Pollock, K. 2001. *Kants Metaphysische Anfangsgründe der Naturwissenschaft: Ein kritischer Kommentar*. Hamburg.
———. 2004. *Locke in Germany: Early German Translations of John Locke 1709–61*. Bristol.
Posy, C. 1992. "Mathematics in Kant's Critique of Pure Reason." In *Kant's Philosophy of Mathematics*, 1–17. Edited by C. Posy. Dordrecht.

Pozzo, R. 1989. *Kant und das Problem einer Einleitung in die Logik.* Frankfurt am Main.

———. 1991. "Catalogus praelectionum academiae regiomontanae 1719-1804." *Studi Kantiani* 4: 163-87.

———. 1995. "Tracce zabarelliane nella logica kantiana." *Fenomenologia e società* 18: 58-69.

———. 1998a. "Kant within the Tradition of Modern Logic: The Role of the Introduction: Idea of a Transcendental Logic." *Review of Metaphysics* 52: 295-310.

———. 1998b. "Res considerata and modus considerandi rem: Averroes, Aquinas, Jacopo Zabarella and Cornelius Martini on Reduplication." *Medioevo* 24: 151-76.

———. 2000. *Georg Friedrich Meiers "Vernunftlehre": Eine historisch-systematische Untersuchung.* Stuttgart-Bad Cannstatt.

———. 2001. "Dall''intellectus purus' alla 'reine Vernunft': Note sul passaggio dal latino al tedesco prima e dopo Kant." *Giornale critico della filosofia italiana* 90: 231-45.

———. 2002. "Melanchthon and the Paduan Aristotelians: The Shift from the Topics to the Analytics." In *Melanchthon and South-West Europe*, 53-65. Edited by G. Frank and K. Meerkhoff. Stuttgart.

———. 2003. "Ramus and Other Renaissance Philosophers on Subjectivity." *Topoi* 22: 5-13.

———. 2004a. "Logic and Metaphysics in German Philosophy from Melanchthon to Hegel." In *Approaches to Metaphysics*, 61-74. Edited by W. Sweet. Dordrecht.

———. 2004b. "Kant on the Five Intellectual Virtues." In *The Impact of Aristotelianism on Modern Philosophy*, 173-92. Edited by R. Pozzo. Washington.

———. 2007a. "La logica di Wolff e la nascita della logica delle facoltà." In *Christian Wolff tra psicologica empirica e psicologia razionale*, 45-52. Edited by F. L. Marcolungo. Hildesheim-Zürich-New York.

———. 2007b. "The Epistemic Standpoint from Kant to Hegel." *Internationale Zeitschrift für Philosophie* 2: 52-66.

———. 2007c. "Umdeutungen der aristotelischen Habituslehreder Renaissance." In *Aristotelismus in der Frühen Neuzeit*, 259-72. Edited by G. Frank and A. Speer. Wiesbaden.

———. 2008. "Aristotelismus und Eklektik in Königsberg." In *Die*

Universität Königsberg in der frühen Neuzeit, 172–85. Edited by H. Marti and M. Komorowski. Köln-Weimar-Wien.
———. 2012. Adversus Ramistas: *Kontroversen über die Natur der Logik am Ende der Renaissance*. Basel.
Quarfoord, M. 2004. *Transcendental Idealism and the Organism: Essays on Kant*. Stockholm.
Riedesel, E. 1937. *Pietismus und Orthodoxie in Ostpreußen: Auf Grund des Briefwechsels G. F. Rogalls und F. A. Schultz' mit den Halleschen Pietisten*. Königsberg.
Risse, W. 1963. "Zur Vorgeschichte der cartesischen Methodenlehre." *Archiv für Geschichte der Philosophie* 45: 268–91.
———. 1964. *Die Logik der Neuzeit (1500–1640)*. Stuttgart-Bad Cannstatt.
———. 1970. *Die Logik der Neuzeit (1640–1780)*. Stuttgart-Bad Cannstatt.
Ritschl, A. 1844. *Geschichte des Pietismus*. Bonn.
Rockmore, T. 2006. *In Kant's Wake: Philosophy in the Twentieth Century*. Oxford.
———. 2007. *Kant and Idealism*, New Haven.
———. 2011. *Kant and Phenomenology*. Chicago.
Rohls, J. 2012/2013. "Der Aristotelismus an den reformierten Ausbildungsstätten." *Wolfenbütteler Renaissance-Mitteilungen* 34: 65–84.
Rompe, E. 1968. *Die Trennung von Ontologie und Metaphysik*. Bonn.
Rosales, A. 2000. *Sein und Subjektivität bei Kant:. Zum subjektiven Ursprung der Kategorien*. Berlin–New York.
Rossi, P. 1960. Clavis Universalis: *Arti mnemoniche e logica combinatoria da Lullo a Leibniz*. Milan-Napels.
Rumore, P. 2007. *L'ordine delle idee: La genesi del concetto di "rappresentazione" in Kant attraverso le sue fonti wolffiane (1747–1787)*. Florence.
Santozki, U. 2006. *Die Bedeutung antiker Theorien für die Genese und Systematik von Kants Philosophie*. Berlin–New York.
Schönfeld, M. 2000. *The Philosophy of the Young Kant*. Oxford.
Schumacher, B. 1913. *Katalog der Lehrerbibliothek des Königlichen Friedrichs-Kollegiums zu Königsberg*. Königsberg.
Schuurman, P. 2004. *Ideas, Mental Faculties and Method: The Logic of Ideas of Descartes and Locke and Its Reception in the Dutch Republic, 1630–1750*. Leiden.

Schwarz, G. 2001. "Der Vorrang des Erkenntnisganzen in Georg Friedrich Meiers Theorie des Systems." In *Kant und die Berliner Aufklärung: Akten des IX. Internationalen Kant-Kongresses* 5: 85-93. Edited by V. Gerhardt, R.-P. Horstmann and R. Schumacher. Berlin-New York.

Sgarbi, M. 2009. "Kant, Rabe e la logica aristotelica." *Rivista di storia della filosofia* 2: 289-313.

———. 2010a. *La* Kritik der reinen Vernunft *nel contesto della tradizione logica aristotelica*. Hildesheim-Zürich-New York: Georg Olms Verlag.

———. 2010b. *Logica e metafisica nel Kant precritico: L'ambiente intellettuale di Königsberg e la formazione della filosofia kantiana*. Frankfurt am Main: Peter Lang.

———. 2010c. "Abraham Calov and Immanuel Kant: Aristotelian and Scholastic Traces in Kantian Philosophy." *Historia Philosophica* 5: 55-62.

———. 2010d. "Matematica e filosofia trascendentale in Kant: Nota a margine di una fonte dimenticata della *Kritik der reinen Vernunft*." *Philosophical Readings* 1: 209-24.

———. 2010e. *The Kant-Weymann Controversy: Two Polemical Writings on Optimism*. Verona.

———. 2011. "The Historical Genesis of Kantian Concept of Transcendental." *Archiv für Begriffsgeschichte* 53: 97-117.

———. 2012. "Il risveglio dal sonno dogmatico e la rivoluzione del 1772." *Archivio di storia della cultura* 25: 237-49.

———. 2013. "Königsberg University in Transition (1689-1722): Aristotelianism and Eclecticism in Johann Jakob Rohde's *Meditatio Philosophica*." *Studi Kantiani* 26: 125-135.

Sloan, P. R. 2002. "Preforming the Categories: Eighteenth-Century Generation Theory and the Biological Roots of Kant's A Priori." *Journal of the History of Philosophy* 40: 229-52.

Smith, N. 2000. "Plato on Knowledge as a Power." *Journal of the History of Philosophy* 38: 145-68.

Sommerfeldt, G. 1918. "Die pietistische Bibliothek zu Königsberg." *Zeitschrift für Kirchengeschichte* 37: 443-63.

Sparn, W. 1976. *Wiederkehr der Metaphysik*. Stuttgart.

———. 2001. "Die Schulphilosophie in den lutherischen Territorien." In *Grundriss der Geschichte der Philosophie: Die Philosophie des 17. Jahrhunderts. Band 4, Das Heilige Römische Reich*

Deutscher Nation. Nord- und Ost Europa, 475–606. Edited by H. Holzhey and W. Schmidt-Biggemann. Basel.

Stark, W. 1994. "Wo lehrte Kant? Recherchen zu Kants Wohnungen." In *Königsberg: Beiträge zu einem besonderen Kapitel der deutschen Geistesgeschichte des 18. Jahrhunderts*, 81–109. Edited by J. Kohnen. Frankfurt am Main.

———. 1999. "Hinweise zu Kants Kollegen vor 1770." In *Studien zur Entwicklung preussicher Universitäten*, 113–62. Edited by R. Brandt and E. Werner. Wiesbaden.

Stich, T. 2004. "Die Bibliothek Andreas Hedio." In *Königsberger Buch- und Bibliotheksgeschichte*, 417–36. Edited by A. Walter. Köln-Weimar-Wien.

Thompson, M. P., ed. 1991. *John Locke und Immanuel Kant: Historische Rezeption und gegenwärtige Relevanz*. Berlin.

Tolley, C. 2012. "The Generality of Kant's Transcendental Logic." *Journal of the History of Philosophy* 50: 417–46.

Tommasi, F. V. 2003a. "Franz Albert Aepinus, l'aristotelismo tedesco e Kant: Un contributo per la storia e il senso della filosofia trascendentale tra metafisica ed epistemologia." *Archivio di filosofia* 71: 333–58.

———. 2003b. "Kant di fronte alla tradizione del trascendentale: Stato della ricerca e prospettive alla luce di un nuovo particolare." *Studi Kantiani* 16: 53–66.

———. 2005. "Michael Piccart, Kant, e i termini primi: Il trascendentale nel rapporto tra filosofia e linguaggio." *Archivio di filosofia* 73: 369–90.

Tonelli, G. 1956a. "L'origine della tavola dei giudizi e del problema della deduzione delle categorie in Kant." *Filosofia* 7: 120–39.

———. 1956b. "Zabarella inspirateur de Baumgarten ou l'origine de la connexion entre esthétique et logique." *Revue d'Esthétique* 9: 182–92.

———. 1958. "La tradizione delle categorie aristoteliche nella filosofia moderna sino a Kant." *Studi Urbinati* 32: 121–43.

———. 1959a. *Elementi metodologici e metafisici in Kant dal 1745 al 1768*. Turin.

———. 1959b. "Der Streit über die mathematische Methode in der Philosophie in der ersten Hälfte des 18: Jahrhunderts und die Entstehung von Kants Schrift über die Deutlichkeit." *Archiv für Philosophie* 9: 37–66.

———. 1959c. "Eclettismo di Kant precritico." *Filosofia* 10: 560–73.

———. 1959d. "La question de bornes de l'entendement humain au XVIIIe siècle et la genèse du criticisme kantien, particulièrement par rapport au problème de l'infini." *Revue de Métaphysique et de Morale* 65: 396–427.

———. 1962. "Der historische Ursprung der kantischen Termini 'Analytik' und 'Dialektik.'" *Archiv für Begriffsgeschichte* 7: 120–39.

———. 1964. "Das Wiederaufleben der deutsch–aristotelischen Terminologie bei Kant während der Entstehung der 'Kritik der reinen Vernunft.'" *Archiv für Begriffsgeschichte* 9: 233–42.

———. 1966. "Die Voraussetzungen zur Kantischen Urteilstafel der Logik des 18. Jahrhunderts." In *Kritik und Metaphysik: Studien. H. Heimsoeth zum achtzigsten Geburtstag*, 126–144. Edited by F. Kaulbach and J. Richter. Berlin–New York.

———. 1971. "A priori/A posteriori II." In *Historisches Wörterbuch der Philosophie*, vol. 1, c. 467–69. Edited by Joachim Ritter. Basel.

———. 1974a. "Kant's *Critique of Pure Reason* within the Tradition of Modern Logic." In *Akten des 4. Internationalen Kant-Kongresses Mainz April 6–10, 1974*, vol. 3, 186–91. Berlin–New York.

———. 1974b. "Leibniz on Innate Ideas and the Early Reactions to the Publication of the Nouveaux Essais (1765)." *Journal of the History of Philosophy* 12: 437–54.

———. 1975. "Conditions Königsberg and the Making of Kant's Philosophy." In *Bewusst-sein*, 126–44. Edited by A. J. Bucher, H. Drüe and T. M. Seebohm. Bonn.

———. 1976a. "Analysis and Synthesis in XVIIIth Century Philosophy prior to Kant." *Archiv für Begriffsgeschichte* 20: 178–213.

———. 1976b. "Kategorie; Kategorienlehre III." In *Historisches Wörterbuch der Philosophie*, vol. 4, c. 725–27. Edited by J. Ritter and K. Gründer. Basel.

———. 1994. *Kant's* Critique of Pure Reason *within the Tradition of Modern Logic*. Hildesheim–Zürich–New York.

Vaihinger, H. 1922. *Kommentar zu Kants Kritik der reinen Vernunft*. Stuttgart.

Van Cleve, J. 1999. *Problems from Kant*. Oxford.

Vasoli, C. 1968. *La dialettica e la retorica dell'Umanesimo*. Milan.

Vollrath E. 1962. "Die Gliederung der Metaphysik in eine *Metaphysica generalis* und eine *Metaphysica specialis*." *Zeitschrift für philosophische Forschung* 16: 258–84.

Von Selle, G. 1956. *Geschichte der Albertus-Universität zu Königsberg.* Würzburg.
Vorländer K. 1924. *Immanuel Kant. Der Mann und das Werk.* Leipzig.
———. 1986. *Kants Leben.* Hamburg.
Wagner, J. 1939. *La méthode chez Christian Wolff.* Leuven.
Walter, M. 2013. "Welche Aristotelesausgabe befand sich im Besitz Kants?" *Kant-Studien* 104: 490–8.
Warda, A. 1922. *Immanuel Kants Bücher.* Berlin.
Watkins, E. 2004. *Kant's Metaphysics of Causality.* Cambridge.
Welch, J.R. 1990. "Llull and Leibniz: The Logic of Discovery," *Catalan Review* 4: 75–83.
Wilson, K. D. 1975. "The Mistaken Simplicity of Kant's Enthymematic Treatment of the Second and Third Figures." *Kant-Studien* 66: 404–17.
Wotschke, T. 1928. *Georg Friedrich Rogalls Lebensarbeit nach seinen Briefen.* Königsberg.
Wubnig, J. 1969. "The Epigenesis of Pure Reason." *Kant-Studien* 60: 147–52.
Wundt, M. 1939. *Die deutsche Schulmetaphysik des 17. Jahrhunderts.* Tübingen.
———. 1945. *Die deutsche Schulphilosophie im Zeitalter der Aufklärung.* Tübingen.
Yolton, J. 1955. "Locke and the Seventeenth-Century Logic of Ideas." *Journal of the History of Ideas* 16: 431–52.
———. 1975. "Ideas and Knowledge in Seventeenth-Century Philosophy." *Journal of the History of Philosophy* 13: 145–65.
Zammito, J. H. 2002. *Kant, Herder, and the Birth of Anthropology.* Chicago.
———. 2003. "The Inscrutable 'Principle' of an Original 'Organization': Epigenesis and 'Looseness of Fit' in Kant's Philosophy of Science." *Studies in History and Philosophy of Science* 34: 73–109.
Zippel, G. O. 1898. *Geschichte des Königlichen Friedrichs-Kollegiums zu Königsberg Pr. 1698–1898.* Königsberg.
Zöller, G. 1988. "Kant on the Generation of Metaphysical Knowledge." In *Analysen-Probleme-Kritik*, 71–90. Edited by H. Oberer and G. Seel. Würzburg.
———. 1989. "From Innate to a priori: Kant's Radical Transformation of a Cartesian-Leibnizian Legacy." *The Monist* 72: 222–35.

INDEX

Abrusci, V.M., 263
Adam, C., x
Adickes, E., 24, 60, 237, 261
Aepinus, F.A., 13, 15, 273
Agrippa von Nettesheim, H.C., 98
Allison, H.E., 225, 261
Alsted, J.H., 26-27, 30, 40-41, 82, 97-98, 237, 239, 244, 257
Ameriks, K., 225, 261
Arnauld, A., 19, 236, 257
Arndt, H.W., 246, 262
Arnoldt, D.H., 226, 233, 257
Arnoldt, E., 228, 262
Auroux, S., 19, 236, 262
Ayers, M., 269

Bacon, F., 97, 176, 196, 227, 229
Barone, F., 237, 245, 247, 262
Baumeister F.C., 13, 45-46, 235-236, 240, 257
Baumgarten, A.G., 14-15, 45-46, 80, 92, 102-107, 149, 189, 214-215, 238, 240, 245, 256-257, 273
Baumgarten, C.F., 230
Bazan, B.C., 236, 262
Beck, J.S., 127

Beck, L.W., 225, 248, 255, 262
Bernini, S., 263
Bernoulli, Jo., 108
Bernoulli, Ja., 108-110, 116, 118, 246-248, 257, 263
Berti, E., 250, 262, 266
Bianchi, M., 266
Bird, G., 4, 225, 262
Blumenbach, J.F., 59
Bochenski, I.M., 245, 262
Boh, I., 236, 262
Böhm, P., 242, 262
Böhme, J., 98
Bök, A.F., 110, 247, 257
Bolton, R., 250, 262
Bonnet, C., 59, 65
Böse, J., 9, 230
Brandt, R., 23-24, 141, 146, 225, 237, 241, 249-250, 262, 273
Brucker, J.J., 6, 8, 102-103, 152, 160, 163, 226-227, 245, 249-251, 257
Bruno, G., 97-98
Buck, F.J. 10, 14, 235-236
Buickerood, J., 19, 236, 262
Burckhard, T., 229, 231-234
Buzzetti, D., 263

Calov, A., 8, 11, 15, 18, 27–32, 34, 41–44, 74, 82, 86, 172–174, 203, 215–216, 218–219, 221–222, 227, 230, 237–239, 244, 252, 255–257, 272
Campo, M., 225, 246, 254, 262
Capozzi M., 151, 237, 241–242, 245–248, 250, 263
Carboncini, S., 250, 262
Casari, E., 263
Cellucci, C., 263
Christiani, K.A., 234–236
Cicero, ix, 43
Clauberg, J., 182
Cohen, H., 255, 263
Conrad, E., 237, 250, 263
Copernicus, N., 20, 196–197, 222
Corr, C.A., 246, 263
Corsi, G., 263
Couturat, L., x
Crusius, C.A., 14, 24, 50, 52-53, 60–63, 83, 102, 106–107, 136, 186, 192, 200, 205, 235–236, 244, 246, 248, 254–255, 258
Crusius, G., 10, 226
Cunde, J., 265

Darjes, J.G., 116, 119–120, 149, 151, 160, 162–163, 220–221, 247, 250, 258
De Pierris, G., 241, 263
De Vleeschauwer, H.J., 70, 244, 263
Delfosse, H., 264
Descartes, R., x, 19, 98, 108, 174, 176–180, 182, 185, 199, 221, 227, 237, 271
Devereux, D., 262
Di Maio, M.C., 263
Dieter, T., 226, 263
Dreier, C., 7–8, 226–227, 258
Duchesneau, F., 238, 264
Dutens, L., 56

Easton, P., 236, 268
Eberhard, J.A., 17, 56, 58–59, 108, 242, 258
École, J., 238, 264

Eifler, M., 40, 172, 218, 226,
Engfer, H.-J., 254, 264
Engmann, J., 249, 264
Erdmann, B., 228, 264
Erdmann, J.E., x
Erler, G., 264
Ertl, W., 248
Euler, L., 87, 88, 90, 244–245, 258

Falkenstein, L., 236, 241, 244–245, 264
Fano, V., 263
Feder, J.G.H., 52, 84
Fehr, J.J., 234, 264
Ferrarin, A., 255, 264
Ferriani, M., 263
Finster, R., 250, 262
Fischer, C.G., 9, 12, 230–231
Flottwell, C.C., 235
Frängsmyr, T., 254, 264
Frank, G., 270
Frederick II, 13–14, 241
Freedman, J., 226, 264
Friedman, M., 199, 244, 255, 265
Fries, E., 225, 245, 265
Fromme, V., 8, 27, 40, 237, 239, 258
Funaki, S., 250, 265
Funke, G., 264, 268

Garber, D., 269
Garve, C., 128, 140
Gassendi, P., 160, 163, 268
Gehrke, M., 230–231
Geilfus, J.G., 40, 258
Genova, A.C., 242, 243, 265
Georgi, H., 218. 227–230, 258
Gerhardt, C., x, 246, 258
Gerhardt, V., 272
Gilbert, N.W., 252, 265
Gilde, L., 249, 265
Gómez Tutor, J.I., 254, 265
Gorgias, 160
Gotthold, F.G., 228, 265
Goubet, J.-F., 254, 265
Gravesande, W.J. 's, 122
Gregoire, P., 98

INDEX 279

Gregorovious, A., 232, 234
Gründer, K., 274
Gutke, G., 8, 27, 30, 40, 237, 239, 258
Guyer, P., 225, 265

Harnack, A., 236, 255, 266
Hedio, A., 82, 161, 218, 222, 226–228, 232, 235, 251, 258, 273
Hegel, G.W.F., x, 268, 270
Heineccius, J.G., 235
Herz, M., 36, 49–50, 54, 60, 129–130, 212
Hinske, N., 151, 225, 250–251, 256, 264, 266
Hobbes, T., 101–102, 106, 245, 258
Holland, S., 113
Hollmann, S.C., 105, 107, 136, 149, 234, 246, 249, 255, 258
Holzhey, H., 273
Horkel, J., 228, 266
Hume, D., 4, 128–129

Ingesiep, H.W., 69, 242–243, 266

Jagenteufel, N., 226
Jungius, J., 98, 182

Kahn, C., 236, 266
Keckermann, B., 20, 40–41, 236, 239, 258
Kemp Smith, N., 256, 266
Kitcher, P., 225, 266
Klemme, H., 228
Knutzen, M., 10, 14, 16, 83, 85, 229–230, 234–237, 241, 244, 258, 264
Kohnen, J., 266, 273
Komorowski, M., 271
Kowalewski, M.C., 253
Kreuschner, J.H., 230
Krollmann, C., 256, 267
Kühn, M., 228, 234, 256, 267
Kuhnert, E., 256, 267
Kypke, G.D., 14, 242, 259
Kypke, J.D., 10, 12–13, 16, 218, 228, 232–235

La Crousaz, J.-P. de la, 229, 232, 235
La Mettrie, J.O., 15
Lambert, J.H., 8, 88, 113–116, 118, 120, 133, 136, 193–194, 202, 213–215, 220, 226, 247–248, 256–257, 259, 263, 266
Lange, J., 231
Langel, H., 106, 267
Lauben, M., 226
Lavrinovic, K., 256, 267
Laywine, A., 225, 267
Le Clerc, J., 231–233
Lee, S.-K., vii, 132, 248, 267
Leibniz, G.W., v, x, 4, 17, 34, 50–53, 56–57, 60, 63–64, 82–83, 85, 87–88, 94, 97–100, 102, 107–108, 112–113, 116, 119–120, 127, 134, 178–182, 185, 191, 199, 219–220, 241, 243, 247, 258–259, 262–263, 268, 271, 274, 275
Leinsle, U.G., 227
Linder, J.G., 235
Llull, R., 96, 98, 245, 259, 275
Locke, J., v, 4, 14–17, 19, 21, 25, 35, 49, 51–55, 57–58, 60–61, 69–70, 72–73, 97, 101–102, 104, 111, 114, 121, 219, 229, 230, 236, 241–242, 245, 259, 262, 269, 271, 273, 275
Lohr, C., 38, 239, 267
Longuenesse, B., 140, 242, 249, 267
Lu-Adler, H., 240, 249, 267
Lugarini, L., 249, 267
Lull, R., 96, 98, 245, 259, 275
Luther, M., 6, 263
Lysius, H., 12

Malebranche, N., 16, 19, 49–50, 54, 60, 109, 229, 241, 259
Malzkorn, W., 245, 267
Manchester, P., 213, 256, 267
Mangione, C., 263
Marcolungo, F.L., 254, 268, 270
Marquardt, K.G., 10, 13, 16, 233–235
Marti, H., 271
Martin, G., 245, 254

Martin, W., 226, 249
Martini, C., 270
Maupertuis, P.-L.M., 15
McDowell, J.H., 225, 268
McRae, R., 236, 268
Meerkhoff, K., 270
Meier G.F., 15, 46–47, 80, 84, 107, 133, 149, 151, 162, 211, 215, 240–241, 246, 250, 256, 259, 270, 272
Meier, G., 32, 227, 239–240, 259
Melanchthon, P., 6–8, 23–25 30, 42, 218, 229, 237, 259, 270
Mendelssohn, M., 194, 255, 259
Menne, A., 245, 268
Mensch, J., 242–243, 268
Mercer, C., 265
Merleker, C.F., 228
Merten, R., 242
Michael, F.S., 19, 26, 268
Michelangelo, 106
Micheli, G., 160, 225, 251, 255, 268
Moretto, A., 268
Morhof, D.G., 8, 227, 259
Mori M., 52, 57, 245, 268
Muchnik, P., 267
Mugnai, M., 263

Newton, I., 185, 187, 190
Nicole, P., 19, 236, 257
Nöbe, G., 31, 238, 259
Nolle, H., 40, 239, 259
Nuchelmans, G., 236, 244, 269
Nuzzo, A., 241, 269

O'Neill, E., 265
Oberer, H., 275
Oberhausen, M., 229, 231, 238, 241–242, 264, 269
Oelmann, H., 9, 230–232
Owens, J., 249, 269

Pace, G., 128, 148, 220, 249, 259
Pantän, L., 226
Paolinelli, M., 254, 269
Pascal, B., 108
Paton, H.J., 55, 241, 249, 269

Pellegrin, P., 262
Peters, W.S., 255, 269
Petersen, P., 226, 269
Piaia, G., 268
Piccart, M., 273
Piché, C., 243, 269
Pisanski G.C., 228–229, 269
Plato, 20–21, 34, 49–50, 52–53, 57, 60–61, 63, 98, 103–105, 159–160, 167, 222, 236, 272
Ploucquet, G., 110–113, 121, 125, 220, 257
Pollock, K., 242, 269
Posy, C., 199, 255, 269
Pouchen, L., 226
Pozzo, R., vii, 255–226, 228–231, 234, 236–237, 240, 244, 246, 249–250, 264, 269–270

Quandt, J.J., 11–12, 147, 223, 265
Quarfoord, M., 69, 242–243, 271
Quintilian, ix

Rabe, P., 9, 11, 18, 82, 128, 147–150, 156–158, 161–163, 172, 174–175, 218, 220–222, 226–234, 249–251, 253, 259–260, 272
Ramée, P. de la, 97
Rappolt, K.H., 233–235
Raspe, R.E., 56
Riehl, A., 128
Reimarus, H.S., 24
Riedesel, E., 232, 271
Risse, W., 249, 252–253, 271
Ritschl, A., 232, 271
Ritter, J., 274
Rockmore, T., 225, 269, 271
Rogall, G.F., 12, 229, 232, 275
Rohde, J.J., 8–9, 11, 13, 227, 229, 231–234, 260, 272
Rohls, J., 226, 271
Rompe, E., 238, 271
Roncaglia, G., 263
Rosales, A., 242, 271
Rossi, P., 245, 268, 271
Rousseau, J.-J., 15

INDEX

Rüdiger, A., 205, 229, 254
Rudolph, O.-P., 265
Rumore, P., 241–242, 244, 271

Salthenius, D., 263
Santozki, U., 225, 271
Schmid, C.C.E., 58, 242, 260
Schmidt-Biggemann, W., 273
Schneider, J.F., 232–233
Schneiders, W., 264
Schönfeld, M., 225, 271
Schultz, F.A., 12, 264, 266, 271
Schultz, J., 126, 248, 262
Schumacher, B., 228, 271
Schuurman, P., 19, 236, 271
Schwarz, G., 256, 272
Scrinius, M., 226
Seel, G., 275
Segner, J.A., 109–110, 116, 118, 121–122, 132, 199–200, 220, 246–248, 260, 263
Sgarbi, M., vii, 227–229, 236, 238, 246, 255, 272
Sloan, P.R., 61–63, 242–243, 272
Smith, N., 236, 272
Sommerfeldt, G., 228, 272
Sparn, W., 226, 237–238, 272
Speer, A., 270
Stanzione, M., 263
Stark, W., 228, 234, 255, 273
Steger, L., 8, 226–227
Stich, T., 256, 263, 273
Stolzenberg, J., 265
Sulzer, J.C., 117–118, 125, 247, 260
Sulzer, J.G., 122, 186, 248, 260
Syrbius, J.J., 233, 241

Tannery, P., x
Tarozzi, G., 263
Teske, J.G., 10, 16, 263
Tetens, J.N., 64–69, 136, 185–186, 243, 254, 260
That, T.R., 230
Thegen, G., 12
Thomasius, C., 12, 124–125, 136, 175, 229–231, 248–249, 253, 255, 260

Thümmig, L., 10, 14, 234–235, 260
Timpler, C., 29, 40, 238–239, 261
Tolley, C., 249, 273
Tommasi, F.V., 225, 273
Tonelli, G., 5, 29, 56, 136, 147, 150–151, 158, 160, 195, 213, 215–216, 225–226, 229–230, 236, 238, 241–242, 248–251, 253–256, 273
Tschirnhaus, E.W. von, 229

Vaihinger, H., 242, 274
Van Celve, J., 75, 225, 244, 274
Vasoli, C., 252, 274
Viano, C.A., 268
Vollrath E., 238, 274
Von Geldern, J., 226
Von Haller, A., 59
Von Selle, G., 228–229, 232, 275
Vorländer, K., 228, 275

Wagner, G., 32, 40, 227, 239, 261
Wagner, J., 254, 275
Wagner, R.C., 98
Walch, J.G., 233
Walter, A., 267, 273
Walter, M., 225, 250, 275
Warda, A., 246–247, 250, 275
Watkins, E., 225, 275
Watson, M.F., 235
Watts, I., 229
Weger, L., 8, 27, 226–227, 237, 261
Weise, C., 149, 231
Werner, J.F., 235, 273
Weymann, D., 14, 192
Wilson, K.D., 245, 275
Winter, M., 158, 193, 226
Wolf, A., 12, 231
Wolff, C., 10, 12, 14–15, 24, 29, 34–25, 42–45, 48, 65, 80, 107–108, 150, 181–183, 186–187, 211–215, 221, 232–235, 237–238, 240–241, 244, 246, 251, 254, 256–258, 260–265, 268–270, 275
Wolff, C.F., 59
Wotschke, T., 232, 275
Wubnig, J., 242–243, 275

Wundt, M., 14, 226–227, 230, 236–237, 275

Xenophanes, 160

Yates, F.A., vii
Yolton, J., 236, 275

Zabarella, J., 8, 11, 16–17, 20, 25–28, 38–39, 41, 44, 74, 82, 85, 94, 97, 128, 148, 169–174, 208, 218–221, 226, 237, 239, 244, 252, 256, 261, 270, 273
Zammito, J.H., 60, 67, 242–243, 275
Zeidler, M., 8, 11, 32, 82, 172, 218, 226–227, 229–231, 238, 261
Zeno, 159-160
Zippel, G.O., 228, 275
Zöller, G., 241–244, 275

www.ingramcontent.com/pod-product-compliance
Lightning Source LLC
Chambersburg PA
CBHW030528230426
43665CB00010B/807